FROM MY OLD
STAMP
ALBUM

From My Old Stamp Album

Exotic Tales of Lost Countries

STUART LAYCOCK
AND CHRIS WEST

First published 2017 as *Lost Countries*
This paperback edition published 2023

The History Press
97 St George's Place, Cheltenham,
Gloucestershire, GL50 3QB
www.thehistorypress.co.uk

British Library Cataloguing in Publication Data.
A catalogue record for this book is available from the British Library.

ISBN 978 1 80399 376 8

Typesetting and origination by The History Press
Printed and bound in Great Britain by TJ Books Limited, Padstow, Cornwall.

Trees for Life

Contents

Introduction   9
A note on 'Stamp-speak'   11

Alaouites and Hatay   15
Allenstein and Marienwerder   18
Amoy   21
Austrian Italy   25
Azad Hind   28
Batum   31
Biafra   34
Bohemia and Moravia   37
Canal Zone   41
Cilicia   44
Confederate States of America   47
Cundinamarca   50
Cyrenaica   53
Danish West Indies   56
Danzig   59
Dedeagh   63
Don, Kuban Republic, United Russia   66
East India Postage   69

Eastern Rumelia	72
Epirus	76
Federation of South Arabia	79
Fernando Poo	83
Festung Lorient	86
Fezzan	89
Fiume	92
French India	95
French Territory of the Afars and Issas	99
German Austria and Carinthia	102
Great Barrier Island Pigeongram Agency	105
Heligoland	108
Herceg Bosna	111
Hyderabad	115
Icaria	118
Inini	121
Italian Social Republic	124
Katanga and South Kasai	127
Kiautschou	131
Kurland	134
League of Nations	137
Manchuria Manchukuo	140
Memel	143
Moldavia and Wallachia	147
North Ingria	150
Nossi-Bé	153
Nyassa Company	156
Obock	158
Patiala and Nawanagar	161
Quelimane	164
Rhodesia	168
Río Muni	171
Ryukyu Islands	174
Saar	178
Sedang	181

Senegambia   185
Serbian Krajina   187
Shan States   191
Siberia, Far Eastern Republic and Priamur   194
Silesia   198
Slesvig   201
Sopron   204
Spitsbergen   207
Stampalia and the Dodecanese   210
Stellaland   213
Straits Settlements   216
Thurn und Taxis   219
Tibet   222
Transcaucasian Socialist Federative Soviet Republic   226
Trans-Juba   229
Transkei, Bophuthatswana, Venda, Ciskei   232
Tripolitania   235
Tuva   238
United Arab Republic   242
United States of the Ionian Islands   245
Upper Yafa   248
Victoria Land   251
Zapadna Bosna   254

Appendix: The Story of Stamp Collecting   258
Acknowledgements   260
Index   261

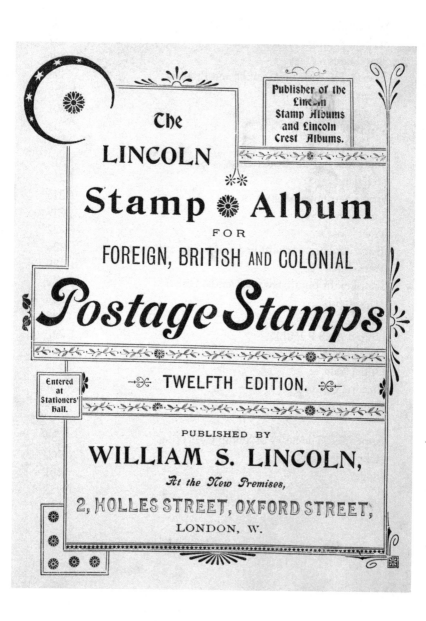

The
LINCOLN
Stamp ✸ Album
FOR
FOREIGN, BRITISH AND COLONIAL
Postage Stamps

Publisher of the
Lincoln
Stamp Albums
and Lincoln
Crest Albums.

Entered
at
Stationers'
Hall.

TWELFTH EDITION.

PUBLISHED BY
WILLIAM S. LINCOLN,
At the New Premises,
2, HOLLES STREET, OXFORD STREET,
LONDON, W.

Introduction

Many of us have them sitting in drawers or attics – old stamp albums that we filled eagerly as children, or that our parents or relatives did. Many of these will have attractive covers, which themselves will speak of bygone times (the one shown opposite comes from the turn of the last century). Inside the older ones, there will be adverts in once-fashionable typefaces for cheap packets of 'assorted foreign stamps' or for 'philatelic accessories' (where would any self-respecting Edwardian collector have been without a Lincoln Transparent Perforation Measure?)

Then there are the stamps themselves. These can be objects of great beauty. They can, if you are lucky, be valuable, though most aren't. But where are these stamps from? Among the familiar issuing places, you will probably find ones you have never heard of. What and where were Cundinamarca, Fiume, Dedeagh or Fernando Poo? What happened to them and their people? Old stamp albums hint at fascinating stories.

This isn't a comprehensive history of every country, island, colony, territory or city state that once produced stamps and no longer does. That would be a rather bigger book. Instead, we have set out to find some of the most fascinating of these and to investigate their past. A few still exist under the same names, though they no longer issue their own stamps. A few still exist and issue stamps, but under different names. Many no longer exist at all as independent entities, except in the pages of history and, of course, of old stamp albums.

Their stories include tragedy, drama, glory, despair and comedy. They often shed light on why parts of the modern world are as they are; places that few people have now heard of can prove to be missing jigsaw pieces that, when found, help make sense of much bigger pictures.

Any stamp from an entity that no longer exists has poignancy to it. Optimistic new countries used stamps to announce their arrival on the world stage. Imperial powers used them to stake their claim to legitimacy in their colonies. A stamp meant that the issuer believed that they were here to stay. Things didn't always work out quite like that, however, as many of these stories show. Above all, perhaps, an old stamp album is a witness to the perpetually changing patterns of power that make up history.

If you try to acquire other official items from many of these lost entities, you may have to search long and hard and pay substantial amounts of money. But often stamps can be bought for very little. We hope you enjoy reading the amazing stories in this book as much as we enjoyed researching and writing them. If it prompts you to go and acquire a few of these remarkable paper scraps of history yourself to hold in your own hands, then that would be an added pleasure.

A Note On 'Stamp-Speak'

Stamp collecting abounds with technical terms. We shall keep their use to a minimum, but a few will crop up in the text. First is the word *philately* itself, which is neatly defined as 'the collection and study of postage stamps' (thus giving it two totally separate meanings!). There is an implication that a philatelist is a rather serious collector.

Stamps essentially come in two conditions, *mint* (unused) and *used* (they have been on an envelope that has gone through the post). With older issues, mint stamps tend to be more rare and thus more valuable. With some modern issues, this is not the case, as many postal authorities have realised that collectors are a source of revenue, and produce 'collectable' stamps, which are sold straight to them. Few actually get used in the post. Few are worth much, either.

Stamp issues can be classified into two types, as well. *Definitive* stamps are the everyday ones, always on sale at your post office. Since 1967, UK definitives have been based on a 'low relief' bust of the Queen by sculptor Arnold Machin, a design classic that hasn't aged over four decades. *Commemorative* stamps are issued to celebrate particular events or anniversaries, or just to create a nice series for people to

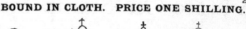

use (and, of course, collect). They are only on sale for a short time. The term 'commemorative' gets stretched somewhat. The year 2016 saw a commemorative issue for the 350th anniversary of the Great Fire of London, but also one featuring landscape gardens. Logically, the gardens stamps weren't 'commemorating' anything, but that is what they are called.

Any writing on a stamp is usually referred to as the *inscription*, and any visual element as the *image*. The value of the stamp (for postal use), almost always stated on it, is the *denomination*.

Overprints are when an extra layer of text or graphics is added to an existing stamp issue by the postal authority. For example, in Germany in 1923, prices roared up faster than new stamps could be produced, so old ones simply had new values printed on them. Examples include a 40 Mark stamp overprinted '8 thousand' and a 5,000 Mark stamp overprinted '2 million'.

Overprints are often the first stamps a new government can issue: it takes time to design and print new stamps, but new regimes don't want reminders of the old order dropping onto people's doormats. For example, after the overthrow of the Portuguese monarchy in 1910, that nation's old stamps were immediately overprinted with 'Republica'. Colonial powers sometimes just issued general-purpose colonial stamps for their entire empire and overprinted the name of each particular colony for local use.

Overprinting is not the same as the *postmark* on a stamp, which is a cancellation mark put on every item sent through the post by the postal service, to stop the stamp being reused. It also often provides information about when and where a letter was posted: postmarks have been the key to many a classic murder mystery.

Finally, when is a stamp-like piece of paper officially a proper stamp? There is a debate about this, usually decided by the magisterial, six-volume Stanley Gibbons 'Stamps of the World' album (or by the Scott Catalogue if you live in the USA). Stamps not listed in these are known as *Cinderellas*. Some have wonderful stories, and have sneaked into this book.

Alaouites and Hatay

THE TRAGEDY OF the Syrian Civil War has recently focused much attention on the complexities of Syria's more recent political and cultural history. Stamps cast an interesting light on some of it.

Syria, of course, has a long, varied and rich history. Damascus is often quoted as the oldest inhabited city in the world, and the area has seen a vast cavalcade of invaders come and go. Some of them are well known: Egyptians, Assyrians, Persians, Alexander the Great, Romans, Arabs etc. Some of the invasions are rather less well known, like the attempt to build a Crusader empire stretching deep into Syria's interior that was limited by the defeat of Bohemond of Antioch at the Battle of Harran fought somewhere near modern Raqqah. Or like the Mongolian invasions of Syria that hit the area a number of times in the thirteenth century.

However, by the beginning of the twentieth century Syria was a key part of the Ottoman Empire, which meant that in the First World War it would become a target for Allied invasion.

Ottoman advances into Sinai in the early part of the war were soon reversed, and by 1917 British and other Allied forces were advancing through what was then Ottoman-occupied Palestine. In autumn they took Beersheba and in December, in time for Christmas, General Allenby entered Jerusalem on foot.

The chaos caused by Germany's Spring Offensive on the Western Front helped call a temporary halt to Allied advances in the area, as Allied resources and attention were firmly focused there. But in late summer Allenby once again had the opportunity to advance north. His forces scored a major victory at the Battle of Megiddo, in September 1918, fought near the site of a number of ancient battles and near the site of Har Megiddo, the hill of Megiddo, also known as Armageddon.

More victories for Allenby would follow, and also advancing against the Ottomans were the forces of the Arab Revolt with, yes, Lawrence of Arabia himself. Australian cavalry and Lawrence and the Arab rebels entered Damascus on 1 October. On 25 October, the advancing Allies captured Aleppo. Turkey had had enough. On 30 October it signed the Armistice of Mudros. Less than two weeks later Turkey's ally Germany would also sign an armistice.

The question now for the Allies was what to do with the remains of the Ottoman Empire. The Arab rebels believed that their assistance to the Allied cause would ensure a new era of Arab self-rule was about to begin. In Syria they were going to be disappointed. Britain and France, however, had already pretty much agreed under the Sykes–Picot Agreement that Britain would get Palestine and France would get Syria.

A lot of locals were extremely unhappy about the situation. In March 1920, the Syrian National Congress declared Hashemite Faisal King of Syria. But in April, the San Remo Conference established a French mandate over Syria. In July, advancing forces clashed with Syrian forces at the Battle of Maysalun and defeated them. Shortly afterwards, French forces entered Damascus and started to implement the French mandate. Faisal himself ended up as King of Iraq after the British who were in control there decided that he would be handy to help them stabilise the situation there.

The French set about organising their mandate and split Syria into several entities. One area, centred on Beirut, where many Christians were concentrated, would eventually become the modern state of Lebanon. To the north of that was an area, centred on Latakia, where the religious community the Alawites were strong, that became the Alaouite state (French spelling for Alawite). To the north of that was another area, centred on the ancient city of Alexandretta, which became the Sandjak of, yes, Alexandretta.

The Alaouite state never issued its own stamps, but a series of overprints, first on French stamps, then on Syrian ones.

The separate Alaouite state would not last for the entire time of the French mandate in Syria. Responding to those who wanted to see a more unified Syria, the French first changed the entity's name to Latakia and then, in 1936, as France negotiated a deal to help protect its presence in the area after the expiry of the mandate, it was incorporated again into Syria.

Tensions over the status of the Alawites would, however, re-emerge. Both the previous and current presidents of Syria and some key members of their administrations have been Alawite, and resentment by members of the Sunni community, which forms the largest religious community in Syria, has been a key element in the Syrian Civil War.

At the same time as they yielded ground over the Alawites, the French authorities were also coming under pressure over another part of the territory they controlled – the area to the north based around Alexandretta.

As well as others, the area contained a significant Turkish population, and Turkey's new leader Mustafa Kemal Atatürk had never accepted that the region was part of Syria. He was determined that the international community would accept it as part of Turkey. He too had been planning for what happened after the expiry of France's mandate in Syria.

Turkey pressed the League of Nations to get involved in the area it referred to as Hatay. In response, a new constitution was prepared for the territory and in 1938 it became the Republic of Hatay.

Hatay had its own stamps. As is often the case, in such instances the first ones (in early 1939) were overprints (on Turkish stamps), but proper Hatay stamps soon followed, an attractive set of fourteen denominations featuring four designs: a map of the republic, its flag, two stone lions from the ruins of ancient Antioch and (for the highest denominations) Antioch's modern Post Office.

The Hatay Republic did not, however, have a long future ahead of it. In June 1939, with the international community's attention focused firmly on the threat of war in Europe, and amid suspicions that France was siding with Turkey in the hope that it would side with France in any new major world conflict, the Hatay parliament voted to join Turkey. In July, the Republic of Hatay became the State of Hatay (the republic's stamps were reissued as overprints celebrating this fact).

French forces would leave Syria in 1946 but even today, many Syrians do not regard the question of the status of Hatay as settled forever.

Somewhat bizarrely, the State of Hatay is the name of a key location in the movie *Indiana Jones and the Last Crusade*.

Allenstein and Marienwerder

ALLENSTEIN AND MARIENWERDER sounds like a particularly old and reputable company. In fact, these are the names of two eastern European cities. Or at least they were. The towns are now called Olsztyn, basically the Polish version of Allenstein, and Kwidzyn, which doesn't sound anything like Marienwerder at all.

Olsztyn is a city in north-eastern Poland not far south of the Kaliningrad enclave, part of Russia situated on the Baltic coast but with no land connection to the rest of Russia. It was badly damaged during the Second World War but has been repaired and rebuilt, and today has some interesting sights, including a castle, town walls, a cathedral, some museums and a university.

As is not unusual for this part of the world, Olsztyn has a history that has seen it connect at different times with both German and Polish identities. The Teutonic Knights constructed a major castle there in 1334 and by 1353 the town that had grown up around it had developed sufficiently to get municipal rights.

The Teutonic Knights and the Polish Crown didn't exactly get on with each other very well at the time. A series of wars took place between the two parties with varying fortunes for each, and Allenstein/Olsztyn occasionally got caught up in these. In 1466, a peace deal that ended the Thirteen Years' War that had featured, yes, the Teutonic Knights and Poland, but also the Prussian Confederation allied to the Poles, put Allenstein/Olsztyn under the authority, ultimately, of the Polish crown.

However, the Teutonic Knights had not yet entirely finished with Allenstein/Olsztyn. In 1519, they were at war with Poland yet again and in 1521 they laid siege to Allenstein/Olsztyn. Fortunately for the inhabitants, and unfortunately for the Teutonic Knights, Allenstein/Olsztyn had a genius in charge of organising its defences, a certain Nicolaus Copernicus, mathematician, astronomer, economist, scientist, diplomat and generally a very useful chap to have around for a wide variety of reasons. The Teutonic Knights failed to take Allenstein/Olsztyn and after a while gave up and made peace.

The town had a nasty time with the plague and also a nasty time with some Swedes who insisted on sacking it during assorted wars. Then, in 1772, as Poland was divided yet again and Prussia expanded, Allenstein was made part of the Kingdom of Prussia. And in 1871, with the declaration of the German Empire, it became part of Germany, which is where it still was as the first shots of the First World War were fired in 1914.

Marienwerder/Kwidzyn has in many senses a rather similar history to Allenstein/Olsztyn. It's situated almost on the same latitude as the other place, but a little further to the west. Once again it's the site of a major castle built by the Teutonic Knights, and once again the place got caught up in the series of wars between the Teutonic Knights and Poland. In 1440, it was the location for the creation of the Prussian Confederation, which would ally itself with Poland against the Teutonic Knights in the Thirteen Years' War. Again, like Allenstein/Olsztyn, it would end up under the authority, ultimately, of the Polish crown after that war. And like Allenstein, Marienwerder would become part of the Kingdom of Prussia, as Poland was split up, and then part of the German Empire, where it too was, at the outbreak of war in 1914.

Almost as soon as the war had broken out, the Russians launched a huge invasion of East Prussia. However, in late August, German forces almost destroyed the Russian Second Army in one of the most decisive battles of the First World War. It prevented what could have been a vital Russian breakthrough in the east, even before the war had really got going. The battle was actually fought pretty much at Allenstein, and yet it has gone into the history books as the Battle of Tannenberg because the Germans were, for nationalistic reasons, keen to see the battle as revenge for the 1410 Battle of Grunwald or Tannenberg in which the Teutonic Knights were decisively defeated by Poles, Lithuanians and a variety of other east Europeans.

In the end, of course, victory at Allenstein/Tannenberg in 1914 would not prevent the defeat of Germany in 1918. And as the victorious Allies looked over the map of Europe and tried to decide how its borders should be changed, the question arose of what to do with Allenstein and Marienwerder, which were originally envisaged as being put in Polish territory. Should they become part of the new state of Poland that was being created, or should they remain part of Germany? In the end, it was decided that a plebiscite should be held. Allied commissioners and British and Italian troops entered the area in order to organise the plebiscite and the vote was held in July 1920 as the Polish–Soviet War was raging. The result of the plebiscite was strongly in favour of Allenstein and Marienwerder remaining in German territory. Which they did.

For the philatelist, Marienwerder is the more interesting of the two cities. A special stamp was designed for it, featuring the allegorical figure of a lady decked with various Allied flags, and with the inscription *Commission Interallièe* and the town's German name. Fourteen different denominations, in different colours, were issued. A later issue changed the inscription to 'Plebiscite' and added the Polish name. Allenstein, by contrast, only managed overprints, on German stamps, one marked 'Plebiscite' and the other, intriguingly, '*Traité de Versailles*'.

The plebiscite is not the end of the story. By 1945, Germany had once again been defeated in a world war and the victorious Allies were changing borders in Europe. This time there would be no plebiscite. As the maps changed, Allenstein and Marienwerder would now be located deep inside Polish territory and be known by the Polish names Olsztyn and Kwidzyn. That is how they remain today.

Amoy

AMOY IS KNOWN to the modern world as Xiamen (pronounced 'Sheeya-men'), a bustling port city 300 miles north-east of Hong Kong and at the heart of China's modern economic miracle. Our word 'Amoy' comes from its name as spoken in local Hokkien dialect, *Ē-mûi*. It sits on an island known as Egret Island, from the birds that used to be found here in profusion, though the city has now spread onto the mainland, to which it is now joined.

Amoy has a full history. In the seventeenth century, a pirate rebel called Koxinga used it as a base for his attempt to drive out China's new Manchu dynasty – he failed, but decamped to nearby Taiwan, from which he continued to harass the new dynasty until he was driven out by combined Dutch and Manchu forces.

In the early eighteenth century, Amoy became a major port, though it declined after 1757, when the Qing emperors decreed that all foreign trade (except for that with Russia) was made to be carried out through Guangzhou (Canton), where it could be more closely monitored under a system known as the *Vigilance Towards Foreign Barbarian Regulations*.

In 1842, the Opium Wars broke out. Britain's role in these is not exactly elevating – maybe we deserved the title of 'barbarian'. Essentially, we wanted to sell drugs to the Chinese; they tried to stop us, so we sent in gunboats. Guangzhou was the main target but we also sent a force to Amoy. The fortified city initially resisted the shelling, but when a land force tried to enter, on the morning of 27 August, it met very little resistance. The inhabitants had abandoned it in one night, having smuggled everything of value out of it in advance (gold items were hidden in hollowed-out logs). Just as well, as the invaders ransacked the city.

Under the Treaty of Nanking that followed this one-sided war, Amoy became a 'Treaty Port', one of five along the Chinese coast, where foreign merchants could do business with anyone they chose, selling whatever they chose. It began to boom again – Amoy's inhabitants have a reputation for entrepreneurship. Foreigners were allowed to live in an international settlement where Chinese law did not apply. Amoy's settlement was on Gulangyu Island. This still boasts magnificent colonial architecture. In the twenty-first century, it has become such a popular tourist attraction that visitor numbers are controlled. (150 years ago it was the British telling the Chinese they could not visit.) For a number of years there were only two such settlements in China: Gulangyu and the Concession in Shanghai.

Life in the settlement was run on Western lines. Churches, parks, schools and hospitals were built. Some of the schools specialised in music: Gulangyu Island still has more pianos per head of population than anywhere else in China.

There was also a Post Office. The settlement had its own postal system, which initially used stamps from Hong Kong or Shanghai. In 1894, Gulangyu's Municipal Council – which now involved people from thirteen nations – decided to have its own stamps. A set was designed and printed in Germany. The stamps feature the same design, two egrets on a marsh, in different colours. The first ones carried denominations of ½, 1, 2, 4 and 5 cents. When the local post ran out of ½-cent stamps, the postmaster, John Philips, improvised, printing 'Half Cent' on 4- and 5-cent stamps. Stamps worth 3, 6 and 10 cents were later produced by the same method, and higher denominations were printed: 15, 20 and 25 cents.

There are also Postage Due overprints, for stampless mail arriving from Taiwan, which was then being invaded by the Japanese and where the postal system had broken down. These are the most valuable for the collector, especially the 2c blue.

An old stamp album will have spaces for the stamps of other Treaty Ports, too. Foochow (modern Fuzhou) is 200 miles up the coast from Amoy: its stamps feature a busy port, with Chinese junks, western sailing vessels and a 'Dragon Boat' used for races. Chefoo (modern Yantai) is in Shandong Province, about half-way between Shanghai and Beijing: its stamps (for some reason) feature a 'smoke tower' used for curing meat. Shanghai, of course, was the most successful of these ports, and issued a range of stamps.

These were all seaports. Your old album might well also feature spaces for later treaty ports that were founded along the Yangtze (Yangzi) River: Chinkiang (modern Zhenjiang), Chunking (now the vast city of Chongqing), Hankow, Ichang (Yichang), Kewkiang (Jiujiang), Wuhu and Nanking (Nanjing). Perhaps the most evocative of these are from Hankow: most of the Treaty Port stamps have a romantic feel to them, show-ing China as an exotic place. On Hankow's stamp, a coolie lugs two huge loads over his shoulder – the reality of life for most of China's inhabitants at the time.

But back to Amoy … The port flourished in the new century. Between the wars, Gulangyu became known as a place to party for Westerners and wealthy Chinese. However, this lifestyle was rudely interrupted by the Imperial Japanese Army, who invaded the island the day after Pearl Harbour. And after the war, it was not long before the Communists came in 1949.

In that year, China's former ruler, Chiang Kai Shek, fled, as Koxinga had done, to nearby Taiwan. Xiamen, now called by its Mandarin name, became a focal point for tension between the two Chinas. The Jinmen (Quemoy) and Matsu islands are only a few miles off Xiamen, but are claimed by Taiwan. In 1954, Chiang began garrisoning large numbers of soldiers on them, intending to use them, so it seemed to the authorities in Beijing, as a stepping stone to an invasion. Mainland China responded by bombarding the islands. Taiwan had a defence pact with America, and in September, the US Joint Chiefs of Staff recommended using nuclear weapons to retaliate. President Dwight D. Eisenhower thought otherwise. However, the sabre-rattling from the US continued, and in the end the mainland Chinese ceased the bombardment. A second, similar crisis followed in 1958. After this, the bombardments continued, but only in the form of propaganda leaflets. There would also be the occasional commando excursion (by either side) to kill sentries or indulge in a little sabotage.

Mainland China's dictator Chairman Mao died in 1976; in 1978 Deng Xiaoping came to power. Deng understood the need to ditch Mao's extreme ideas and create a modern economy. He did so slowly – it was an enormous cultural change. Xiamen was one of the earliest places for this to happen. In 1980, it became one of four Special Economic Zones, where economic decisions would be 'primarily driven by market forces' and where foreign firms would be encouraged to form 'joint ventures' with Chinese businesses.

Since 2016, relations between Taiwan and mainland have deteriorated, with Taiwan declaring ever more robustly that it values its independence and China insisting that Taiwan is still its property. In the last two years, China has carried out major military operations threatening the island state (and especially the Jinmen and Matsu Islands). There is renewed talk of an invasion. For many years, Xiamen/Amoy has been quietly getting on with the business of making money. If such an invasion were to happen, the world's spotlight would suddenly be on it again.

Austrian Italy

ONE THINKS OF Austria and Italy as two separate European countries, with very separate identities, but they have at times controlled – or aspired to control – chunks of each other's territory. Austria had a long involvement with Italy via the Holy Roman Empire.

After the Battle of Waterloo in 1815, Europe craved peace. At the Congress of Vienna, its leaders got together and tried to draw boundaries that would last. As usual, what happened was that the most skilful and forceful diplomats got the best deals. One such man was Klemens von Metternich, the representative of the Austrian Empire.

Before the Congress, various parts of northern Italy had been ruled by Austria through various dukes. After it, these were lumped together into the Kingdom of Lombardy–Venetia – a kingdom in theory; in practice a 'crown land' (in other words, part) of the Austrian Empire. It was a big territory. Lombardy is in the middle of the most northerly part of Italy, the area around Milan. Venetia no longer exists, but its former extent is similar to that of modern Veneto, the province at the top left of the Adriatic, of which Venice is the capital. A third modern Italian province, Friuli-Venezia Giulia, to the east of Veneto, was also part of this 'kingdom'.

It was never very Austrian. Veneto had traditionally been part of the territory of the Republic of Venice. Lombardy had been under Austrian rule for a long time, but the culture was Italian.

As the nineteenth century progressed, new ideas came to the fore. Nationalism, and a sense that nations were defined by language and culture rather than whose army was biggest, became a liberal cause.

The year 1848 was the 'year of revolutions' all around Europe, especially central Europe. In Milan, it kicked off with a boycott of government monopolies (gambling, tobacco), which soon descended into street violence. Then in March, Metternich, who had become Austrian chancellor, was thrown out of office. Cue more unrest in Milan: five days of street fighting, during which several hundred people were killed. The Austrians retreated from the city and the Lombardy Provisional Government was formed. However, the Austrians regrouped, and next year won their territory back.

The Kingdom of Lombardy–Venetia got its first stamps the year after that. There is nothing Italian about them at all, apart from the denomination, which is in local currency. Otherwise they were of the same design that Austria used throughout its empire, showing the Austrian coat of arms and bearing the inscription KK Post – *kaiserlich und königlich*, Imperial and Royal.

In 1858, special stamps for the delivery of newspapers in the kingdom were produced. Though only issued in Lombardy–Venetia, they were, again, totally Austrian, with the inscriptions in German and even the Austrian currency used. Three denominations were issued. The highest, the 4 Kreuzer, was bright red and featured the god Mercury. The 'Red Mercury' is now extremely rare: in 2015, one was sold for 40,000 Euros.

Despite Austria's victory in what is now called the First War of Italian Independence, the momentum of '*Risorgimento*', the move to create a united Italian nation, had merely stalled. A second War of Independence broke out in 1859, and this time the nationalists played a better game. Led by Count Cavour, who was prime minister of both Sardinia and Lombardy–Venetia's neighbour Piedmont (the western part of northern Italy, around Turin), they allied themselves with a major European power, France. Cavour then goaded the Austrians into attacking him by organising large military manoeuvres near his border with Lombardy – an attack which brought the French into the conflict.

There were no French forces in Piedmont at the time, but their army was soon taken there by railway – the first time that this means of transport had played a major role in a war. Austria was defeated at the Battle of Solferino on 24 June 1859. The battle was a vicious one, with several thousand soldiers killed and 20,000 wounded. The businessman and writer Henry Dunant saw the aftermath, and went on to become a founder of the Red Cross. He was instrumental in drafting the Geneva Convention on the rules of war.

Solferino did not mean the complete end of Austrian rule in Italy. However, much of Lombardy now became part of the expanding 'Kingdom of Sardinia'. Austria still controlled Venetia – and showed it by issuing more stamps. Again these were standard Austrian ones, made local only by the currency (the soldo and the florin were not used anywhere else in the Austrian empire).

Elsewhere in Italy, the country was uniting. By the end of 1860, it was effectively one nation – the Kingdom of Italy was formally proclaimed on 17 March 1861.

Venetia was still under Austrian rule, however – but not for long. The last stamps for 'Austrian Italy' came out in 1863. In 1866, Austria got into another war, this time with Prussia. Eager for Venetia, Italy allied itself to Prussia. Apart from Garibaldi's 'Alpine hunters', the Italian forces did not distinguish themselves, but the Prussians did, and when peace was negotiated, Austria had to cede Venetia, first to France (Austria refused to hand it directly to Italy, because it did not feel that Italy had defeated it in battle), then to Italy. A plebiscite in Venetia in October of that year confirmed what everyone knew: the vast majority of the population wanted to be part of Italy.

The tension between the two nations continued into the twentieth century. In the First World War, Italy joined the Allies, and launched a series of mountain offensives against the Austrians. Fought in harsh conditions – avalanches were a perpetual threat – the battles, though vicious and costly, were mostly indecisive or led to small territorial gains for Italy (even after a victory, it is hard to sweep through mountain terrain). Then Germany entered on Austria's side, and the tide turned. In October 1917, they won the Battle of Caporetto – during which poison gas was used – and advanced into Italian territory. Overprint stamps for the newly occupied region were issued.

However, the British and French then joined the Italians and stopped the advance. In 1918, Germany withdrew much of its support, needing to concentrate its resources on the war in France. The Austrian forces were defeated at the Battle of Vittorio Veneto and driven back. After the war, the current borders between Italy and Austria were drawn.

Azad Hind

AZAD HIND MEANS Free India. It was the name taken by the Indian government-in-exile set up by the Japanese in occupied Singapore in 1943. Its aim, as one would expect, was to end British rule in the subcontinent.

The Japanese had begun trying to subvert the loyalty of Indian servicemen before the outbreak of war. In late 1941, Mohan Singh, a former captain in the Punjab Regiment, agreed to lead an 'Indian National Army' (INA) of deserters. As the Japanese swept through Malaya in late 1941/early 1942, rather than being treated as prisoners of war, captured Indian troops were put under Singh's command.

When Singapore fell on 15 February, over half the 80,000 captured defenders were Indian. They were offered the chance to serve under Singh and fight alongside the Japanese. Many accepted. At its height, the INA numbered 35,000 men.

Singh soon found himself at loggerheads with his new masters, however – he wanted his army to be autonomous, but the Japanese insisted that they must retain overall command. He was removed from power and arrested. Instead of simply replacing him with another, more compliant, commander, the Japanese built a political structure around the new army. It needed a 'government' to serve, and this government should be Indian. How much autonomy that government would have, of course, would be a different matter …

Enter Subhas Chandra Bose. Bose had been a senior member of Congress alongside Gandhi, but had no time for the latter's non-violent methods. He had been under house arrest in India, but in 1940 he escaped, via a dramatic trek across Afghanistan, to Germany, from which he broadcast propaganda for his new hosts and began recruiting Indian soldiers captured by the Germans to fight against the British in India.

Around 3,000 signed up, swearing, 'I will obey the leader of the German race and state, Adolf Hitler, as the commander of the German armed forces in the fight for India, whose leader is Subhas Chandra Bose.'

The aim was that these men would be parachuted into India – but before this could happen, Hitler invaded Russia. Bose, a Communist sympathiser, was dismayed. He quit Germany, leaving his legion leaderless – they were subsumed into the German army – and made his way, first in a German submarine then in a Japanese one, to Japanese-occupied Sumatra. Here, he was given a new role: to lead 'the Provisional Government of Free India', the political leadership of the Indian National Army.

A theme running through this book is the role of stamps in asserting the legitimacy of a political entity. Bose understood this well. His new government issued its own currency (a central bank was set up in 1944), had its own courts – and issued stamps (though, as we shall see, they were never used).

The stamps, designed and printed in Germany, range in value from ½ Anna to 1 Rupee. Designs show rural life (a peasant ploughing a field beneath a range of mountains), a nurse, a map of India with a chain breaking across it, a Sikh solider firing a German MG 34 machine gun, and three soldiers under the Azad Hind banner. Apart from the last of these, the stamps were printed in simple, clear monochrome. The last one is mainly black, but the orange and green of the banner also feature. This stamp is also much rarer, as only 13,500 were printed.

Some feature a surcharge: these are the ones intended for use in parts of India occupied by the Japanese. The Japanese did effect such an occupation (see below) – but the stamps did not get used.

No way could be found of getting them from Berlin to Singapore or to Port Blair, capital of the Andaman Islands, so they actually sat the war out in the *Reichsdruckerei*.

As Japan conquered formerly Indian territory, Azad Hind was given formal control over it. This mainly meant the Andaman and Nicobar Islands, two archipelagos in the Bay of Bengal (actually much nearer Burma than India), where an INA major-general, A.D. Loganathan, was made governor. However, he soon found out that he had no real power. The Imperial Japanese ran the place and soon began to exhibit the brutality that they showed to all other subject people. The vicious circle common to inept, authoritarian governments followed: 'spies' and 'traitors' were blamed for inefficiencies, given show trials and executed (forty-four of them on one day, many of whom had been supporters of the new administration but who had expected genuine independence). Forced labour was used in the construction of military projects like a new airport. There are stories of women forced into prostitution.

The islands were only reconquered in October 1945. Meanwhile, of course, Imperial Japan had been defeated. On that defeat, Bose, based in Singapore, had tried to flee to Russia, but was killed in an air crash in Taiwan. Naturally, conspiracy theories abound, some of which say he survived. The truth seems to be more prosaic. The plane was overladen to start with, and then developed engine trouble. Nobody survived. The Indian National Army and Azad Hind, featured on its confident stamps, died with him.

People still argue about the legacy of Azad Hind. In modern India, Bose is seen by many as a freedom fighter. Two stamps were issued in 1964 to celebrate the sixty-seventh anniversary of his birth (quite why such an odd figure was chosen, we don't know), and another one in 1968 to commemorate the twenty-fifth anniversary of the founding of the Azad Hind government. A popular film in 2005 celebrated him as *The Forgotten Hero*.

On Andaman and Nicobar, however, people disagree. To them, the Azad Hind administration failed its own people. It seems hard to use the term 'freedom fighter' for Bose, who propagandised for Hitler, fought for the people responsible for the Rape of Nanking and, when they were beaten, tried to run to Stalin for support. But such is history. What you see, and certainly what you make of what you see, at least partially depends on where you stand.

Batum

UNLIKE MANY OF the locations in this book, Batum is still a name you can find on the map today. On the eastern shores of the Black Sea coast, a short distance north of the Turkish border, is situated Batumi, a port and the second-largest city in Georgia. It has beaches and modern skyscrapers but the region also has a long, long history.

In ancient times the legendary land of Colchis, home to the Golden Fleece, was located in this area. Home to the Golden Fleece that is, until, according to the legend, one Jason turned up with his Argonauts and nicked the fleece after seducing Medea, the daughter of the King of Colchis. Ancient Greeks were among the first foreigners to descend fully armed on the region, but far from the last. For instance, in the fifteenth century a bunch of Burgundians who were far, far distant from Burgundy, under the command of one Geoffroy de Thoisy, himself a knight of the Burgundian Order of the Golden Fleece, made an attempt to raid the region, only to find themselves ambushed, with Geoffrey taken prisoner.

In ancient times, the area lay on the border between the Roman Empire and the lands to the east, and later it would lie near the boundary between the Russian Empire and the Ottoman Empire. Which is just about where the British come in. Because yes, even though Batum is situated deep in the Caucasus, thousands of miles from Whitehall, it was the British who secured Batum's place in stamp albums and stamp catalogues across the world.

Russia basically won the Russo-Turkish War of 1877–78 and as part of the peace deal that ended the war it sent its troops into Batum. As the Caucasus oil boom took off in the late nineteenth century, Batum became a key component in the infrastructure of the area, with a railroad and oil pipeline running from Baku, on the Caspian Sea across the Caucasus to Batum from where oil and its products could be shipped elsewhere.

But the region was about to see changes, big changes. The same year that Russian troops entered Batum, to the east, was born one Iosif Vissarionovich Dzhugashvili. He is rather better known by his alias, Stalin, the man of steel.

In 1901, early in his revolutionary career, Stalin got a job at an oil refinery in Batum. After a fire, he led strikes at the plant which eventually led to his arrest. In 1903, he ended up in Siberia.

But, of course, this was not to be the end of attempts at revolution in the Russian Empire. In 1914, with the outbreak of the First World War, Russia joined the Allies, with Turkey siding with Russia. The Caucasus became a war zone again. Russia scored some successes in the war, but the cost in men and money was dreadful, and it suffered many defeats as well. In early 1917, the February Revolution (actually in March by the current calendar) led to the abdication of Tsar Nicholas II. The later October Revolution (actually in November by the current calendar) of the same year saw the Bolsheviks come to power. In March 1918, desperate to relieve themselves of the burden of war against Germany and its allies, the Bolsheviks signed a peace deal at Brest-Litovsk. Under its provisions, Russia gave up claims to Batum, and in April, Turkish forces moved into the city.

However, Turkish dominance of the region was to be short-lived. By October of that year, with German forces starting to collapse on the Western Front, it was Turkey that found itself looking for an exit from an unwinnable war. On 30 October, the Armistice of Mudros was signed and Turkey was out of the war. But war was definitely not at an end in the Caucasus.

Local nations, including Georgia and Armenia, took the opportunity presented by the collapse of the Russian Empire to declare independence, and fighting followed as new states battled to define borders in a chaotic regional mix that also included Turkish forces, German advisers, Red Russian forces and White Russian forces. Then into this violent, confusing and rapidly evolving regional situation strode the British. The British government thought intervening in the area would be a good idea. It wasn't.

British forces seized the oil-rich areas around Baku and, in December 1918, Britain also sent troops in to seize Batum. General James Cooke-Collis became Governor of Batum. Just like British intervention elsewhere in the chaos that followed the collapse of the Russian Empire, British intervention in Batum achieved very little. One of its few lasting achievements, in fact (apart from instilling in the Soviet government a long-term suspicion of British intentions) was to get Batum listed in stamp albums. By February 1919, the city was running out of stamps. It was also running out of quite a lot else, but at least stamps were something the British occupation force could do something about. An attractive set of six stamps was produced, featuring an Aloe tree and inscribed *Batumskaya Pochta* in Cyrillic. Unfortunately, inflation set in, and various sets of overprints were soon needed, on both the 'Aloe tree' series and on Russian stamps. The latter are rare – but sadly also much forged, as are all Batum stamps. Buyer beware!

The end of British power in the Caucasus was not, however, far off. In the summer of 1920, British forces left the city and after being disputed between Turkish and Georgian troops, Batum finally came under control of Soviet forces, where it was to remain for many decades. Meanwhile in 1922, Stalin, the Georgian who had once led strikes in Batum, took control of the Soviet Union after Lenin's death. Georgia would remain part of the Soviet Union until, after a referendum in 1991, it declared its independence.

Biafra

BIAFRA IS ONE of those names that is chillingly familiar for people who were adults during the 1960s. It is a name that they associate with pain, war and tragedy, a bit like people who were adults in the 1990s think of Bosnia.

Yet the name Biafra is an old one. It derives from the gulf off the coast of what is now Nigeria, called the Bight of Biafra (also called the Bight of Bonny). And for part of the 1850s and 1860s Britain had a Bight of Biafra Protectorate. Eventually it was merged with other territory into the Oil Rivers Protectorate. This had its own stamps, or at least British stamps overprinted with 'British Protectorate Oil Rivers'. In 1893, these overprints were themselves overprinted with new values – these 'double overprints' are serious collectors items. The name subsequently changed to Niger Coast Protectorate, and this entity got its own stamps: two designs featuring an older Queen Victoria than ever appeared on British stamps.

However, it is what happened in 1967 that really brought the name Biafra to the world's attention, and it is the reason its name is found in stamp albums and in this book.

In 1960, Nigeria became independent from Britain. By 1966, it was in turmoil as coup and counter-coup struck and ethnic tensions within the country erupted, particularly involving two groups, the Hausa, mainly located in Nigeria's northern regions, and the Igbo, mainly located in the more prosperous east (which also contained much of the nation's valuable resources of oil).

In September 1966, thousands of Igbo were massacred in Hausa regions and large numbers of Igbo fled to the Igbo areas in the east of the country. Some non-Igbos were then killed in the Igbo east or expelled from the area.

Peace talks in Ghana in early 1967 failed to reach a solution to the problems and, in May 1967, the head of Nigeria's Igbo-majority Eastern Region, Lieutenant Colonel Odumegwu Ojukwu, with the support of a local assembly, declared the region independent as the Republic of Biafra. General Yakubu Gowon, Nigeria's leader, refused to accept Biafra's secession and by July the Biafra War, or the Nigerian Civil War, had broken out.

An initial federal 'police action' had little success and by contrast the early stages of the war saw some Biafran military successes. In August 1967, Biafran troops advanced into Nigeria's mid-Western region.

The Biafran government went ahead with creating the structures and symbols of an independent state, and that, of course, included stamps. The first stamps, a set of four, came out in 1968. Another set appeared later that year, commemorating the country's first year of independence. One, the 1s, features probably the most horrific image ever portrayed on a stamp: a decapitated body, with the inscription 'May 29, July 29, September 29. Nigerian Pogrom 1966, 30,000 massacred'.

France would offer some limited diplomatic and secret military support to Biafra; nevertheless, only a small number of countries would actually recognise Biafran independence and it soon became apparent that without major international political and military support, Biafra would struggle to defend its claimed borders against the much larger forces and resources of the rest of Nigeria. Britain continued to supply large quantities of arms and ammunition to the Nigerian government with which, as the former colonial power, it had strong links. The Soviet Union also supplied significant quantities of weapons and munitions to the Nigerian government.

Nigerian forces soon retook the area occupied by the Biafrans in their offensive, and began to launch attacks into Biafra itself from a number of directions. In the north, Nigerian federal forces captured Enugu, the capital of Biafra, in October 1967. In the south, Nigerian federal forces fought to seize key oil areas and key ports. In July 1967, they seized Bonny Island in the Niger Delta. And in October, Operation Tiger Claw saw Nigerian forces land on the Biafran coast and capture the key Biafran port of Calabar. Then, in May 1968, the Nigerians captured Port Harcourt as well.

The Biafrans, unable to get open military assistance from foreign powers, sought military help from foreign mercenaries and foreign volunteers. Nonetheless, Nigeria's capture of ports and vital supply routes meant that getting supplies in to the population of Biafra became increasingly hard and starvation increasingly widespread. This caused massive international sympathy and led to efforts around the world to get aid to the suffering. The starvation caused by the Biafran War was one of the first major international humanitarian crises that was televised and it created something of a pattern for future international responses to such incidents – for instance, the Biafran airlift involved church groups and NGOs, with some support from foreign governments, flying aid into Biafra. The NGO Médecins Sans Frontières, for example, was born out of the Biafra experience.

In 1969, Biafran forces supported by mercenary pilots launched a number of counter-offensives which achieved some limited temporary success. Nevertheless, the long-term outlook for Biafra was not at all good. In December 1969, Nigerian forces launched a major offensive into the shrunken territory still held by Biafran forces. The Nigerian offensive succeeded in splitting what was left of Biafra-held territory in half. On 11 January 1970, one of the last Biafran strongholds, provincial capital Owerri, fell to Nigerian forces and Biafran leader Ojukwu escaped by plane to the Ivory Coast. On 14 January 1970, the Biafran surrender was signed in Lagos, bringing the war to an end. In all, somewhere between half a million and several million people had died, a huge number of those killed by severe malnutrition.

Ojukwu did not return from exile until 1982, when he was pardoned and went home to Nigeria. He died in 2011. Gowon was removed from power in 1975 by the Nigerian army while he was in Uganda for an Organisation of African Unity summit meeting. He went into exile in Great Britain but has sometimes returned to Nigeria.

In recent years a number of groups have once again started pressing for Biafran independence. Among them is MASSOB, the Movement for the Actualisation of the Sovereign State of Biafra.

Bohemia and Moravia

THE MODERN CZECH Republic is essentially made up of two former areas, Bohemia (the western part) and Moravia, to the east. In the early Middle Ages, Moravia was the dominant power – there was an empire known as 'Great Moravia', though historians are still debating exactly what its boundaries were. Around the end of the tenth century, that empire began to break up. Bohemia became an independent kingdom, one of its rulers being Good King Wenceslas of Christmas carol fame (he was actually only a duke, but has been promoted posthumously). By 1200, Bohemia had its own king, Ottokar, and ruled over its eastern neighbour. A hundred years later, it had its own empire. This reached its peak under King Wenceslas II – then, like all empires, began to shrink.

In 1526, Bohemia became part of the Habsburg Empire – between 1583 and 1611, Prague was even made the capital of that empire. It would remain Habsburg for nearly four centuries, despite the best efforts of nationalist movements, which were especially militant in the nineteenth century (our word 'bohemian', for an unconventional artists' lifestyle, dates from that era – but comes from a mistake: early nineteenth-century Parisians thought that the capital's Romani inhabitants had come from Bohemia). When the Austro-Hungarian Empire fell apart after the First World War, the nation of Czechoslovakia was created.

Bohemia and Moravia's centuries-long cultural link with Austria meant that there were many German speakers in their northern, western and southern parts (German speakers made up nearly a quarter of the population of the new nation). This area became known as the Sudetenland, after a range of mountains on the Czech–Polish border.

With the rise of Hitler, many of these German speakers became vociferous in their demands to be united with Germany. By 1935, a pro-Hitler party had become the second biggest in Czechoslovakia. The demands became louder when Hitler annexed Austria in 1938. Apart from its border with Moravia, the old kingdom of Bohemia was now almost totally surrounded by the Third Reich.

Hitler threatened to invade, using the usual excuses of 'atrocities' against German speakers by the Czechoslovak authorities. A flurry of diplomacy in September 1938 tried to stop this, but ended up with Italy, France and Britain caving in to Hitler's demands at the notorious Munich Conference, an event at which the Czechs weren't even represented. Neville Chamberlain returned from it waving his piece of paper and promising 'peace in our time'. Hitler, it had been agreed, could have his German-speaking areas and would leave the rest of Czechoslovakia alone. German troops moved in at once.

Most of Czechoslovakia's border defences and much of its resources and industry were in these areas: once they were under Nazi control, the rest of the country was easy prey. Hitler invaded the rest of Bohemia and Moravia on 15 March 1939 (Slovakia declared itself 'independent' on the same date, but was actually just a puppet Nazi state). Chamberlain realised, too late, that Hitler had been lying to him, and the Second World War became inevitable.

New regimes issue stamps as soon as possible. The first ones for the new 'Protectorate of Bohemia and Moravia' were over-prints on old Czech stamps. In July 1939, the first original design appeared, featuring linden leaves. Pictorials of local landmarks soon followed. Both of these featured the protectorate's name (Bohemia and Moravia) in German and Czech.

In 1942, the stamps changed. Suddenly the inscription across the top, in big letters, read 'Deutsches Reich', with any mention of Bohemia and Moravia banished to the bottom of the stamp. The old pictorials were replaced with an image of Hitler from a photograph by his 'court photographer', Heinrich Hoffmann.

This reflects a new intensity of the German occupation. On 27 September 1941, Reinhard Heydrich had been put in charge of the protectorate. Unlike many Nazis, Heydrich came from a cultured background, his parents both being musicians (he himself played the violin well). He possibly had Jewish ances-tors. Yet as a young man he became involved in ultra-right, anti-Semitic politics, and as he made his way up the Nazi Party ladder, he gained a reputation for ruthlessness. Even Hitler called him 'the man with the iron heart'. In Prague, he began a campaign against Czech cultural institutions, which had had some freedom up to that point. The capital's Jewish community was ruthlessly targeted.

On 27 May 1942, Heydrich was assassinated by Jozef Gabčík and Jan Kubiš, two Czech agents parachuted into the country by the British Special Operations Executive. The Nazis ordered massive reprisals in which an estimated 5,000 people died. The village of Lidice (initially linked, via false intelligence, to the attack) was razed to the ground and its inhabitants murdered or sent to death camps. Gabčík and Kubiš, who had fled after the assassination, were hunted down by the Gestapo, taking final refuge in Prague's cathedral of Saints Cyril and Methodius, and committing suicide to evade capture.

The Nazis issued a stamp commemorating the first anniversary of Heydrich's death.

The last stamps from the protectorate date from 1944. As the war drew to a close, Czech resistance underwent a resurgence. Battles were fought in the streets of Prague between partisans and Nazis, before the Soviet army arrived to set the seal on the city's liberation.

The Sudeten Germans paid a high price for their treachery. Three million of them were driven out of Bohemia and Moravia, leaving a few hundred thousand behind (largely individuals deemed to have 'useful skills' by the country's new rulers). They joined a sea of fellow German-speakers evicted from Poland, creating vast logistical and humanitarian problems for the Allied occupying powers in Germany itself. In the expulsion from the Czech lands, many scores from the occupation were violently settled – it is estimated that around 20,000 people died in this way. Compared with Nazi atrocities, this is, of course, a small figure, but it still means a lot of suffering: such is the grim arithmetic of war.

Bohemia and Moravia were reunited with Slovakia, as Czechoslovakia was reconstituted after the war. Elections were held in 1946. In February 1948, the Communists seized power with a coup.

Canal Zone

YES, THERE ARE plenty of canals around the world, and plenty of zones, too. But the Canal Zone that appears on these stamps refers to one canal and one zone in particular.

Once Europeans had worked out quite how narrow the Isthmus of Panama was, they soon began to think of methods of exploiting that fact. After all, if crossing the Isthmus of Panama meant you could get travel between the Atlantic and Pacific oceans without having to go as far as the bottom of South America and then up again, then it was worth considering.

In 1698, Scotland made one of its few independent colonial attempts. They thought it would be a good idea for them to establish a Scottish colony on the Isthmus, controlling a land route between the two oceans. It didn't turn out that well. In fact, it turned out disastrously. The settlers themselves experienced a wide range of problems including disease and, in particular, Spanish hostility. In the end, a Spanish military force besieged the colony and the colonists eventually gave up and went home. The hugely expensive disaster did, however, have enormous unexpected side-effects in Britain. The cost of the failed expedition had such a disastrous financial effect on Scotland that it made many Scots see an advantage in union with England and helped ensure acceptance of the Act of Union in 1707 which made Scotland and England parts of the same kingdom.

In the mid-nineteenth century, the US was keen to ease sea traffic between its western and eastern seaboards by building a railroad across the Isthmus. However, from the sixteenth century onwards, assorted people could see that the ideal solution would be a canal across the Isthmus. It was after the explosion of canal-building in the eighteenth and nineteenth centuries that interest in the idea of building a Panama Canal really began to get very serious.

The successful completion of the Suez Canal gave particular impetus to plans and, in fact, it was Frenchman Ferdinand de Lesseps, the Suez Canal conqueror himself, who in 1881 set out to conquer the Isthmus of Panama as well. Instead, it conquered him. Once again disease became a major problem. A staggering 20,000 lives may have been lost, and generally speaking progress was slow, inefficient and hugely expensive, none of them adjectives you really want to hear describing a major engineering project. In the end, the project collapsed and construction of the canal halted.

It was time for the Americans to step in. They were already deeply involved with the area because of the railroad they had built across the Isthmus, and now their involvement was about to get a whole lot deeper. In 1902, the US Congress passed the Spooner Act, authorising the buying of the French company and the construction of a canal.

This, however, would be dependent on successful negotiations with the government of Colombia which at that stage controlled the area. The negotiations were not successful, but, as it turned out, that wasn't going to stop the project. Colombia might not offer the Americans what they needed, but a new country would. Panama declared itself conveniently independent of Colombia, with some American assistance, and the United States rushed to recognise its new friends. A deal was quickly done between the United States and the new country, and in 1904, the Canal Zone was established. This was a strip of land across the Isthmus that the US controlled in return for annual payments to Panama and on which it would be able to build and operate the canal.

Work quickly began. Even with the improvements in medical science and engineering that had taken place since the disastrous French effort, building the canal still cost thousands of lives. Nevertheless, the canal was finally finished and open for traffic on 15 August 1914. It was a huge engineering achievement and would have been an even bigger news story than it was if the

Austro-Hungarian army hadn't just entered Serbia three days earlier, in the opening campaign of the First World War.

The Canal Zone was 10 miles wide and the United States exercised power there under the original deal 'as if it were the sovereign'. This included stationing troops there. The zone became home to Fort Gulick, the location for the School of the Americas, a military training installation that became famous, and in the eyes of critics, infamous, for training thousands of military personnel from Latin-American countries during the Cold War period (it was celebrated on an Airmail stamp in 1961). Whole communities developed in the Canal Zone.

The first stamps for the zone were sets of overprints, on stamps of both Panama and the United States, in 1904. Two decades of overprints on Panamanian stamps followed, then in 1924 overprints on US stamps, then, in 1928, the zone's own definitive stamps, designed and printed in the US. These featured various individuals who had been influential in building the canal. A 1931 Airmail series shows a plane flying over the canal. A 1939 series celebrating the twenty-fifth anniversary of the canal's opening shows key parts of the canal.

After the war, the zone tended to issue single commemorative stamps rather than sets (as did the US at this time). One showed the Thatcher Ferry Bridge (now known as the Bridge of the Americas), and is famous for an 'error'. A sheet of stamps was issued missing a rather important ingredient – the bridge itself. The postal authorities then tried to issue more errors, to drive down the price of the original errors, but were taken to court by a Boston stamp dealer to stop them.

US control of a strip of the Canal Zone caused extensive resentment in Panama over the years, and in the end, in 1977, the US agreed a new deal with Panama. This recognised Panama as sovereign in the territory of the Canal Zone, but allowed the US to remain involved in managing and operating the canal for a further period of twenty years.

The new deal came into operation in 1979, terminating the Canal Zone as it had existed. The last Canal Zone stamp, showing an electric towing locomotive, dates from 1978. Nevertheless, the US remained deeply involved in the Panama Canal, and when it invaded Panama in December 1989, part of its rationale for doing so was that Panama's dictator General Noriega was a threat to US rights and interests in the Panama Canal area.

However, despite swift American success in the war, the end of American power in the canal area was not far off. Finally, in December 1999, Panama took full control of the canal.

Cilicia

IT SOUNDS SOMEWHAT classical and indeed it is. As people who have holidayed on Turkey's beautiful southern coast may know, Cilicia is a part of southern Anatolia with a long history, including some very interesting classical bits, and plenty of others, too.

Cilicia sits in a key strategic location, at the meeting place of Asia Minor and the Levant. Not surprisingly, therefore, it has seen plenty of invaders come and go. Long before classical times, for instance, the mighty Hittite Empire seized control of the region. When Greeks first arrived in the region, they were probably Mycenaean Greeks. But other mighty Asian empires would soon develop an interest in the area. The Assyrians, for instance, would invade and occupy. And then the Achaemenid Persian Empire, one of the world's most spectacular, would seize the region. Under the Achaemenids the area enjoyed limited autonomy.

But more Greeks were coming from the west. At the end of the fifth century BC, the soldier and author Xenophon marched through Cilicia with the famous 10,000 Greek mercenaries en route to the Battle of Cunaxa near present-day Baghdad in an attempt to seize the throne for Cyrus the Younger from his brother Artaxerxes II. They won the battle, but lost the war. Cyrus the Younger was killed and the Greeks were left with a long march north to the Black Sea Coast and eventual escape.

Less than a century later, however, another army from the west would erupt into Cilicia. Yes, Alexander the Great passed through en route to even greater conquests. And eventually, after Alexander's early death, Cilicia would end up as part of the Seleucid Empire, under a dynasty founded by Seleucus, one of Alexander's generals.

And then it was the turn of the Romans. A key point in the rise of Pompey the Great was the defeat of the Cilician pirates who had been plaguing shipping, at the Battle of Korakesion, modern-day Alanya, in 67 BC. Among many visitors to the great cities of Roman Cilicia would be St Paul himself.

After the end of the Western Roman Empire in the fifth century AD, Cilicia continued to be a part of the Eastern Roman Empire, or as we tend to know it from that period on, the Byzantine Empire. In the seventh century, however, Muslim Arab armies invaded the area and used it as a base for raiding further north into Anatolia. But it was not to be the end of Byzantine power in the region. Around 964, Nicephorus II Phocas reconquered the region for Byzantium.

And soon, another Christian power would emerge to challenge Byzantine authority in the region. In the eleventh century, fighting in their homeland to the north prompted the beginning of a move by Armenians into the region. In 1080, Armenians set up a principality that would eventually develop into the Armenian Kingdom of Cilicia, or, as it was also known, the slightly less grand-sounding Little Armenia. The Rubenids were first barons and then kings from 1199 to 1226. They were followed by the Hethumids.

The Kingdom of Cilicia played a major role in assisting the Crusades and Crusader states but eventually Christian political and military power disappeared from the Holy Land, and the Armenian Kingdom of Cilicia would eventually come to an end, too. In 1375, Muslim Mamluks took the area, and they were followed by Turks. By 1515, Cilicia was part of the Ottoman Empire.

The city of Adana saw a massacre of Armenians in 1909, and worse was to come for the Armenians elsewhere in Turkey during the First World War. However, by late 1918, the Ottoman Empire was under intense pressure from advancing Allied forces and after it eventually signed an Armistice with the Allies, part of Cilicia came under French control. Troops from the French Armenian Legion landed at Mersin in November 1918 and, after that, the French expanded their control across the area. The French saw the area as something of a safe haven for Armenians in the region, and yes, they made sure that it had stamps with the name Cilicia, or at least its French version – Cilicie – printed on them. There are a range of overprints, first on Turkish stamps, then, once the Turkish ones ran out, French ones.

The French occupation of Cilicia was in line with other Allied occupations of parts of the Ottoman Empire after the end of the war. However, while the French managed to consolidate their hold on neighbouring Syria, in Cilicia they were going to have a few more problems. Well, a lot more problems actually.

As Mustafa Kemal led the resurgence of Turkish nationalism after the collapse of the Ottoman Empire, the French suddenly found, to their surprise, that there was significant resistance to their rule in Cilicia. The Battle of Marash, in early 1920, saw a disastrous defeat for French and Armenian forces by Turkish nationalist forces. After bitter fighting, French forces were pushed out of the city. And worse was to come for the French.

In the end, the French had had enough and they decided to cut their losses in Cilicia, concentrating on their other holdings in the region, particularly in neighbouring Syria. In early 1922, French forces finally withdrew. Many Armenians had already gone as well. And Cilicia remains a part of Turkey today.

Confederate States of America

AMERICA, FAMOUSLY, DOES not feature living people on its stamps, even presidents. Recently, this rule has been eroded somewhat: a 2013 series featured actors from the Harry Potter films – the US Postal Service argued that the stamps portrayed the roles rather than the actors. Nonetheless, Daniel Radcliffe managed to do something that Theodore Roosevelt, Dwight Eisenhower and JFK failed to, appear 'live' on an American stamp.

However, when the South split from the North back in 1860/61, this rule was broken, and the South's leader Jefferson Davis featured on the stamps of the Confederate States of America. He would later be joined by George Washington, Thomas Jefferson and Andrew Jackson – all safely dead; their images were also used by the Union in a philatelic propaganda war, whereby each side claimed to be representing the true spirit of these great men.

Jefferson Davis was not a firebrand secessionist. He once said that the day Mississippi seceded from the Union was the saddest one of his life. Rather than make a grab for power, he simply offered his services to the new Confederacy and was surprised to find himself elected its leader. But he was, and duly appeared on a stamp in October 1861, six months after General PGT Beauregard opened fire on Fort Sumter and began the American Civil War.

By that time, the South had already attempted a quick win. Their forces had marched north and met and defeated the Union at the Battle of Bull Run, but rather than press on for victory, they had been forced by their own losses to retreat. They were now digging themselves in for a longer struggle, during which they hoped to get the European powers to put diplomatic pressure on the North to come to the negotiating table.

Europe, especially Britain, did a lot of business with the South. This was exemplified by the Confederacy's stamps, which were designed by a Frenchman, Jean Ferdinand Joubert de la Ferté, and of which several printings were made by Thomas de la Rue in London (London printings are particularly popular with philatelists). Europe needed the South's cotton; the South needed Europe's money.

Lincoln brilliantly cut off this source on 1 January 1863 with his Emancipation Proclamation, a presidential Executive Order which formally abolished slavery. Slavery had always been the underlying cause of the conflict, but neither side would face the issue in such bald terms. Instead, the war was claimed to be (and partially was) about the integrity of the Union against the concept of States' Rights. This was essentially a domestic American matter, so Europe could trade with either side with at least a pretence of conscience. The proclamation made it clear: the Union was fighting to abolish slavery. Once it was apparent that this was the central issue, it became morally much harder to trade with the South. Public opinion in Britain was particularly strong on this matter.

As the trade dried up, the Confederacy began to finance its war by printing money, and inflation soon resulted – later Confederate stamps have higher denominations than earlier ones.

They battled on, however. Davis was not a particularly effective president, but he was good at choosing generals: for the first part of the war, Robert E. Lee, Thomas 'Stonewall' Jackson and Nathan Bedford Forrest outsmarted and outfought their northern rivals. However, Jackson was killed – by friendly fire – in May 1863, and the North began to find its own military leaders, William T. Sherman and Ulysses Grant. These men were aided by the fact that, without European support, the South was getting ever weaker economically. It also had a smaller population.

July 1863 saw the two events generally agreed to have been the military turning points of the war. The Battle of Gettysburg was followed two days later by the fall of the Confederate stronghold of Vicksburg on the Mississippi (Confederate bonds, still traded on European markets, collapsed in value after these events). Gettysburg shattered the Southerners' morale and meant they never attacked the North again; Vicksburg opened the great waterway to the south to the Union navy. A year later, General Sherman began his 'scorched earth' march through Georgia, the background to *Gone with the Wind*, and the game was up.

The American Civil War is, like the First World War, a classic example of a war that nobody expected to last long but which degenerated into horrific slaughter. This was largely due to the new military technology that was not understood at the outbreak of hostilities. New rifles were much more accurate; new types of bullet could inflict much more vicious wounds – but systems for caring for the injured remained unchanged. Estimates of losses vary, but a figure of 750,000 dead is possible. This is fifteen times the number that had died in the total of all America's wars up to that point, and more than that nation lost in both twentieth-century world wars added together.

Post was another new factor in this war, not strategically but for the historian. The American Civil War was the first major conflict where ordinary combatants could write home to their loved ones. Many of the letters that have survived are heartbreaking, written, as many were, by men who did not survive. Intriguingly, though the war was in many ways about a moral issue, few from either side seem to dwell on these big topics: family love, comradeship and fatalism, not tub-thumping rectitude, are the overriding themes of these letters.

After the war, Jefferson Davis was imprisoned but never tried for treason. A general amnesty for Southern leaders was announced in 1868, and Davis lived for another twenty-one years. His opposite number in Washington was, of course, not so fortunate.

Cundinamarca

ONE OF THE themes of this book is that the settled-looking atlas in which we find fixed 'countries' is actually just a snapshot of something that is perpetually changing. It's a bit like Alfred Wegener's discovery of continental drift – beneath what looks like something immutable, there is unending motion. Nowhere is this truer than South America in the nineteenth century.

Look at Colombia, for example, which the modern atlas shows as a squarish country wedged neatly into the top left of South America. It wasn't always like this.

Before the Conquistadors arrived, of course, it was simply home to a range of indigenous peoples: coastal dwellers like the Wayuu, rainforest people like the Barasana and the Nukak, mountain people like the Kagaba or the Muisca. Europeans started appearing on its northern coast in 1499. Stories of fantastic hordes of gold soon gripped the new arrivals – none more alluring than that of the native king whose coronation involved his being covered in gold dust. Unlike many of the stories, this one was true: the king was the leader of the Muisca, who lived in what was later Cundinamarca. The Spaniards called him the Gilded One, or El Dorado. This name later mutated to a place, which became a magnet for explorers and adventurers. One of these, Francisco de Orellana, became the first man to traverse the continent: starting from Quito, he crossed the Andes and followed the east-flowing rivers that he found. At one point, he was attacked by fierce female warriors, and named the river he was on at the time for them: the Amazon. He did not find El Dorado, though.

The Conquistadors, who arrived in the early sixteenth century, enforced their rule brutally. The last Muisca king, Aquiminzaque, was decapitated in 1540. An old Muisca village called Bacatá was destroyed and a new city built on the spot: this became Santa Fe de Bogotá, capital of 'New Granada'.

In 1717, New Granada became a viceroyalty of the Spanish Empire. It included modern Colombia, Ecuador, Panama and Venezuela, though Venezuela split off from it in 1777. However, the mother country of this empire was growing ever weaker. In 1808, Spain was taken over by Napoleon, who dethroned its king, Ferdinand VII, and replaced him with his own brother Joseph Bonaparte, making it effectively a French client state. Rebellions began all over its South American empire.

Cundinamarca declared itself a 'Free Independent State' in 1810. It initially swore loyalty to King Ferdinand, but in 1813, it declared total independence. Three years later it lost that independence again: Ferdinand had been restored in 1813, and Spain soon launched an expedition to reclaim its territories. In 1816, General Pablo Morillo recaptured Bogotá for the old rulers.

Enter Simón José Antonio de la Santísima Trinidad Bolívar y Palacios, or, more simply, Simón Bolívar (a man featured on stamps all round South America). Bolívar was born in Venezuela in 1783. Like many great anti-imperialists, he was the product of the system he set out to destroy. His father was a colonel (though both his parents died when he was young, and he was largely brought up by a family slave, Hippolyta). He studied with the liberal educator Simón Rodríguez, then at military academies, first in Venezuela and then in Spain. Once in Europe, he travelled widely and witnessed the coronation of Napoleon.

Back in South America, he continued his military service. Venezuela saw a series of coups and countercoups in the 1810s, which Bolívar managed to ride out, despite his clear anti-colonial views. In 1819, he turned his attention to neighbouring New Granada. A series of battles against the Spanish and their allies followed; the one fought at Boyacá, north-east of Bogotá, on 7 August 1819 was the decisive one (the day is still a national holiday in Colombia). New Granada became the 'Republic of Greater Colombia' (*Gran Columbia*, named after Christopher Columbus), with Bolívar as its president.

Bolívar might have been a liberator, but he wanted a powerful centralised government. Other people, including his deputy, Santander, wanted more local rule. The cracks in the new regime soon opened and Ecuador went its own way. In 1857, the nation (soon renamed the Granadine Confederation) split into seven states. Cundinamarca was one of these – a rectangular strip across the middle of the country, mountainous in its west, the Orinoco basin in its east. In 1861, the Granadine Confederation underwent another rebrand, and became the United States of Colombia.

Cundinamarca's first stamps were issued in 1870, featuring the state's coat of arms. Further values, with similar images, were issued in 1877, 1884 and 1885. Other 'united states' produced their own stamps, too. Antioquia, the area around Medellín, is of particular philatelic interest due to the rarity of its 1868 issue.

In 1886, the states were reined in and became departments of a new, federal, centralised republic. They continued to issue stamps for two decades, though the republic also issued its own national ones from that date.

In 1899, Colombia collapsed into civil war. The conflict was essentially a rerun of that between Bolívar and Santander, one side wanting a strong central state, the other wanting more liberalism and democracy. The war ended in 1902 (Cundinamarca issued its last, and fullest, set of stamps shortly afterwards), but Colombian society divides along these lines to this day. Violent civil conflict has erupted on several occasions since 1899, most notably in the 1950s, during a period known as *La Violencia*, and in the battle with the FARC, a far-left guerrilla group, which has been operating since 1964. The booming demand for drugs in the USA has created a third party in these struggles.

At the time of writing, Colombia appears to be moving towards peace. In 2016, a deal was signed between the government and FARC, but this was then rejected in a referendum. Shortly after that, Columbia's president, Juan Manuel Santos, was awarded the Nobel Peace Prize. A second deal was then negotiated, after which Santos decided to avoid the potential pitfalls of referenda and simply had the treaty ratified in the country's congress. FARC members are currently handing over their weapons and moving to 'transition camps', where they will live until re-entering civil society. One must hope that the peace holds in this fascinating, war-torn country.

Cyrenaica

SOME OF THE entities in this book are short-lived; some of the names are modern inventions. Cyrenaica definitely falls into neither category.

Cyrenaica ultimately gets its name from Cyrene, a Greek colony established on what is now the eastern Libyan coast, allegedly in 631 BC by settlers from the Greek island of Thera, or as it tends to be better-known in Britain, Santorini, the stunningly beautiful island that is the possible origin of the Atlantis stories and, in more recent times, that has become a major destination for cruise liners.

Cyrene wasn't the only Greek colony in the area, by any means, but it was the major one, so, not unreasonably, they named the area after it. It became a key centre of Greek life and culture. It had its own school of philosophers, again named, not unreasonably, the Cyrenaics. It had its own celebratory classical author, Callimachus (although he doesn't top many best-seller lists these days). And its own celebratory mathematicians, including, of course, Eratosthenes – a man who, among other achievements, calculated the circumference of the earth and came up with the famous Sieve of Eratosthenes, less metal implement with holes in, and more something to do with finding prime numbers. Yes, ancient Cyrene was quite a place. Although to be fair, both Callimachus and Eratosthenes legged it to the even more exciting Alexandria in Egypt when they got the chance.

Persian invaders turned up and after Alexander, the Ptolemaic dynasty from Egypt took an interest. Then in 96 BC, one Ptolemy Apion, who'd ended up as King of Cyrene, died without children and left Rome in his will, not something like a few books and a picture of himself, but instead Cyrene. Cyrenaica was a place under the Romans, appearing, for instance, in the name of a Roman province 'Creta et Cyrenaica'. This province combined as you've probably now guessed the Greek island of Crete and Cyrenaica. The geographic logic of this isn't exactly obvious and eventually the Romans had had enough of the strange arrangement and administratively separated the two territories. If the Romans had printed postage stamps we would probably have some of theirs with Cyrenaica on.

Ancient Cyrene had a flourishing Jewish community and Simon of Cyrene is said in the gospels to have been forced to carry the cross of Jesus. A major rebellion among Jewish communities in the eastern Mediterranean region in the early second century AD saw heavy fighting in Cyrenaica.

In the seventh century, Arab armies conquered the area, and in the sixteenth century it became part of the Ottoman Empire.

Then in 1911 erupted one of those wars that very few people (outside Italy, Turkey and Libya) have actually ever heard of. Yes, it's the Italo-Turkish War of 1911–12. With Italy only just having been reunified in the nineteenth century, it was, in the late nineteenth century, for understandable reasons, quite far behind long-standing imperial powers like Britain and France in the empire-building race. For a people who would soon start seeing themselves as, in some sense, heirs to the imperial heritage of ancient Rome, this was somewhat humiliating, and with Britain and France eyeing up assorted bits of the now-enfeebled Ottoman Empire, Italy started eyeing up Libya, including Cyrenaica. It was conveniently located not far across the Med, and it had been a key part of the Roman Empire. It was expected among many Italians to be a nice, easy invasion for their forces. It wasn't.

Italians deployed huge forces and their latest military technology including aircraft. In fact, the war saw the very first use of bombardment from the air. Nevertheless, they found it hard to push far inland from the coastal cities and they suffered some significant defeats, including in Cyrenaica. For instance, the young Mustafa Kemal, who eventually, as the founder of modern Turkey would become known as Atatürk, led his forces to a victory over the Italians at the Battle of Tobruk. Eventually, however, a war broke out in the Balkans, and Turkey agreed to a peace deal. Many of the locals, however, weren't so happy with the deal and would continue to resist Italian control and fight for autonomy instead. Ahmed Sharif as-Senussi united Cyrenaican tribes against the Italians and, during the First World War, attacked British positions in Egypt. His nephew and successor, Idris, by contrast, made peace with the British and tried to carve out an autonomous realm for himself within the context of Italy's efforts in Libya. However, Idris was not able to achieve this and he went into exile in Egypt. The Italians proceeded with a brutal campaign to impose their rule on the whole of Cyrenaica.

The Italians printed stamps for Cyrenaica, beginning with simple overprints in 1923. A 1926 series featured St Francis of Assisi, not a figure usually celebrated on the stamps of Islamic countries. In the same year, Italy issued special stamps for its colonies, and in 1928 the first ones with 'Cirenaica' printed on them appeared. These were largely still about Italy and its achievements.

In 1934, Italy united Cyrenaica with its other colonies into one colony of Libya. However, Italian control of Cyrenaica was not to last long. In 1940, Italian troops invaded Egypt, setting off a North African branch of the Second World War that would drag in Rommel and his Afrika Korps and see campaigns smash across Cyrenaican territory a number of times in both directions. The port of Tobruk in Cyrenaica became one of the focal points of this North African war and, indeed, one of the most familiar names from the entire history of British operations in the whole of the Second World War. In the end, of course, the Axis powers lost, and after Britain took control of the region suddenly Cyrenaica was in the news again and so was Idris. In 1949, with British support, Idris declared the Emirate of Cyrenaica with himself as emir. A handsome series of definitive stamps, featuring an Arab horseman in a desert setting, was issued in 1950. However, in 1951 the Kingdom of Libya became independent and Idris became King of all Libya.

Idris was toppled in 1969 in a coup led by Gaddafi. And recently the fluid and volatile situation in Libya after Gaddafi's toppling had seen something of a resurgence of Cyrenaican demands for autonomy.

Danish West Indies

YES, DENMARK AND the West Indies doesn't at first seem a natural fit. You know that the Vikings went to loads of places you didn't entirely expect, and even made it as far as Newfoundland, but surely even they couldn't have made it as far as the Caribbean.

Well no, they didn't, but some other Danes did. Eventually.

Already in the sixteenth century, assorted European powers had established bases for themselves in the region, and the Danes didn't want to be left entirely behind. It was, to put it mildly, a bit of a slow start. The Danish king granted a permit for trading in the region as early as 1625, but then not much happened, partly because Denmark decided to get deeply involved in Europe with the mass slaughter instead now known as the Thirty Years' War.

However, in the second half of the seventeenth century, the situation began to look a bit more hopeful for Denmark in the Caribbean, for a while that is. Captain Erik Nielsen Smit made some successful trading voyages to the area, and other Danes started to join in. Then war and the weather temporarily stepped in to thwart plans again.

Finally, when it seemed like Denmark might never become a major Caribbean power, it did. Well, sort of. For a short time. It was Captain Erik Smit to the rescue again. In 1665, with a Royal Commission tucked under his arm, and despite storms and a war between England and the Netherlands raging both in the Caribbean and elsewhere, Smit established a Danish colony on the island of St Thomas. Some English and Dutch even joined in to help establish the new colony. And then, having planted the Danish flag firmly in the Caribbean, Smit promptly died, privateers promptly attacked, the weather promptly turned foul and disease soon struck, resulting in the collapse of the colony. The English departed for St Croix, the Danes went home and the Dutch stole what had been left behind.

You'd almost have thought that the Danes might have given up on their Caribbean dreams entirely at this point, but the inheritors of a Viking tradition had other ideas.

This time the Danes did a deal with England to ensure that Denmark could establish colonies on uninhabited islands, and in 1671 the Danish West India Company got its royal charter from the Danish king, along with two ships and a load of criminals and prostitutes whom the king felt Denmark could spare. In 1672, a Danish colony was established, again on St Thomas. Eventually, after a slight dispute with local British authorities, St John also came under Danish control. In 1733, the Danes added St Croix to their Caribbean collection after buying it from the French. And they even had designs on Crab Island. A slave rebellion on St John in 1733 was eventually crushed with the help of French and Swiss troops from Martinique.

At some points it looked like it might be going well for the Danish West India Company. But in the end, it wasn't. The company went bankrupt, so the King of Denmark, Frederick V, took direct control instead.

Would the islands now have a bright long-term golden future under the control of the Danish throne? Well, in a word, no.

War had caused problems with the initial establishment of the Danish presence in the Caribbean, and it was about to cause a few more problems with the ongoing health and wealth of that presence. Napoleon was setting Europe alight and the Danish West Indies were not going to escape the consequences entirely.

In 1801, a British fleet turned up and demanded that the Danish West Indies surrender. It seemed to the Danes the sensible option was to comply, so they did. The British left the islands in 1802. But not for long. In 1807, they returned. Once again, it was a very civilised invasion, with not a shot being fired. This time, however, Britain kept the islands rather longer. Until 1815, in fact.

Then in 1848, another slave rebellion erupted, leading to the governor freeing the slaves. The introduction of sugar beet also led to the near economic collapse of the islands. By 1852, the Danes had, finally, just about had enough and the Danish parliament for the first time debated selling the islands to someone looking for some desirable, pre-owned property with stunning Caribbean views.

However, fortunately for the purposes of this book, the Danes did, in the end, hang on long enough to start producing stamps for the Danish West Indies, thus securing for them a kind of perforated immortality in stamp albums and stamp catalogues across the world. The first postage stamp for the Danish West Indies was produced in 1865, with new issues following in 1873 and 1900. The 1900 series was rather dull, featuring a coat of arms, but in 1905, the colony produced its most attractive issue. The lower denominations feature a cameo of King Christian IX surrounded by art nouveau frame and lettering, and the upper ones a picture of the training ship *Ingolf* in the islands' main harbour, Charlotte Amalie.

Sadly for the Danish government, not even revenue from sales of Danish West Indies stamps to stamp collectors could make the colonies attractive in the long term to Denmark and soon the islands would be under new management. In 1867, the US had already tried to buy the islands, but the Danes wanted $7.5 million and the US Senate turned down the deal. In the early twentieth century, the US offered $5 million for the islands and the Danish parliament turned down the deal. Denmark finally managed to offload the islands onto the United States, which was interested in the islands' strategic significance, for $25 million in 1917.

The USA then renamed the islands the United States Virgin Islands, leading to much schoolboy laughter over the years ahead. The name had, however, nothing to do with the level of sexual experience of the islanders and everything to do with the fact that Christopher Columbus, on first encountering the numerous islands of the region, had named them after Saint Ursula's Eleven Thousand Virgins.

Today, the United States Virgin Islands are considerably more American than they are Danish, but elements of the islands' history under the Danes still remain, including, for instance, the names of towns like Frederiksted and Christiansted on St Croix, and, of course, the section for the Danish West Indies in stamp albums across the world.

Danzig

DANZIG IS A name that seems at the same time familiar and unfamiliar. All those who have looked at the origins of the Second World War will know the name well. And yet not all those people could probably locate it on a modern map and many of them won't know that it had a long and fascinating history prior to 1939.

Danzig is the German name of the city in Poland now known by its Polish name Gdańsk. It is a port on Poland's Baltic Coast and is situated on the west side of a massive bay or gulf, known not surprisingly as Gdańsk Bay or the Gulf of Gdańsk. On the east side of the same gulf is Kaliningrad, now in Russia, previously Königsberg in East Prussia.

Considering most people will know of the city because of twentieth-century events, it may come as something of a surprise to know that the city may be about a thousand years old. Its exact origins are somewhat hazy but, in fact, it celebrated its millennium in 1997 based on the evidence of the Life of Saint Adalbert. Saint Adalbert is said to have baptised people in a place that sounds like Gdańsk, shortly before his missionary efforts in the area were somewhat prematurely terminated by martyrdom.

Certainly, in the thirteenth century it acquired municipal autonomy and was fast emerging as a major trading centre. In 1308, King Władysław of Poland was having a bit of trouble with Gdańsk. Władysław did have some significant achievements as a king, even though he was not one of history's towering figures physically. In fact his rather graphic nickname was Władysław Elbow-High. The Teutonic Knights, an order of knights that became powerful and rich through crusading and other activities, in the Baltic region, went into Gdańsk to 'restore order', which they did with a certain amount of slaughtering and destruction. Having arrived there, they liked the look of it and decided that, in the absence of a juicy deal with the Poles, they would keep it. Not only that, but they'd seize more territory around it.

Not surprisingly, the Poles weren't hugely keen on this and, in general, the situation between the Teutonic Knights and Poland was about to hit a rocky patch – so rocky, in fact, that a large number of Polish-Teutonic wars were to follow over the next

two centuries as the two sides tried to sort out various griev-
ances and borders.

The Teutonic Knights managed to hold onto Gdańsk/Danzig
for most of this time. They improved its fortifications and developed its German side. And the city became part of the Hanseatic
League, a league that had basically nothing to do with football
and everything to do with mutual self-interest between a bunch
of merchant cities on the Baltic and North Sea coast.

By the mid-fifteenth century, however, Gdańsk/Danzig had
had enough of the Teutonic Knights and joined in a Prussian rebellion against them. This led to yet another war between Poland
and the Teutonic Knights, which the Knights lost, and when the
war ended in 1466 Gdańsk/Danzig was confirmed as part of the
Kingdom of Poland, but it was given extensive autonomy.

Gdańsk/Danzig entered a golden Renaissance age when it
was the most thriving port in the Baltic. Not that there weren't
the occasional hiccups. For instance, the Danzig rebellion over a
disputed succession to the throne led to the Siege of Danzig in
1577, which ended in a sort of score draw for the two sides.

However, the city suffered rather more when it fell to the
Russians after the 1734 Siege of Danzig, and in 1772 it was seized
by the rising power Prussia and annexed to Prussia in 1793. The
city saw assorted actions during the Napoleonic Wars and found
itself made a free city by Napoleon in 1807. Nevertheless, at the
end of the Napoleonic Wars, Danzig was restored to Prussia.

Meanwhile, Poland had been going through even worse
times. The late eighteenth century saw a process of gradual dis-
mantling and partitioning of Poland by its powerful neighbours.
Even though Napoleon temporarily restored a client Polish state,
the Duchy of Warsaw, after the fall of Napoleon the only focus
for Poles' dreams of freedom was mainly assorted rebellions. But
the First World War was to change all that and was also to make
Danzig a name in stamp albums around the world.

Huge numbers of Poles fought for the Allies in the First
World War, and Point Thirteen of Woodrow Wilsons's famous

14 Points demanded a new independent Polish state with access
to the sea. At the end of the war, the Poles got their independent
country, and they got their access to the sea through the Polish
Corridor. They also wanted Danzig, but because the city itself
had a German majority, they didn't get that. Instead, the Allies
made Danzig once again a Free City. Well, it was freeish. It was
under the protection of the League of Nations but the Poles had
some rights within the city, including having a post office and a
garrison at Westerplatte.

Danzig had its own stamps, too. The early 1920s saw a flurry
of them. First, as usual, overprints. Then its own definitives,
featuring a Hanseatic 'cog' (ship). Airmail stamps followed, then
another definitive set. As inflation, imported from Germany,
kicked in, further stamps were created – one of which shows,
perhaps, the effects of the inflation, being for the Poor People's
Fund. Overprints followed, then monetary order was reasserted
with fresh definitives.

The Free City solution, however, did not solve the problem of tensions in the area between Germans and Poles. In the
end, the Poles built their own port, Gdynia, within the Polish
Corridor and in Danzig, the Nazis won the 1933 and 1935 elections. A 1937 stamp shows traditional German houses with a
swastika flag flying from one of them.

The status of Danzig and the Polish Corridor became a major
grievance for Hitler. Hitler demanded the return of Danzig to
Germany and also German access across the Polish Corridor.
Tensions with Poland mounted and on 1 September German
troops invaded Poland. One of their key initial targets was
Danzig. Poles inside the Polish Post Office in Danzig bravely
held off German attacks for a whole day before the building
fell. The Polish garrison at Westerplatte courageously held out
for seven days. However, in the end all of Danzig fell and was
annexed to Germany. However, in March 1945, Danzig was captured by the Red Army and in the settlement of territory after
the war, it became Polish Gdańsk again, and remains that to this

day. In 1980, the trade union Solidarity that played such a role in the collapse of Communism in Poland was born in Gdańsk shipyard. Its leader, Lech Walesa, would go on to become president of Poland in 1990.

Dedeagh

WITH A LOT of the locations featured in this book, even if one is not 100 per cent sure where the place is or was, it is at least possible to have a guess roughly on the globe where it might have been. Dedeagh is one of the places that for many would be pretty hard to guess. You sort of either know or you don't. In fact, Dedeagh is the French spelling of the Turkish name Dedeağaç. The fact that it's Turkish via French partly explains why it's hard to guess its location. Another reason is that the place isn't even called Dedeağaç anymore on most maps. Instead it's called Alexandroupoli.

Now Alexandroupoli, as anybody with a bit of knowledge of Greek will know, means the city of Alexander. Probably the most famous Alexander, Alexander the Great, rather famously was very well travelled, if you can call invading a large chunk of Asia travelling. Alexander left behind him a number of cities named after him, including, of course, Alexandria in Egypt, but the Alexander after whom the Dedeagh Alexandroupoli was named is someone else entirely.

The Dedeagh Alexandroupoli is located in Thrace in Greece, just a short distance from Turkey's European border.

It is an area that has seen many invaders come and go over the centuries. For instance, even before Alexander marched his troops through the region en route to Asia, Persian armies had marched past it in the opposite direction en route to cities of classical Greece to the south. Later would come the Romans.

To the west of the future site of Dedeağaç, Thessalonica would become one of the great cities of the Roman Empire, seat of one of the four tetrarchs, and to the east, Constantine would re-establish the Greek city of Byzantion/Byzantium as Constantinopolis, the city of Constantine, and the eastern capital of the Roman Empire.

In 378 at Adrianople (now Edirne in Turkey, on the other side of the border with Greece, and a sister city of Alexandroupoli), the Emperor Valens was killed in battle along with a big chunk of his army by Germanic invaders from the north. But in the fifth century, as the western Roman Empire crumbled, the eastern Roman Empire – or the Byzantine Empire as we tend to call it in this period – lived on.

There were assorted forces moving to the north and one force in particular would play a major and extended role in the region's history – Bulgaria. Many outside Bulgaria will know of it as a place for both winter and summer holidays. Not as many will know about the might of the Bulgarian empire, which was a major force in the region for much of the Middle Ages. For instance, in the ninth century Krum, Khan of Bulgaria, had already taken Adrianople. And the following centuries would see a varied cast of powers competing for control in the region, including – in addition to the Bulgarians – Byzantines, Crusaders, and the Despotate of Epirus.

In the fourteenth century, though, a new power was going to transform power politics in the region. Sultan Murad I came to the Ottoman throne in 1362, and under him Ottoman forces advanced through Thrace, taking Adrianople and then advancing into Bulgaria and seizing Sofia. In 1430, they would take Thessaloniki, too, and in 1453, they took Constantinople itself.

For the next few centuries the area would remain part of the Ottoman Empire, and towards the end a little fishing village called Dedeağaç began to expand when the Istanbul–Thessalinki rail route was built through it in 1896. It also acquired something else, a French post office. This, at first, it is true, seems somewhat unlikely. The Thracian coast of the Ottoman Empire doesn't immediately seem the sort of place you would find a French post office. However, France was one of the European powers that had acquired in the nineteenth century the right to run its own post offices within the Ottoman Empire. It set up a string of them, including another at Thessaloniki, but the one at Dedeağaç was special because it was one of the offices that got its own stamps – or at least overprints on French stamps, with two sets being issued in 1893 and 1902. The 1893 set, of seven denominations, is of interest to collectors as it is reasonably rare.

Dedeağaç/Dedeagh would not have its own stamps for long because the situation in the region was about to see huge geo-political changes again. Already the area had seen the temporary presence of Russian troops during the Russo-Turkish War of 1877–78. And in 1912 the First Balkan War broke out. In November of that year, Bulgarian troops – with Greek assistance – captured Dedeağaç. However, in 1913, during the Second Balkan War, Bulgaria, wanting more territory, attacked Greece and Serbia. This time it was the Greeks who captured Dedeağaç, in July 1913, though Bulgaria got it again in the peace deal that ended the war. In the First World War Bulgaria found itself on the losing side, and a French force occupied the territory while it was decided what the future of the area would be. In the end it was given to Greece and, shortly after, the King of Greece made a visit to the town. The king's name was Alexander and the town's name was changed from Dedeağaç to the much more Greek Alexandroupoli in his honour. Not that it did the king himself that much good: shortly after he was bitten by a monkey and died of septicemia.

During the Second World War, the Bulgarians arrived again. As Germany invaded Greece in 1941, Bulgaria joined in and sent troops into Thrace, retaking land there, including Alexandroupoli, which gave it access to the Mediterranean. Bulgarian troops withdrew from Greece in 1944. The area did see some fighting during the Greek Civil War, but today Alexandroupoli is peacefully part of Greece.

Don Republic, Kuban Republic, United Russia

RUSSIA'S 1917 REVOLUTION is often presented as a kind of instant turning point: one moment the tsar was in charge, the next Russia was Communist. The truth is far messier. There were, of course, two revolutions. The first one, in February, dethroned the tsar and set up the provisional government (elections were planned for 1918), but made the fatal error of not taking Russia out of the First World War, a conflict that was by now loathed by that country's long-suffering citizens. Lenin made no such mistake when he seized power in October 1917. However, even that seizure was provisional. It could be argued that the October Revolution plunged Russia into anarchy rather than created a new order. The next few years would see the country engulfed in civil war.

Numerous forces piled into the power vacuum. There were foreign powers. There were freedom fighters from parts of the old tsarist empire: Poland, Finland, Ukraine, the Baltic states. A Czech army marooned in central Russia got involved in the fighting. There were anarchists, monarchists, moderate socialists – and people who didn't know what the hell was going on, but had been told that their families would be killed if they didn't enlist. A simplified view presents the civil war that followed October 1917 as a battle between the Red Army, led (utterly ruthlessly) by Trotsky, and the Whites, which was actually a loose configuration of groups who had one thing in common, dislike of Bolshevism. A simplified view also sees the war as being fought on three main fronts, north-east, south-east and south-west. As this is not a book on the Russian Revolution, we shall buy into this simplification. This piece focuses on the south-western front.

The initial focus for resistance to the October Revolution came from the Cossacks of South Russia. The Cossacks were not an ethnic or religious group – what bound them together was a sense of belonging to a tribe, or 'Host', of warlike outsiders, with shared customs (including bringing up male children as warriors: by the age of 5, a Cossack boy could ride well and shoot a bow and arrow). Over the centuries, many serfs had run away to join these tough, independent people. The authorities in Moscow had long had an ambivalent attitude to them, using them to keep their borders secure or to extend those borders, but encountering fierce resistance when they tried to tie them down with too much bureaucracy. Rebellious in some ways, Cossack culture is also deeply traditional and religious. They were natural opponents of the atheistic, controlling Bolsheviks.

There were two main Cossack areas in South Russia. Kuban, the most southerly, was across the Sea of Azov from Crimea. Its capital was Yekaterinodar (modern Krasnodar), which means 'Catherine's Gift': the great eighteenth-century empress granted the city and its surroundings to the local Cossack Host. Directly above Kuban was a more nebulously defined area, around Rostov-on-Don and spilling over into modern Ukraine's Donbass region. This was home to the Don Cossack Host.

Kuban's *Rada* (parliament) declared its independence after the February Revolution. However, there was little internal agreement. The October Revolution split Kuban further, into traditionalists and radicals. Alongside these feuding locals was the growing White Army of General Anton Denikin, who had been fighting Germany and its allies in Romania when the revolution happened and was now trying to assemble an anti-Bolshevik force.

The *Krug*, the assembly of the Don Host, declared independence after the October Revolution. However, the Red Army soon overran the area, and let loose a campaign of terror. This, in turn, alienated people so much that an uprising occurred, driving the Bolsheviks out. A second *Krug* announced a new leader, Pyotr Krasnov, who led his forces to a series of military victories. These events and the ones that followed form the background to Mikhail Sholokhov's novel *And Quiet Flows the Don*.

Denikin tried to unify anti-Communist forces in the area, with moderate success. He also proved himself as vicious as his enemies, carrying out his own terror, in his case against Jews, against whom he was violently prejudiced. But in the end, the well-organised Red Army began to prove too much. In 1920, Denikin was replaced by General Pyotr Wrangel, who, despite his nickname of the Black Baron, was a much more humane individual than Denikin. By then the Whites were losing both military initiative and popular support, however. Wrangel's main job turned out to be organising the evacuation of the White Army. The remainder of the Imperial Russian Navy ferried them across the Black Sea to Turkey, with Wrangel leaving on the last boat on 14 November 1920. He became a leading light in the huge and eccentric Russian émigré population, until he was murdered by a Soviet agent in 1928.

All the main players in this drama issued stamps. Kuban's are the least interesting, being overprints onto old Imperial Russian definitives. Most of the Don Republic's are the same, though it did issue a 20 kopek featuring Yermak, a Cossack warrior from the sixteenth century, who had helped Ivan the Terrible drive the Tatars out of Siberia. The stuff of schoolboy romance (unless you're a Tatar), Yermak and an army of under 1,000 men ventured deep into uncharted territory and fought a string of battles with the incumbent rulers. The unpleasant General Denikin issued the most interesting stamps, a series of eleven, printed in Yekaterinodar, bearing the inscription 'United

Russia'. The more decent General Wrangel could only manage a few overprints.

The reprisals of the Red Army against the defeated Cossacks were vicious. A process known as *Raskazachivaniye*, or 'decossackisation', was instigated. Towns were burnt, senior figures in Cossack society murdered, and humbler Cossacks sent into forced exile into other parts of Russia, where many died of starvation. Enmity between the Cossacks and the Soviets continued during the Second World War, when some of them fought for the Nazis. Of these, some fell into British hands as POWs. They were handed over to the Soviet authorities after the conflict, an act that remains controversial to this day, as they were obviously being sent to their deaths (defenders of the act say that it had been agreed with an essential ally, so we could do little else). Modern Russia, with its new nationalist, martial, traditionalist mindset, treats the Cossacks with respect.

East India Postage

IT SEEMS SO bizarre – India, now a massive nation of over a billion people and a rising global economic superpower, was once part of an empire that belonged to Britain. But that's how it was.

Even stranger, British rule in India wasn't even built by the nation and its armies, but by a commercial organisation, the East India Company. 'John Company', as it was known, effectively ran huge parts of the country from 1765 to 1858, which gave it just enough time to issue its own stamps.

The company was founded in 1600, when Elizabeth I was on the throne and Shakespeare was packing audiences in at the Globe with his new hit, *Twelfth Night*. It was a 'joint stock' company with limited shareholder liability – a relatively new invention at the time, but one that changed the world, being the forerunner of the modern PLC. It had a share capital of £75,000; a governor, Sir Thomas Smythe; twenty-four 'committees' (not groups of people but individual directors); and 215 shareholders, drawn from the knights, squires and burgesses of Elizabeth's booming new nation.

Ships were sent east, initially intending to buy spices from what is now Indonesia. They found the Dutch already active in this trade and not welcoming competition. India, however, where the company originally had a simple supply point for 'Indies'-bound vessels at Surat in modern Gujarat, was another matter. Trade took off.

The business of the company quickly became entwined in that of India itself. In 1612, King James I sent an ambassador to the Mughal Emperor Jahangir, asking for special trading rights for it. Jahangir's empire was massive at the time: his capital, Agra, was four times bigger than London. But a deal was struck. By the middle of the century, the company had 'factories' around the Indian coast. The term is misleading: they didn't make things but were simply trading posts, run by a 'factor'. The biggest ones were in Goa, Chittagong, Madras (modern Chennai), Bombay (modern Mumbai) and three small villages, one of which was called Kalikata. The main items traded were cotton and silk, in bolts or as 'piece goods' (curtains, tablecloths, carpets, bedding), indigo, saltpetre and spices from South India. The providers largely received payment in silver.

The situation with the Mughals ebbed and flowed – after the British pirate Henry Avery raided a Mughal treasure ship on which the Emperor Aurangzeb's granddaughter was travelling, the company nearly lost all its rights. But British diplomacy won the day, and the ban was rescinded.

The Mughal Empire began to collapse in the eighteenth century, and in 1739 invaders from Persia overran it, took away most of its treasures and left a virtual power vacuum. The company eagerly expanded into this – rivalled only by the French. The two nations battled over India for two decades, before the French and their allies were defeated at the Battle of Plassey in 1757. The East India Company effectively had India to itself. In 1765, it did a deal with the weakened Mughal emperor to collect his taxes for him (and take a cut, of course).

A famine struck Bengal in 1770 – but fabulous wealth kept flowing into Britain, courtesy of company 'nabobs' (the equivalent of modern oligarchs). Some of that wealth went into keeping parliament sweet, which in turn ensured that British armed forces kept India under control and that the company would be bailed out if it got into financial trouble (which it did in 1772: the notion of 'too big to fail', applied to modern banks, is not new). At its height, John Company carried out half the world's trade, ruled 90 million people, controlled 243,000 square kilometres of land, issued its own coins and could field an army of 200,000 men.

By 1784, public opinion was turning against its abuses of power. Parliament passed the India Act, which increased governmental control over the company. Four years later, its former governor, Warren Hastings, was impeached. Hastings dragged the process on, hoping to wear down his opponents. He was right; once the French Revolution had begun, the trial came to be seen as a sideshow, and he was acquitted. This was probably a fair result – unlike other nabobs, Hastings hadn't grown ridiculously rich from his time in India. (By contrast, Clive, victor of Plassey, made a fortune and founded an aristocratic dynasty.)

The company continued to trade, though now as part of an imperial machine. After the 'Indian Mutiny' of 1857 – more a revolution than a simple mutiny – the British government took over all administrative duties. The East India Company paid its last dividend in 1873 and was wound up the next year.

It just managed to squeeze in two stamp issues before its demise – in 1855 and, as a swansong, in 1860. Values ranged from

8 Pies to 1 Rupee (there were 12 Pies to the Anna, and 16 Annas to the Rupee). Both issues, of course, feature Queen Victoria. Despite the fact that they are over 150 years old and ooze history, some examples are not expensive to collect.

The East India Company is often seen as a kind of bizarre historical relic. However, aspects of its story have a decidedly modern ring to them. In Britain, it mastered the art of lobbying, of influencing a nation's decision-making machinery for its own ends. In India, it found the barriers between business and politics permeable in other ways. It made allies of local rulers with offers of money (in its early days, it offered to provide an English virgin for a Sultan's harem). Those rulers who didn't want to do deals with it tended to have redcoats arriving at their palaces. It was arguably the world's first multinational, with all the political and moral issues associated with such organisations. At the same time, its later, quasi-governmental self can also be seen as a forerunner of the modern 'state corporation' – huge companies like Russia's Gazprom or China's Sinopec, that combine commerce with national politics.

The East India stamps are a last tangible relic of this once mighty organisation. Up until 2006, another was Adwaita, a giant Aldabra tortoise that had reputedly been given to Robert Clive by the crew of a British ship. Adwaita lived in the zoo in one of the world's greatest cities, which had once been the obscure village of Kalikata but which the East India Company made into Calcutta.

Eastern Rumelia

RUMELIA WAS NEVER really a country, though its name appears in old stamp albums. It was a term used by the Ottoman Empire to describe those parts of Europe that it had conquered

– it means 'Land of the Romans'. So 'Rumelia' covered modern Bosnia, Serbia, Montenegro, Albania, Hungary, Greece and Bulgaria, during various eras of that empire.

The story of the Ottoman Empire begins around 1300, when Turkey was a patchwork of small *beyliks* or principalities. One of these was in the area around Söğüt, a town that now boasts a population of 20,000, and wasn't any bigger then (imagine a transcontinental empire starting in Market Harborough). But its ruler Osman and his son Orhan were determined to expand. In 1326, Orhan captured a neighbouring, much bigger city, Bursa (the equivalent, perhaps, of capturing Leicester) and made it his capital. From there, he conquered much of north-west Turkey – but he had his eyes on Europe. In 1354, he secured his first piece, the Gallipoli peninsula.

Using this as a beachhead, Orhan's son Murad marched into Europe. The Byzantine city of Adrianople (modern Edirne, on the border of Greece and Turkey) fell in 1361. Philippopolis, the modern city of Plovdiv, followed two years later: by 1386, the ancient kingdom of Bulgaria was part of the new empire. It would remain that way until the events at the end of this chapter.

By 1450, the Ottomans effectively ruled a Balkan Europe south of the Danube, except Constantinople, the last vestige of the Roman Empire, which they had bypassed. In 1453, this fell into their hands. It became their new capital, Istanbul, straddling Europe and Asia. The fortification built by the victors on the European side of the Bosporus is called *Rumelihisarı* or the Rumelian Castle.

The empire reached its height in the sixteenth century, under Suleiman the Magnificent, when it stretched from Algiers all the way round the Mediterranean to the Adriatic, up to just short of Vienna, to Budapest, across to the Caspian Sea, down to the Persian Gulf via Baghdad and along the coast of modern Arabia and Yemen to the Arabian Sea.

The naval battle of Lepanto in 1571, in which the writer Cervantes fought and lost an arm, marked the end of Ottoman seaborne expansion. On land, they continued to be a massively powerful force until an attempt to capture Vienna failed in 1683. After this, they didn't go into terminal decline so much as stagnate. It was only in the nineteenth century, when new notions of nationalism arose in western Europe, that the Ottomans faced a serious challenge. The independence of Greece became a fashionable cause in the 1820s – Lord Byron died fighting for it (or at least died of inept treatment of minor ailments while waiting to fight for it). Nationalist movements, backed by Russia, began to emerge in the empire's Orthodox Christian provinces: Serbia, Montenegro, Romania and Bulgaria.

In 1875, there were uprisings in Serbia and Herzegovina. Ottoman forces moved in to quell these. When another uprising took place in Bulgaria, the Ottomans were so stretched that they sent in irregular forces, known as bashi-bazouks. These were basically undisciplined thugs, and tales of atrocities soon began emerging. The media spotlight – something we consider quintessentially modern, but which was already a powerful force in late Victorian times – turned on Bulgaria, particularly through the efforts of *New York Herald* war correspondent Januarius MacGahan, whose report of a massacre at the village of Batak grabbed the world's attention.

Nowhere did this create more rage than in Russia, where the ideology of pan-Slavism was powerful. At the end of Tolstoy's *Anna Karenina*, set around this time, Anna's lover Vronsky emulates Byron and goes off to Serbia to fight as an irregular and probably die for Slav freedom.

Russia declared war on the Ottomans on 24 April 1877. They marched through Romania (itself a nominal Ottoman territory which immediately declared independence) and crossed the Danube, besieging the city of Pleven. After six months, this fell, after which the Russians fought their way across the Balkan Mountains, taking Sofia, Plovdiv and Edirne. The Ottomans sued for peace.

A grand congress was called in Berlin to create a new, peaceful Balkans. Unfortunately, it turned into a game between the Great Powers of the time, and largely ignored local realities. Russia was particularly poorly treated – Britain and France, still smarting from the Crimean War two decades earlier, did not let Slav Bulgaria become a free nation again but split it in half. The top half would become The Principality of Bulgaria, which had the bizarre status of being a 'suzerain' of the Ottomans, with independence in internal matters but no control over its foreign policy. The bottom half was effectively returned to the Ottomans as a province. This was Eastern Rumelia.

As a new political entity, Eastern Rumelia soon issued stamps. The first ones were the letters RO overprinted onto the Turkish 'Empire' stamp issue of 1876. In 1881, Eastern Rumelia got its own stamps, though they were still essentially the Turkish Empires, now expanded to include the name of the new province in French, Greek and Bulgarian. As such, it is a testimony to the cultural mix of the area – but also a reminder of who was supposed to be boss.

The new entity did not last long. A powerful revolutionary movement built up, and a coup was launched in September 1885. It was unopposed by the Rumelian government, who were half-hearted in their loyalty to the *Sublime Porte* – and by the time the news had reached Istanbul, Western powers had been alerted, who told the Ottomans to stay out.

The new government quickly issued its own stamps: overprints of the Empires again, but now with Bulgaria's heraldic lion and (in some cases) the words 'Bulgarian Post' on. These are now the most valuable of the stamps of this area, but, like many overprints, have been much forged. Eastern Rumelia soon announced a merger with the Principality of Bulgaria, and moved to simply using Bulgarian stamps like the one above, a clear sign that, after nearly 500 years, it was now *de facto* no longer part of Osman's empire.

Epirus

EPIRUS IS A term that describes an area that stretches across a part of what is now north-western Greece and part of what is now southern Albania. It is a region with huge amounts of history and, yes, stamps shed an interesting light on some of that history.

Epirus first makes a really big impact on ancient history in the fourth century BC. The early part of the century saw the royal house of the Molossians, who claimed descent from Achilles, expanding their area of control and becoming richer and more powerful. Other states began to pay them more attention, and in 356 BC Philip II of Macedon married the daughter of King Neoptolemus (named after the son of Achilles). Philip and Olympias would shortly have a rather well-known son, yes, Alexander the Great, although obviously, it was some time after he was actually born before he became Great.

In 334 BC, Alexander headed east to conquer Asia. In the same year, his uncle, King of the Molossians, also called Alexander, headed west from Epirus to conquer Italy. Alexander the nephew had rather more success than Alexander the Uncle. Alexander the nephew ended up the Great. Alexander the Uncle, after some initial success, ended up dead rather quickly, killed in 331 BC.

However, this was not to be the end of Molossian military efforts in Italy. The reign of Pyrrhus didn't have a great start. After coming to the throne rather young, he was toppled by a rebellion, but in 297 BC, he was restored to the throne of Epirus. He had some success in fighting in Macedonia and Greece, but it was what was to happen in Italy that would make him famous and still, in some sense, a household name today (even if many of those referring to him don't actually know they are or who he was).

In 281 BC, the Greek city of Tarentum in Italy asked for his help against Rome, so he set off to help. The help he gave consisted of defeating the Romans, in 280 BC at Heraclea and in 279 BC at Ausculum but at very heavy cost. He suffered heavy losses again against the Romans at Beneventum in 275 BC before finally being killed in fighting in Argos in Greece in 272 BC. The experience of Pyrrhus, of defeating the Romans but at very heavy cost, has given rise to the expression 'Pyrrhic victory'.

It would not be long before the Romans got their revenge on Epirus. In 167BC, the Romans took Molossia and enslaved many thousands of the people who lived there. Epirus would become part of the Roman Empire, with flourishing cites like Buthrotum (now Butrint), the impressive ruins of which are now located in southern Albania. After the collapse of the western Roman Empire, Epirus remained a part of the eastern Roman Empire, or as we tend to call it for the period after the fall of the western Roman Empire, the Byzantine Empire.

The Middle Ages, however, were going to be fairly chaotic in the region, with a number of powers including the Venetians, Serbs, Albanians, Byzantines and Ottomans fighting over it. It is particularly worth looking at the Despotate of Epirus in this chapter, both because it has Epirus in the title and, being honest, because it just sounds interesting. And in fact it is interesting.

Despotate doesn't sound a good place to live, but in this instance, it's more of a reference to the Greek word *despotes*, meaning lord, rather than any particular judgement on the place. In 1204, a bunch of Crusaders, instead of fighting in the Holy Land, seized wealthy (and Christian) Constantinople. The Byzantine Empire was temporarily fragmented and one of its fragments was a state that included Epirus and surrounding territories, ruled by a family with imperial Byzantine connections and claiming continuity from the legitimate Byzantine Empire. It expanded gradually and eventually took Thessalonica, with plans to advance further eastwards and liberate Constantinople. Theodore declared himself emperor. However, its forces were decisively defeated by the Bulgarians at the Battle of Klokotnitsa in 1230, and after that the future didn't look quite so bright for the dynasty from Epirus. A rival Byzantine dynasty from Nicaea instead became more prominent and it would be that which would restore the Byzantine Empire, not the team from Epirus.

The Despotate of Epirus did manage to last a little longer but eventually disappeared under pressure from Byzantines, Serbs, Albanians, assorted Italians etc. Then, in 1430, the Ottomans annexed the area. They would not find the locals always easy to control.

In the eighteenth century, Albanian warlord Ali Paşa Tepelenë established himself as a semi-independent ruler. The Ottomans recognised him as governor of Ioannina in 1788 and from there he spread his territory far and wide, even as far as the Peloponnese. However, eventually the Ottomans had had enough of him and he was killed in fighting in 1822, just after the Greeks had also risen against the Ottomans and started the Greek War of Independence.

The Greek War of Independence left, obviously, much of Greece independent, but at the beginning of 1912 almost all of Epirus was still under Ottoman control. But that was all about to change.

That year, revolution broke out in Albania and the First Balkan War began, which saw Greece and a number of other local nations defeating the Ottomans. Greece advanced into Epirus but the peace deal that ended the war awarded northern Epirus to a newly independent Albania. This caused resentment among the local Greek population, who rebelled and declared the Autonomous Republic of Northern Epirus.

This issued its own stamps in 1914. The first, roughly drawn, featured a skull and crossbones and the exhortation 'Freedom or Death! Defend our country!' A more restrained set of definitives, printed professionally in Corfu, followed in the spring of that year. Eight values, from 1 lepton to 5 drachma, show a rifleman in traditional costume. Another series appeared in August, featuring the flag of Epirus in two colours. Various semi-official stamps followed: collecting Epirus is a surprisingly complex business.

Shortly afterwards, however, the First World War broke out, and the Autonomous Republic of Northern Epirus disappeared as Albania collapsed, various Allied contingents, particularly Italians and French arrived in the area, and the Greeks advanced from the south. At the end of it all, and after the Greco-Turkish War had finished as well, a restored Albania got northern Epirus again.

Mussolini then occupied Albania in 1939 and in 1940 his forces from there invaded Greece. The Greeks promptly defeated the Italian forces and advanced again into northern Epirus. They issued overprints for this area: the words for 'Greek Administration' on Greek stamps.

The German invasion of Greece in 1941 forced Greek troops in the area to surrender and Italy occupied all of Epirus – until 1943, when it signed an armistice with the Allies and the Germans took over. The Greek Civil War subsequently saw heavy fighting in the area, and the Cold War saw tension in the area and, indeed, a formal end to the state of war between Albania and Greece was not signed until 1987.

Federation of South Arabia

THE FEDERATION OF South Arabia sounds something rather grand, big and stable, and probably that was what it was intended to sound like. In fact, the South Arabian Federation was small, vulnerable and unstable, and was gone a few years after it was created. But at least, before it disappeared, it did manage to get some stamps out.

The particular bit of South Arabia that we're focusing on in this chapter is a bit in the bottom left hand of the Arabian peninsula, now part of Yemen, and including the famous port city of Aden.

The area has, of course, a long and fascinating history. For instance, the ancient Sabaean kingdom was located in this region. And during the reign of Augustus, a Roman expedition under Aelius Gallus almost made it this far. The land expedition was focused on Ma'rib, slightly to the north of the Federation of South Arabia, but Roman ships attached to the expedition are supposed to have attacked the coast as well, probably including an attack on the port city that would become Aden.

Even in Roman days, the area was vital for shipping and international trade. Trade routes ran from Egyptian ports on the Red Sea through the Bab-el-Mandeb and along the coast of Arabia towards the Indian Ocean and the riches of the east. The area would continue to play a major role in international trade routes for much of its history. In the fifteenth century, for instance, a Chinese fleet is supposed to have reached Aden, as China reached out to explore the world. The Ottomans and Portuguese would both have times in control of Aden. And the neighbouring Omanis would sail south along the East African coast to establish the Sultanate of Zanzibar.

And then, of course, came (as they came to so many places in the world) the British. As early as 1609, an English ship, the *Ascension*, had made it as far as Aden. However, it was at the end of the eighteenth and into the early nineteenth century that British interest in the area was going to get really serious.

In 1798, Napoleon invaded Egypt and Britain started to get nervous about what plans he might have for British influence in India and the vital sea-routes leading there. So British forces were initially dispatched to the island of Perim at the mouth of the Red Sea, and subsequently to Aden where, with the agreement of the local Sultan, they established a base. At this stage, the base was temporary and when the French threat passed, the troops departed elsewhere.

However, a precedent had been established and British involvement in Aden would soon increase substantially. The importance of Aden to Britain was growing and when an agreement with the local authorities for Britain to take control there fell through, the British decided they weren't taking no for an answer. On 19 January 1839, a British force led by HMS *Volage* bombarded Aden and then landed troops. There was some brief resistance, but it was brief, and soon Aden was British. As was a rather impressive cannon of Suleiman-founded Mohammed ibn Hamza in 1530–31, that was 'liberated' by Captain Smith during the capture of the port and subsequently sent to the Tower of London for display.

Aden became a key coaling station and strategic transport centre for the British Empire, and its importance only increased after the opening of the Suez Canal was completed in 1869, once again making the Red Sea a major route for international long-distance trade. Britain began to acquire more land around the port of Aden itself and expand its influence over the local rulers who controlled territory in that part of the Arabian peninsula.

The situation in the area, however, began to change drastically after the Second World War, as around the globe, the inhabitants of the colonies of Europe's empires began more vociferously to demand their independence.

In 1956, the Suez Crisis saw the end of British influence in Egypt. Not only that, but it led to massively increased popularity for Egyptian president Nasser in the region. Nasser began to spread his ideas of left-wing anti-colonialist Pan-Arabism across the region, and one area he had his eyes on, just a little further down the Red Sea from Egypt, was Yemen.

In April 1962, in an attempt to add some stability and sense of permanence to the network of local rulers under British protection in the area, a new entity, yes, the Federation of South Arabia, was formed. Britain announced that Aden would remain a permanent British garrison. But the region was about to explode.

In September 1962, a republican coup attempt, launched with Egyptian support against the royal government in Yemen to the north, started the Yemen Civil War. The same year, the National Liberation Front, NLF, was formed with the intention of expelling Britain from the area.

In 1963, Aden was added to the Federation of South Arabia, and the following year, more little states were added. But already in October 1963 open conflict had broken out, starting with a grenade attack aimed at Aden's British High Commissioner. It was the start of a sustained anti-British guerrilla campaign. In December, a state of emergency was declared. The situation became even more complex and violent when a new rival to the NLF emerged, the Front for the Liberation of Occupied South Yemen, usually known by the acronym FLOSY, which makes it sound a lot more cuddly than it actually was.

The Federation of South Arabia did have stamps made, however. Its definitives featured the federal crest and the federal flag. Commemorative issues celebrated international institutions, or, in one issue, showed their loyalty to Britain by commemorating the death of Sir Winston Churchill. Quite what the local people made of a design featuring the great war leader and a picture of St Paul's Cathedral surrounded by flames and anti-aircraft searchlights is not known. The Federation also sent a team to the 1966 Commonwealth Games. Neither the stamps nor the participation in the games was going to save it.

The security situation got worse and Britain announced that it would be leaving. And then, in June 1967, local police mutinied and forced British troops to withdraw from the old quarter of Aden known as the Crater because it actually is situated in an ancient volcanic crater. What followed is known as the Battle of the Crater, as the British fought to re-enter and eventually managed to recapture the Crater.

However, the British government had had enough. On 30 November 1967, the Federation of South Arabia ceased to exist. The same day, the People's Republic of Southern Yemen came into existence there and in the neighbouring Protectorate of South Arabia.

Fernando Poo

THIS NAME HAS guaranteed mirth to schoolboy (and some adult) collectors over the years. However, a look at Fernando Poo's history provokes little laughter: for many years it was involved in the slave trade, and in the last century it was subjected to a little-known but psychotic dictatorship.

Now known as Bioko, Fernando Poo is an island off the coast of Cameroon, though it is currently part of Equatorial Guinea.

It gets its name from Fernão do Pó, a Portuguese navigator who landed on the island in 1472 and claimed it as a colony of his home nation. Since then, it has been handed round various European powers – the Dutch, the Spanish and the British. It is strategically important, but tropical diseases are rife: nations tended to decide they needed Fernando Poo for geopolitical reasons, then to lose interest when their administrators started dying. Explorer Sir Richard Burton, who was British consul there in 1861, described his workroom as 'a plank-lined coffin containing a dead consul once a year'.

The story of Fernando Poo is tied in with the history of slavery. It's not known if Fernão do Pó took part in the trade, but his countrymen certainly did, shipping slaves to Brazil to work on the sugar plantations that boomed in the seventeenth century. When the Dutch established an outpost on the island, their main interest was in trading slaves. The Portuguese soon threw them out and resumed the trade themselves.

Readers will probably know enough about this unspeakable business, so a few figures can suffice here. It is estimated that over 10.5 million African slaves landed in the Americas during the era of slaving. Add to this 2 million who died on the journey and an estimated 3 million who died in Africa itself, being transferred to slave ports or waiting for shipment there. In addition, an uncountable number of people died in 'slave wars', where African peoples fought each other to enslave the losers and sell them to the slavers ... Fernando Poo was not a major slave port, but played its role in this horror.

After William Wilberforce drove his anti-slavery bill through parliament in 1807, the island began to play a nobler role in this story. It had been ceded to Spain by Portugal in 1778, but the Spanish soon lost interest in it. However, Wilberforce's bill tasked the Royal Navy with suppressing the slave trade, and Fernando Poo was an excellent base from which to do this. Britain leased part of the island, and a port was set up there named Port Clarence – this is now the city of Malabo, capital not just of the island but of Equatorial Guinea.

The noted anti-slaver Captain (later Vice Admiral) William Fitzwilliam Owen based himself here. He pursued what he called the 'hellish trade' with vigour, releasing the slaves onto the island and trying the slavers in a special court.

The island's economy boomed as a result of Owen's attention, and the Spanish reclaimed it in 1855. The first stamps were issued in 1868, featuring Queen Isabella II – who in the same year was ousted from the Spanish throne. After a brief republic, her son Alfonso XII became king: a new set of stamps was issued, featuring him, in 1879. When he died in 1885, his unborn son succeeded him. Fernando Poo's stamps show this youngster growing up, as a baby in 1894, as a curly headed boy in 1899, and as a young man in 1907.

In 1926, the island was united with the mainland colony of Río Muni to form Spanish Guinea, on whose stamps a new leader appeared in 1940: General Franco, victor of the Spanish Civil War. In 1960, Spanish Guinea was split up again, initiating a second phase of Fernando Poo stamps.

By this time, colonialism was in retreat. Britain, France, the Netherlands and Belgium were all divesting themselves of their colonies. Not so Spain, whose traditionalist leader saw them as a continuing source of national pride. The often attractive Spanish Fernando Poo stamps of the 1960s give the impression of a confident, multiracial society. Beneath that, the old system was falling apart. Various attempts were made to put off independence, but in the end, local nationalism and international pressure proved too much. The second-last Fernando Poo issue celebrated the centenary of the island's first stamp back in 1868, but the game was up. On 12 October 1968, the Republic of Equatorial Guinea came into being, with Francisco Macías Nguema as its president.

Celebrations were short-lived. Nguema turned out to be one of the worst rulers in twentieth-century history. The descent into tyranny has a familiar ring to it: the mysterious disappearance of his main political opponent; a 99.9 per cent vote for a new constitution that gave him all power; a personality cult – of the eleven stamp issues made during his time in power, all but two feature him. However, Nguema put his own spin on this dismal story. Like Pol Pot in Cambodia, he had a particular hatred for intellectuals – though among the titles he gave himself was 'Grand Master of Education, Science and Culture' (another one was 'The Unique Miracle'). Like Idi Amin in Uganda, he seemed to revel in killing his opponents (real or imagined) in bizarre ways. On Christmas Day in 1975 he had 150 of them taken to the national football stadium and shot while Mary Hopkin's *Those Were the Days* played over the ground PA. (Some versions of this story add the killers dressed as Santa Claus, but this might be an embellishment.) Other opponents were buried in the ground and left to be killed by ants. During his time in office, a third of the country's population were murdered or managed to flee.

He was kept in power by an elite of his own family and clan, but when he started executing his own supporters in 1979, he was ousted in a coup by a nephew, Teodoro Obiang. Obiang remains president to this day, despite an attempted coup, straight out of Frederick Forsyth, by western mercenaries in 2004.

Festung Lorient

A NUMBER OF intriguing stamps emerged from France's experience of the Second World War, all of which tell stories of the conflict. Probably the best known are the ones from the German-built fortress of Lorient, or 'Festung Lorient'.

Hitler decided to build an 'Atlantic Wall' in 1942. Propaganda proclaimed that this would run from the northern tip of Norway to the Franco-Spanish border, creating 'Fortress Europe'. However, most of the work on it took place in France, where the Axis rightly guessed any Allied invasion would take place. The key points would be massive fortified ports, as Hitler believed that no invasion of Europe would succeed without capturing a major port. There were also to be subsidiary defences along beaches and on places where paratroops or gliders might land (forests of stakes appeared along the Normandy coast, and became known as 'Rommel's asparagus'). Most strongly fortified of all would be the submarine bases, one of which was at Lorient, a port about halfway along the southern coast of Brittany.

The forts were built by Organisation Todt, an arm of the Nazi government headed by Fritz Todt, an engineer and early party member. Before the war, its main work had been building Germany's autobahns. Now it built fortifications, first along the Eastern Front, but from 1942 (the year in which Todt was killed in an air crash and his job taken by Albert Speer) along the Atlantic.

Organisation Todt used vast amounts of resources building the Atlantic Wall – an estimated 1.7 million tons of concrete, a million tons of iron, and the labour of 300,000 people. Technical experts, often German, were well paid; ordinary labourers badly paid – many of these were Frenchmen drafted in by the Germans or by the puppet regime in Vichy. Beneath them was an army of slave labourers paid nothing at all, many of whom came from conquered parts of Eastern Europe. Thousands of the latter died during the construction of the wall, some in accidents but mainly through malnutrition and disease. Todt also used local contractors, some of whom made good money from the work. After the war, this wealth became a matter of national controversy, but in the end no restitution was made.

Hitler's belief that ports were the key to defending Fortress Europe appeared to receive support from the Allies' amphibious raids on Dieppe (a tragedy) and St Nazaire (an amazing piece of bravery that succeeded in causing huge amounts of damage to the enemy), which looked like dry runs. Of course, he was wrong; the Allies landed on the beaches of Normandy, built 'Mulberry harbours' from scratch and marched past the giant forts (the Mulberry harbour at Gold Beach was transited by over 2.5 million men, 500,000 vehicles, and 4 million tonnes of supplies). Brittany, apart from three of Hitler's fortified ports – Brest, Lorient and St Nazaire – was liberated during the first twelve days of August 1944. Once a prime node in a defensive wall, Lorient quickly found itself a strategically irrelevant pocket under siege.

The siege was not a mediaeval attempt to starve the inhabitants into submission: Lorient was bombed (and the submarine pens put out of action), but then became a strange island of Nazi Germany in Brittany, populated by 27,000 German soldiers and sailors and 10,000 locals. The American and Free French besiegers essentially waited for Germany to lose the war.

Life goes on, even in such odd circumstances, and this includes post. In January 1945, Lt Alfons Schmitt was put in charge of the local post office, and decided to produce overprints. This he did, though in small numbers, which means that genuine examples are valuable (and that forgeries abound). The stamps he overprinted are those of Vichy France (no longer valid outside the Festung, of course). The low denomination ones (10 to 50 centimes) featured the god Mercury; the higher denomination ones (60 centimes to 4 francs) featured, as many Vichy stamps had done, Marshal Pétain.

Philippe Pétain was a hero of the First World War. He had been probably the most thoughtful French commander of that war, believing in the power of technology rather than endless frontal infantry attacks: his reluctance to order these led to his being demoted (despite a successful defence of Verdun) and replaced by General Nivelle, who launched plenty. Few of them worked, and the French army came close to mutiny until Pétain's command was restored. He continued to annoy his critics by playing a waiting game till new tanks – and reinforcements from America – came onstream.

When Germany invaded France again in 1939, Pétain was invited into government to oversee the nation's defence. But he could do little. Despite entreaties from Churchill, he capitulated to the Nazis, who had occupied 60 per cent of his country, on 22 June 1940. His defenders say he could have done little else. The remaining 40 per cent, essentially the Riviera, south-east and central areas, became the *zone libre* – in name, anyway.

From a new capital in the old spa town of Vichy, Pétain became the autocratic head of this zone, which he tried to turn into an ultra-traditionalist Catholic regime, similar to that of General Franco. The old French slogan of liberty, fraternity and equality was replaced with 'Work, family and fatherland'. Behind this façade lay increasing German control. The so-called *zone libre* had to pay heavy reparations to Germany. Anti-Semitic propaganda was rife. By 1942, members of the *Milice*, a paramilitary body, were arresting Jews and sending them to camps in occupied France. This still did not satisfy Hitler; in November of that year, Germany marched in and took over the zone. Pétain, who was still popular with many people, was kept on as a figurehead leader of the new occupied France.

Festung Lorient surrendered on 10 May 1945, three days after Hitler. There is film footage of US and Free French troops driving into the ruined centre of the town, to be greeted by (largely female) crowds, some in traditional Breton costume, handing out flowers. The actual surrender document was, bizarrely, signed in a bar, the Bar Breton on the quay of the tiny fishing port of Magouër. A ceremony was then held in a meadow, at which the German commander General Wilhelm Fahrmbacher offered his pistol to US Major General Herman F. Kramer. The Festung Lorient pocket was a pocket no longer.

After the war, Marshal Pétain was tried for treason. He made little attempt to defend himself and was sentenced to death, a sentence commuted by his former student Charles de Gaulle to life imprisonment, in the light of his achievements in the First World War.

Fezzan

FEZZAN ISN'T A place that many people outside the region where it's located could probably find on a map, and yet, as a name, when you find out where it is actually located, it seems somehow appropriate. Fezzan is basically the south-western part of what is now Libya, a land of deserts and oases, of camel trails, ancient towns and villages. The name has nothing to do with the Fez, that symbolic headgear, but instead seems to be derived from a local word meaning, not unreasonably, 'rough rocks'. It is a word in the language that has often been referred to as Berber, like the carpets, but should more accurately be called Amazigh, itself another beautiful word.

In ancient times the Libyan coastline was home to a number of peoples (as well as the Amazigh) including Phoenicians, Carthaginians, Romans and Greeks. Fezzan was a little too remote from the Mediterranean coast to receive that much of this international influence. Instead, it had the mighty Garamantian Empire, inhabited by the Garamantes who were adept at irrigation and were linked into extensive trading networks. They would also raid the coast occasionally, and occasionally the Romans would send expeditions south to 'conquer' the Garamantes. So, for instance, in 19 BC Lucius Cornelius Balbus attacked the Garamantes, 'conquered' them, and celebrated a triumph over them. In reality, however, Roman 'control' of the area was probably always pretty minimal. The Latin for Fezzan is Phazania, which is also a rather beautiful name and sounds like the name of a planet in some sci-fi epic. But the climate was changing and the desert was advancing and, eventually, the power of the Garamantes would disappear entirely.

In time, Arabs would become the new power in the region and they too would endeavour to expand their control over Fezzan. But it was not just powers from north of the Sahara that were interested in the Fezzan – powers from the south were as well. The mighty Kanem–Bornu Empire based around Lake Chad during the Middle Ages at times extended its control north of the Sahara to include parts of the Fezzan.

Eventually the Ottoman Empire would succeed Arab and local dynasties and take control of Fezzan. But in the nineteenth century Europeans would return to the region. For instance, in 1822, the British, Denham, Oudney and Clapperton expedition reached Murzuq in Fezzan after travelling south from the coast. From there they travelled even further south, reaching Lake Chad in early 1823.

It was, however, to be the twentieth century that would eventually see European powers invade the region and, once again, Fezzan would see not just invaders from the north but invaders from the south as well.

In 1911, Italy invaded Libya (see the sections on Cyrenaica and Tripolitania). The invasion was not the easy walk in the park that some Italians had expected but instead involved bitter fighting that resulted in Italian forces struggling to hold coastal enclaves against Ottoman and allied local forces. In the end, superior weaponry and crises elsewhere in the Ottoman Empire led the Ottoman authorities to abandon Libya to the Italians. This was not the same, of course, as meaning that local forces had agreed to abandon their country to the Italians. There would be periods of intense conflict for some time. Eventually, however, Italy began to spread its authority into the further reaches of its Libyan territory, including Fezzan. For instance, a major landmark in Sabha, one of the main towns in Fezzan, is the Italian-built Fort Elena, formerly known (like the pizzas) as Fortezza Margherita.

After the First World War, Italy was aided in its colonial endeavours in the area by its wartime ally France. As a sort of partial quid pro quo for Italy not demanding any colonies of the former German Empire, France handed over some of what it regarded as low-value territory on Fezzan's borders. Though the paperwork on it was never quite concluded, Italy acquired through this process the Aouzou Strip. This has nothing to do with exotic dancing and even less to do with a Las Vegas-type conglomeration of glitzy casinos and hotels. It is instead a strip of desert along the border between the Fezzan and Cyrenaica regions of Libya and Chad. We will return to this later, but not literally, of course, because it's quite hard to get to.

In 1940, Italy declared war on France. Shortly afterwards, the French government fell and was replaced by the pro-Nazi Vichy regime. However, Chad was not going to be any kind of ally of the Germans. In charge of Chad at the time was Félix Éboué, the first black colonial governor in the French empire, and he was not going to make peace with the Nazis. Instead, almost as soon as possible, he joined forces with Charles de Gaulle and Chad became a Free French territory. Which meant it was at war with Italian forces in Libya to the north.

Due to the nature of the terrain this was never likely to be the most active frontline, but in January 1943, Free French forces advanced north into Fezzan and seized Murzuq, a few days before the British seized Tripoli in the north. And as British forces formed administrations elsewhere in Libya, the French formed an administration in Fezzan and the area of Ghadames.

Stamps soon followed. The first ones were overprints, with 'Fezzan, Occupation Francaise' and new denominations on old

Italian Colony of Libya stamps. Genuine examples of some of these are rare and valuable. After the war, a number of attractive issues appeared: one, in 1946, for 'Fezzan and Ghadames' and five, from 1948, just inscribed 'Fezzan'. Like the stamps of France of that time, they have a strong sense of place, albeit a slightly romanticised one.

The days of Fezzan stamps were not, however, to last long. In 1951, France pulled out and Fezzan became part of the Kingdom of Libya. It is still part of Libya, though the Aouzou Strip is, it turns out, not.

Gaddafi's Libya fought and eventually lost a war against Chad before accepting an international judgement that the Aouzou Strip belongs to Chad, not Libya.

Fiume

YOU WON'T SEE the name Fiume on maps today. Or you will sort of, because Fiume means 'river' in Italian and Rijeka means 'river' in Croatian and sure enough, there near the top of the Adriatic, on Kvarner Bay, sandwiched between the Istrian peninsula and the main Croatian coastline, is the ancient port city and shipbuilding centre of Rijeka. Bearing in mind the name of the city, it would be somewhat surprising if there was not also a river associated with the site, and indeed the city is located at the mouth of the River Rječina, which has also been known as the Fiumara.

Over the millennia invaders, including Romans, Franks and Venetians, came and went through the area. In the early fifteenth century it became involved with the Uskoks. Nothing to do with Buzzcocks, these were either Adriatic entrepreneurs or pirates, depending on your point of view and which end of the weapon you were looking at.

In the late fifteenth century it became a key city of the Habsburg dynasty. During the Napoleonic Wars the French came to visit, though on rather more of an invade and occupy basis than a bed and breakfast one. Finally it was liberated in 1813 by an Irish-born general, Laval Nugent, serving with the Austrian army. During the nineteenth century it became a key base for the Austro-Hungarian navy. In the 1860s, a collaboration between Austro-Hungarian naval officer Giovanni Luppis and British engineer Robert Whitehead led to the production of the first self-propelled torpedo and a factory in the city manufacturing them.

However, it was to be the chaos at the end of the First World War that would really put the city on the international political map, and more importantly for this book, of course, into the stamp albums of the world.

Generally speaking, the Austro-Hungarian navy had quite a frustrating time in the First World War. The Allies had constructed the Otranto Barrage across the Straits of Otranto, which meant that the Austro-Hungarian surface fleet spent most of its time cruising up and down the Adriatic trying to find something useful to do. By contrast, someone who had quite a dramatic war was an Italian called Gabriele D'Annunzio.

D'Annunzio was fundamentally a poet of passion, while also a novelist, playwright, reporter, collaborator with Debussy, aviator etc. etc. By the start of the First World War, he had already started a series of affairs and become something of a literary phenomenon.

As Italy threw itself into the maelstrom of the First World War, Gabriele D'Annunzio answered his nation's call. But not for the poet of passion, the mundane task of sweating it out under shellfire in the trenches. D'Annunzio is largely known for two exploits, both of the type you'd imagine really.

A few months after Italy's catastrophic defeat in the Battle of Caporetto, D'Annunzio took part in a raid, in February 1918, on the port of Bakar, coincidentally a few miles distant from Rijeka. Three Italian MAS torpedo boats eluded the Austro-Hungarian defences and slipped in to fire their torpedoes at Austro-Hungarian shipping, then escaped unscathed. Admittedly the torpedoes didn't actually do any damage, but the passion and elan of the attack perfectly suited D'Annunzio's temperament and earned the applause of the Italian nation.

Then in August 1918, he led the famous Flight over Vienna in which Ansaldo planes managed the impressive technical feat of a more than 1,200km round trip to Vienna. While over Vienna, the planes dropped not bombs, but propaganda leaflets, many of them copies of a leaflet written, of course, by D'Annunzio himself. And not translated into German. As Germany and its Austro-Hungarian and Turkish allies started to collapse and the First World War started to come to an end, D'Annunzio was a major Italian celebrity. And he had another major act of dashing military elan yet to come.

As the Austro-Hungarian Empire collapsed, new borders and new nations emerged, among them the Kingdom of the Serbs, Croats and Slovenes, that would later become known by the rather shorter name Yugoslavia. The new nation wanted Rijeka. The Italians wanted Fiume. Both set up rival administrations in the city. Then, to add to the international confusion, a multinational Allied force of British, French, American and Italian troops arrived in the city as well. The question of who ultimately would control the city remained unresolved. Once more, the poet D'Annunzio decided it was time to act.

A majority of the city's population was Italian and in September 1919 D'Annunzio led a bunch of Italian nationalist militiamen on a bloodless invasion of the city. After Italy refused to annex the city, he established a new state in and around Fiume. D'Annunzio's new state was a somewhat eccentric affair. It recognised Soviet Russia but it was also corporatist in nature and in some senses prefigured the rise of Italian fascism. Features that would later become commonplace under Mussolini such as speeches from balconies, parades by uniformed toughs, and the reuse of Roman imagery were all seen in D'Annunzio's Fiume. Music was made an integral part of the state and, of course, it printed stamps.

The first definitive stamps of the new nation were attractive and stylish, featuring images of Liberty, the city's clock tower, with an Italian flag flying from it, a mythical creature symbolising revolution and a sailor raising the flag in the port. Next year, more definitives followed, which were much less attractive: they feature a rather sinister image of D'Annunzio, in theory modelling him as a Roman god but, to modern eyes anyway, making him look more like a villain in a low-budget sci-fi movie. Special military stamps were also printed.

The future was not, however, bright for the new state. An agreement on Fiume was signed at Rapallo in November 1920 between Italy and the Kingdom of the Serbs, Croats and Slovenes, establishing the Free State of Fiume. The deal was not to D'Annunzio's liking and, being a poet of passion, he acted with passion and declared war on Italy. At this point, Italy was one of the key victorious Allied powers. It was something of a mismatch. In December 1920, after an Italian naval bombardment and an advance by the Italian army, D'Annunzio was forced to surrender the city. The D'Annunzio series was replaced by a gentler one featuring a ship in full sail, Saint Vitus, and Roman ruins.

D'Annunzio himself was finally forgiven by the Italian state and he was soon ennobled by the king. The permanently crisis-stricken Free State of Fiume managed to last until 1924 when it was annexed by Italy. After the Second World War, Rijeka would become part of Yugoslavia, and today it is one of Croatia's major cities.

French India

FOR A LOT of people, French and India aren't two words that join up very easily. When they think of French colonies in the east, they think maybe of somewhere like French Indochina. Nonetheless, such an entity as French India did exist and yes, it did have stamps printed, ensuring it a kind of perforated immortality.

One reason, it has to be said, that the French aren't the colonisers of India of whom many people think most readily is that they started late. And slow. Early French efforts had little success.

It wasn't until 1668 that the first French trading post was established in India, at Surat. By that time, Britons, Dutch and Portuguese already all had long experience of operating in the region, and generally speaking they weren't hugely enthusiastic about the idea of the French getting involved in the area; in fact a lot of them were distinctly unenthusiastic and were prepared to show their unenthusiasm in the traditional manner, i.e. colonial warfare. In 1673, the French managed to set up shop at the place that would above all others in India become associated with France: Pondicherry. But even this wouldn't be immune to the ambitions of competitor Europeans. The Dutch, for instance, captured Pondicherry in 1693 and kept it until 1699, after a peace deal had been done.

It was to be the eighteenth century that saw the greatest chance that India might actually become French instead of British. Some able colonial French administrators expanded and developed Pondicherry and other settlements and then, in 1742, Joseph-François, Marquis Dupleix became governor general of all French establishments in India. He had big plans to develop a real French empire in India and he set about developing a local army and building extensive links with local rulers. He had two major obstacles to deal with, a lack of support from others within the French government and colonial administration on one hand, and on the other, the stubborn hostility of the British in India.

One man who was going to prove something of a problem for Dupleix and the French in India subsequently was Robert

Clive. He would become known in more imperial times than our own as Clive of India, and there is still a statue of him in a street next to the Foreign Office in London, even though Clive of India doesn't entirely represent the kind of values our Foreign Office likes to promote around the world these days. Clive became famous in 1751 for his defence of Arcot against besieging French and Allied troops, and when Dupleix's forces also failed elsewhere to make as much progress as he had hoped, the French government gave up, made peace, and had Dupleix replaced.

In 1756, however, war broke out again. And this time Clive scored a decisive victory over a key French ally at the Battle of Plassey. Thomas Arthur, comte de Lally, baron de Tollendal, a French general, but of Irish Jacobite ancestry, arrived in India with the intention of decisively defeating the British instead. He didn't. During an attempt to recover the fort at Vandavasi (called Wandiwash by the British) he was defeated in January 1760 by Sir Eyre Coote. In 1761, the British captured and flattened Pondicherry itself. The French had the (flattened) Pondicherry returned to them in 1763, but the situation for an expansion of French India wasn't looking hopeful. More fighting, however, would follow. Admiral comte Pierre André de Suffren de Saint Tropez, bailli de Suffren, for instance, would fight a naval campaign with some success against British forces, including at the Battle of Cuddalore in 1783.

When war between Britain and Revolutionary France broke out in 1793, British forces quickly moved into French territories in India and in August, Pondicherry itself fell. Again. Napoleon had plans to take an army to India but never did. In 1816, as part of the peace deal that tided up the chaos and carnage of the Napoleonic years, a few small possessions, including Pondicherry, were returned to French control. As alliances and strategic focuses changed and as Britain and France ceased to be each other's main enemies, French India now had a secure, if not particularly successful, future ahead of it for a time. It also, of course, had stamps ahead of it.

The first stamps were the standard French colonial issue of 1892 with 'Etablissements de l'Inde' inscribed on them. But in 1914, the colonies got their own stamps. An issue of eighteen values featured two designs, one the god Brahma, the other the Kali temple near the capital of French India, Pondicherry.

Gradually, as elsewhere in India, in the early twentieth century pressure began to mount in the French establishments in India for independence from European colonial rule. However, for one last time, French India would be dragged (or actually almost dragged) into a war between France and Britain.

On 22 June, after lightning German attacks smashed French and British defences, France collapsed and signed an armistice with Nazi Germany. on 10 July, Pétain was given authoritarian power in France. The Vichy years had begun, and around the globe, France's colonial administrators had decisions to make. Some remained loyal to the Vichy French regime. But not French India.

In June, Louis Bonvin, governor of the French Establishments in India, announced that they would continue to fight alongside Britain. In September, Bonvin announced that French India was part of Free France. New stamps for the region reflected this, first with overprints then with a new design featuring lotus flowers and the Cross of Lorraine.

In 1947, India became independent from Britain. In the years following, French India's few little possessions would also become independent of European rule – though not before one more major stamp issue, in 1948, featuring Hindu deities. In 1954, France's last possessions in the area, including Pondicherry, became de facto part of the modern state of India (though the legal deal took a little longer to finalise).

However, even today, French influence on, for instance, Pondicherry (or Puducherry as it is now more usually known) can be seen in places by visitors, for example in the architecture of the French quarter.

French Territory of the Afars and Issas

NOT THAT MANY people could locate on a globe where the French Territory of the Afars and Issas used to be. But then, to be fair, quite a few people couldn't find its present identity, Djibouti, on a globe either. But before it was called the French Territory of the Afars and Issas, it was called the French Somali Coast or French Somaliland, which would probably be a useful hint. Because yes, the French Territory of the Afars and Issas was on the coast of the Horn of Africa, sandwiched between Eritrea to the north and Somalia to the south, with Ethiopia inland and with Yemen just across the Bab-el-Mandeb, the strait at the mouth of the Red Sea. The Afars and Issas are two of the main peoples living within the territory.

The region, of course, had a long history before the arrival of Europeans in the area. The area known to the ancient Egyptians as the Land of Punt (not a reference to flat-bottomed boats) was probably located roughly in this area. And the middle ages would see battles roughly in the region between the Muslim powers on the coast and the Christian kingdom of Abyssinia inland. Yemen also had an interest in the area, at one stage taking over the port of Zeila a few miles along the coast in Somalia. And then there were the Ottomans and in the nineteenth century once again the Egyptians and, of course, those Europeans.

In the early nineteenth century Muhammad Ali, Pasha of Egypt, not only took control of parts of the Somali coast, including Zeila, but he expanded his reach across the Red Sea into Yemen. But in the end, it turned out he had extended too far, and as the Europeans began to take a serious interest in the Somali coast, Egyptian forces would eventually withdraw.

French explorer Rochet d'Héricourt spent time in the region between 1839 and 1842 and gradually French interest in the area increased. In the 1850s, Frenchman Ferdinand de Lesseps started the business of building the Suez Canal and when it finally opened in 1869 it did so under French management. Suddenly, the Red Sea and its coastline had a whole new strategic significance as the Suez Canal route became a short cut from Europe to the east, cutting out the long journey around the coast of Africa and around the Cape of Good Hope. An area of particular strategic importance was the Bab-el-Mandeb, the narrow southern entrance to the Red Sea. By the middle of the nineteenth century, the British already had a well-established presence in Aden, near the Yemeni side of the strait. However, no European power at this stage firmly controlled the African side of the strait.

The French wanted it. They signed agreements of friendship and assistance with local rulers and then in 1862 they bought the anchorage at Obock. But the French weren't the only Europeans interested in the region. The British had their eyes on it from across the waters in Aden and eventually they would establish the territory of British Somaliland on the coast to the south. Meanwhile, along the coast to the north, the Italians were establishing a presence. And at this stage the Egyptians still had forces in the area.

In the 1880s, the French did more deals with local rulers and expanded their area of control to the Gulf of Tadjoura, as the Egyptians finally pulled out, after fighting with Ethiopian forces. As the Egyptians abandoned Sagallo and Tadjoura, French ships moved in to secure new territory. The little French-held area was now becoming a proper colony.

In 1889, news arrived in Obock that a Russian cossack expedition had arrived just along the coast at the old Egyptian fort of Sagallo. French naval ships were dispatched and the Russians were expelled.

In 1897, the French signed a deal with the Ethiopians, fixing their colony's border on that side, and the same year construction was begun on a rail route from Djibouti to Addis Ababa. It was completed in 1917.

Despite being distant from the major Second World War battlefields, the French Somali Coast/French Somaliland was going to have a comparatively dramatic war.

In 1936, the Italians occupied Ethiopia, meaning that they now almost surrounded the French enclave. In 1938, Italian troops moved into border areas in a dispute over the line agreed under the original deal with the Ethiopians, and later the same year, the Italian foreign minister demanded France cede the land to Italy. In June 1940, as German forces advanced into France, Italy declared war on the country and Italian forces attacked the French Somali Coast/French Somaliland. Italian ground forces clashed with the French defenders and Italian planes hit Djibouti's port and airfield.

However, France's rapid collapse and the signing of an armistice left the Vichy French in control of the little French enclave. So the next attack on it would be a British and Free French one. British forces against the Italians in East Africa meant that eventually they would surround the little French enclave. They imposed a blockade on Djibouti and eventually the Vichy French authorities surrendered and British and Free French forces occupied it.

In 1958, a referendum was held on whether the territory should remain French or unite with soon-to-be independent neighbouring Somalia. Amidst allegations of irregularities, a decision was made to stay French. A second referendum on whether to remain French or become independent again opted, again amidst allegations of irregularities, to remain French. But the name of French Somali Coast/French Somaliland was finally changed to the French Territory of the Afars and Issas in an attempt to distance the territory, in some sense, from Somalia.

Stamps were issued from 1967 to 1977. They make an interesting set. Despite the territory being small, a genuine effort was often made to produce stamps that celebrate the area and its life. While some sets are obviously generic – famous scientists, the Munich Olympics, sea shells – others are not. Subjects include Afar daggers, administrative outposts of the region, and local landmarks. When a small car ferry was set up between Tadjoura and Djibouti in 1970, a special stamp celebrated the fact.

Finally, by a third referendum in 1977, everyone had had enough. Almost everybody voted for independence and the French Territory of the Afars and Issas became independent Djibouti.

German Austria and Carinthia

TO MANY PEOPLE today, German Austria would be a contradiction in terms. For a long time there has been Germany (even though divided during the Cold War) and there has been Austria – entirely separate nations. Or we might think of the German Nazi 1938 annexation of Austria into 'Greater Germany'. But the stamps printed in the name of German Austria come from a somewhat earlier time.

The German collapse at the end of the First World War is a subject that has received a fair amount of attention over the years, largely, of course, because of the chaos that followed it and Hitler's emergence from that chaos. However, Germany didn't fight the First World War on its own. Austria-Hungary or the Austro-Hungarian Empire was there at the start of the war, and it was there almost until the end of it.

As 1918 progressed, it became increasingly clear that Austria-Hungary was in big trouble. Discontent and shortages on the home front had led to strikes and mutinies, and the many of the different peoples who made up the empire were becoming restless. Nationalists across the region were encouraged both by Austro-Hungarian problems on the battlefield and by Woodrow Wilson's Fourteen Points, which among many other points encouraged belief in a right to self-determination.

Large numbers of Czechoslovaks and Poles, for instance, were fighting for the Allies in a belief that an Allied victory would give them the independent countries they aspired to. And in May 1918, there was a Slav national celebration in Prague.

By October, the government was desperately looking for an escape from catastrophe. But October 1918 was not going to be a good month for the Habsburg monarchy. Not good at all. The Emperor Charles, in an attempt to satisfy the new nationalists, announced that Poles would be free to join an independent Poland and that Austria itself would become a federal state, with four elements, German, Czech, South-Slav and Ukrainian. And a plea was made to the Americans to open armistice negotiations on the basis of Woodrow Wilson's Fourteen Points.

It was far too little far too late. That same month, the Poles declared their independence and so did the Czechoslovaks. In Zagreb, a National Council of Slovenes, Croats and Serbs took power. And the United States rejected the armistice nego-tiations, as suggested, because of the new independence of Czechoslovakia. In late October, the inevitable was accepted. Czechoslovak independence was implicitly agreed to and an armistice on 3 November took the Austro-Hungarian armies out of the war.

And if October 1918 had been a bad month for the Habsburg monarchy, then November 1918 was going to be even worse. On 11 November, the same day the armistice between the Allies and Germany came into force, the final Emperor of Austria, Charles the First (and Last) of Austria-Hungary announced his with-drawal from any participation in the administration of the state. Two days later, he did the same for Hungary, where a revolu-tion had broken out. It was effectively an abdication and the end of the Habsburg monarchy. He would be officially deposed by the Austrian parliament in 1919 and his attempts to regain royal authority in Hungary would also be thwarted. Madeira is today a beautiful and popular holiday destination but Charles didn't much enjoy his time in enforced exile there. He died of influenza in 1922.

The break-up of Austria-Hungary and the creation of a bunch of new states left the question of what to call what was left after Hungary and the other new nations had taken their leave.

Parts of the Austro-Hungarian Empire that were not part of the Kingdom of Hungary had been part of the Austrian monarchy. So, when all the other nations had left that entity, what was left was basically German-speaking Austria, so German Austria had seemed a reasonable description of the region. On 18 October, as other peoples within the empire were making their nationalist dreams come true, German-speaking members of the Austrian parliament formed the National Assembly for German-Austria and, on 30 October, they declared an independent state. On 12 November, the day after Charles I had effectively abdicated, the assembly declared German Austria a democratic republic. Even more controversially, it then declared itself, in line with the then widespread redrawing of borders along ethnic lines, as a part of the German republic.

The Republic of German-Austria did produce stamps. First, overprints, with 'Deustschosterreich' on a mixture of Austrian stamps featuring both Franz Joseph and his successor Charles I, then its own definitives, with three designs: a heraldic eagle, a post horn and a fit-looking young man in a loincloth getting to his feet – a symbol of the new nation. Stamps featuring the parliament building in Vienna followed.

It was not, however, to have a long and glorious career as a country. Not even a short and glorious one really. It faced hostility at home from communist attempts at rebellion. And it faced hostility abroad. Having just defeated Germany and with plans to take big chunks of its territory from it, pretty much the last development the Allies wanted now was to see Germany and Austria united in one huge, powerful, central European German megastate.

The peace deal that Austria finally signed with the Allies at St Germain specifically banned Austria from joining Germany without the agreement of the League of Nations. It also forced the Republic of German-Austria to rename itself as the rather less obviously German, Republic of Austria.

There were, however, still some other small details to be sorted out before the Republic of Austria could get on with its life. Or some big details. For instance, the new Kingdom of the Serbs, Croats and Slovenes (soon to be renamed as the rather more catchy and snappy Yugoslavia) had decided it was owed Carinthia and threatened to use military force if it didn't get it. In the end, it was agreed that a plebiscite would be held. The new nation's definitives were reissued as overprints, with 'Karnten Abstimmung' (Carinthian Plebiscite) on them.

When the vote was finally held, on 10 October 1920, almost 60 per cent voted in favour of being Austrian.

Great Barrier Island Pigeongram Agency

POST HAS BEEN carried by various means over the years. In 1959, the US Postal Service experimented with firing a missile with 300 special commemorative envelopes in place of the usual warhead. It landed, safely, where it was supposed to, and Postmaster General Arthur Summerfield proudly declared, 'Before man reaches the moon, mail will be delivered within hours from New York to California, to Britain, to India or Australia by guided missiles'. (Summerfield later became even

more of a comic figure by setting up a museum of porno-
graphic materials sent through the US Mail, with the aim of
shocking people and helping his crusade to clean up the post.
Unfortunately for Summerfield, most visitors came for other
reasons.) Reindeer have been used for deliveries in Alaska.
Mules are still used on one postal route in the Grand Canyon in
Colorado. By these standards, using pigeons is rather mundane.

However, it works. The banking house of Rothschild used
pigeons to convey the news of the Battle of Waterloo to London,
and thus clean up on financial markets. During the Siege of Paris
in 1870, the Parisians sent mail to the rest of the world by pigeon
(the besieging Prussians used hawks to try and stop them). And
in 1896, the Great Barrier Pigeongram Agency was set up.

Great Barrier Island lies off the north-west coast of New
Zealand, about 60 miles from Auckland. Copper was found
there in 1842, and small amounts of gold and silver in the 1870s.
However, the only means of communication with the mainland
was by weekly boat – like the Rothschilds, the mining companies wanted news from the island to travel faster. When a ship,
the SS *Wairarapa*, was wrecked off the island, the Auckland
newspapers demanded a faster news service, too.

Enter Walter Fricker, an entrepreneurial pigeon-fancier. He
created a system whereby for 2 shillings islanders could deliver a
message to the local post office at Okupu. It would be attached
to a pigeon by the postmistress, Miss Springhall, and sent to the
mainland. There would be a daily flight, carrying a maximum of
five messages (they had to be written on special lightweight paper
and became known as 'flimsies'). A return system followed.

A rival service soon sprung up, calling itself, with amusing
effrontery, the Original Great Barrier Pigeongram Service (or
'The Service' for short). This offered two pigeons a day, and,
according to an advert in the *Auckland Observer*, guaranteed
'secrecy and absolute security'. The price was only 1/6. It also
poached the services of Miss Springhall, with whom Fricker
had had a row after a mix-up with rival pigeons (Fricker seems

to have been good at falling out with people: he originally had a partner in the agency, but it soon became a one-man show). Two years later, The Service was taken over by a dynamic young solicitor's clerk named S. Holden Howie, who had even bigger ideas. These included building an aviary on the mainland with an electronic alarm system that would announce whenever a pigeon arrived. He also issued special stamps.

The first stamp, a shilling one, was somewhat basic, with just a line drawing and no real perforations. It appeared in 1898. The next year saw a stamp with a more intricate, but poorly printed design. This bore the words Great Barrier Island Special Post until the New Zealand Post Office – possibly alerted by Stricker – objected, and the stamps had to be overprinted with 'Pigeon Post'. A new service, to Marotiri Island (another mineral-rich island off Auckland) was introduced, and was given its own bright carmine stamp.

Howie soon had 300 birds plying his routes. His loft received a visit from the Governor General, during which Howie tried to interest him in further services to the nation's lighthouses. He received a letter from the Duke of Cornwall (later George V) commending him on his endeavours.

Fricker did not take this competition lying down, however. In 1898, he cut his prices and issued two beautiful stamps. These had much finer engravings, proper perforations (though imperforate examples exist) and were triangular. There were two denominations: 6*d* for post from the island, 1*s* for the journey out there (birds flying the 'out' route required more training). They were designed by Harry Charles Wrigg, a veteran of the Māori Wars – a link to the darker side of New Zealand's history, a set of conflicts which had started in the 1840s as settlers began encroaching on traditional Māori lands (despite a treaty that had promised they would not) and had continued until 1872.

Howie did not respond to Fricker with better stamps. Instead, he decided to expand into other areas. He set off on a world tour to source 'novelties' that he reckoned would prove popular in

New Zealand, including 'cycles and their accessories' and, the latest gadget from America, the phonograph. However, he also visited many 'pigeon-houses', to update himself with 'the latest methods of pigeon management and service'.

He was wise to diversify. In 1908, a cable was laid across the Hauraki Gulf, which lies between Auckland and the island, and the pigeon postal services were no longer needed. The stamps remain popular with collectors, however, and valuable – especially if still attached to a 'flimsy'. In 1997, New Zealand Post reissued the two triangulars as official commemoratives, with modern values of 40*c* and 80*c* (the old NZ pound was replaced by the NZ dollar in 1967). Commentators observed that the originals were the first Airmail stamps ever issued.

Heligoland

HELIGOLAND IS A small archipelago consisting basically of two islands in the North Sea. It used to be just one island until an enormous storm hit in 1721.

Despite being quite close to Denmark and having at times come under Danish control, Heligoland has nothing to do with Legoland. And on the small island of Düne you won't find giant worms, House Atreides, House Harkonnen, the Fremen and all the other details of the classic sci-fi epic.

The name Heligoland sounds like it ought to mean Holy Island, but if it does, nobody seems entirely sure any more to whom it might be holy. Heligoland used to make regular appearances on the BBC Shipping Forecast.

Another place you will find the name Heligoland is, of course, in stamp albums, and fascinatingly, considering the proximity of Heligoland to Germany and Denmark, its first stamps, issued in 1867, had Queen Victoria's head on them.

Somewhat confusingly, the flag of Heligoland is a green, red and white tricolour which is basically the same as the flag of Bulgaria. If Heligoland was in the Black Sea rather than the North Sea, this could have caused no end of problems.

Some sources suggest that an early visitor to Heligoland was Radbod, King of the Frisians, a character not to be confused with Nogbad the Bad, villain of the Noggin the Nog 1960s children's cartoon series. Radbod spent much of his life fighting the advance of Franks into the region and at one point needed to get away for a while after a rather troubling defeat. Later tourists would experience the holiday joys of the island, but before all that some rather less peaceful history was about to happen.

Both the Dukes of Schleswig-Holstein and the Kingdom of Denmark liked the idea of controlling the islands and at one stage the dukes would be in control and then at another the Danes. Finally, in 1714, the Danes took long-term control of the island, long-term, in this instance, being until Britain took a serious interest in the islands during the Napoleonic Wars.

During this long and complex series of wars, Britain fought assorted nations as well as the French. So in 1808, when we happened to be at war with Denmark, British ships arrived at Heligoland and the small Danish garrison decided that instead of death or glory it would choose life and a hasty capitulation. And when a peace deal was signed in 1814 to tidy up some of the numerous messy effects of the conflict, Britain got to keep Heligoland.

It could have been a major strategic naval base, but instead, under Britain, Heligoland started becoming something of an early tourist destination. German intellectuals and revolutionaries could, for instance, get away to enjoy bracing sea air and stunning sea views without the ever-present threat of incarceration. August Heinrich Hoffmann wrote the lyrics to the German national anthem while on holiday in Heligoland in 1841. Heligoland's flag had a Union flag added to its top left corner to show who was boss, and stamps were printed. Heligoland became the Gibraltar of the North Sea – though with somewhat less sunshine and heat, and no apes.

British lieutenant governors of Heligoland had such names as Arthur Cecil Stuart Barkly or Henry Berkeley Fitzhardinge Maxse (a man who prior to his time on Heligoland had managed to live through the Charge of the Light Brigade).

However, Britain's global empire grew rapidly through the nineteenth century and British priorities elsewhere eventually came to outweigh British interest in Heligoland. The islands' stamps show this neatly: a second issue in 1875 now features four designs, but only one of them involves Victoria. The others show arms and emblems of Heligoland. More intriguing still, they are denominated in dual currencies. This makes them members of a very exclusive club: there are a few other stamp issues in dual currencies (examples include ones from Cuba, Persia, Australia and Rhodesia). The 1875 issue was later reprinted. Originals from 1875 are valuable; the reprints aren't.

Swapping stamps has, of course, long been a favourite pastime of collectors and in 1890 the British government decided to go a little further and swap the islands themselves, despite the reservations of Queen Victoria herself. Germany got Heligoland and Britain took over the German interests and rights in assorted bits of Africa including Zanzibar, itself also an island, but otherwise extremely different from Heligoland.

At the time, Britain reckoned it had got a good deal, but as Germany started to turn Heligoland into a massive German naval base, a few Britons must have started to have a few qualms. Rightly so, since Britain would, in the decades after the 1890 deal, spend a lot of time, effort and munitions attacking the area that includes the little North Sea archipelago that it had once controlled.

The Battle of Heligoland Bight on 28 August 1914 was an early British naval victory and, at the end of the war, Britain would assist with demolishing fortifications on the island.

The inter-war years saw something of a renaissance of the Heligoland tourist industry with, for instance, Werner Heisenberg doing some of his key thinking on quantum mechanics on the island.

But the Second World War would once again see bitter combat in the area. In December 1939, another Battle of Heligoland Bight took place, though this was an air battle, as RAF units attempted to attack German surface shipping. This was generally regarded as a German victory. At times during the war, the island was seriously bombed and much attention was paid to laying mines in the waters off it. And when the war ended, Britons once again returned to take control of Heligoland. By now, Britain had got slightly tired of Heligoland and its German naval fortifications. On 18 April 1947, the Royal Navy detonated thousands of tons of explosives on the island in one of the biggest non-nuclear explosions ever. Not surprisingly, the event is known as the 'Big Bang' or the 'British Bang', and it literally changed the landscape of the island.

In 1952, Heligoland was returned to the control of West Germany and today it is, once again, a tourist destination. There is not that much sign today of Heligoland's British past except for a few pointers like a street named after Sir Henry Maxse and, of course, those details in stamp albums and catalogues around the world.

Herceg Bosna

THERE IS THE Bosnian war that almost everybody knows about, the war mainly between Bosnian Serbs and (mainly Muslim) Bosniaks. There is the Bosnian war that few people outside Bosnia have heard about, the strange story of Zapadna Bosna (told in a later section). And there is the Bosnian war that some people have heard about, the story of changing alliances and changing strategies that is Herceg Bosna.

At first sight, the name looks familiar because it looks like Bosnia and Herzegovina, the official full title of the country which is often abbreviated to Bosnia, both because it's shorter and because many people around the world have no idea where Herzegovina actually is. In fact, Herzegovina is a name derived from the word for a count (of the noble rather than the mathematical kind), herceg/herzog, and it refers to a large triangle of land in the south of Bosnia and Herzegovina that is sandwiched between Croatia to the west and Montenegro to the east – sandwiched, that is, except for Neum. One of the delightful (and little-known) eccentricities of geography in this area is Bosnia's beach. Yes, it has a beach, or actually Herzegovina has a beach, a 12-mile strip of Adriatic coastline that separates the very southern bit of Croatia from the rest of Croatia.

Herzegovina is a beautiful land with both rugged scenery and gentler beauty like the valley of the river Neretva, and at its heart is the gorgeous old city of Mostar with its famous bridge. It is a land that has been part of a number of great empires, Roman, Byzantine, Ottoman and Austro-Hungarian.

The name Herceg Bosna looks familiar because, of course, it is basically the same name as Bosnia and Herzegovina, but with the Herzegovina bit given priority over the Bosnia bit, and, as one frequently finds in life, the clue is in the name, because Bosnia and Herzegovina's Croat community, Catholic by religion and identifying ethnically and culturally with neighbouring Croatia, is most heavily concentrated in Herzegovina. Yes, there are Croat communities spread across much of Bosnia and Herzegovina, but Herzegovina, with Croatia just next door, is where they have the most influence.

When many people think of the Balkan wars of the 1990s, they think of the Bosnian war in isolation, as if it happened on its own. But it never was in isolation. The Croatian war which started, as Serb elements in Yugoslavia fought to prevent Croatia leaving Yugoslavia and taking the Serb minorities there with it, had started months before the Bosnian war and lasted basically as long as it, playing a huge strategic role in it.

By the time the Bosnian war started in early 1992, Serb forces were in control of large chunks of Croatia and, with President Slobodan Milosevic offering the Serbs there major political and logistical support, there was no obvious sign that Croatia could regain the lost territory any time soon. In that context, it seemed natural to most at the start of the Bosnian war that the Bosniak and Croat communities there would fight alongside each other to prevent the Serbs doing to Bosnia what they had already done to Croatia. And at the start of the war, Bosniaks and Croats did mainly fight alongside each other. For instance, in the summer of 1992, the HVO (*Hrvatsko Vijeće Obrane*, Croatian Defence Council) and Bosniak forces scored a rare early victory over the Bosnian Serbs by preventing them taking Mostar.

However, there were signs from early on that it could get a whole lot more complicated than that, particularly in Herzegovina. The Bosnian Croat community began to focus more on its Croatian than its Bosnian identity and Croatia, with its hard-won experience of fighting the Serbs, and with easier access to weaponry than the Bosnian government, helped arm and train the Bosnian Croat militia, the HVO which in the badges it used looked more Croat than Bosnian. Despite the efforts of the HVO and its allies in the Bosnian army, in the summer of 1992, Bosnian Serb forces seized a huge part of Bosnia, and already by the autumn of 1992, while the Serbs were still advancing in Bosnia, clashes were already breaking out between Croats and Bosniaks.

To many in the world, and to some within the leadership of both Croatia and the Bosnian Croats, Bosnia Herzegovina seemed like a lost cause at the end of 1992. The Bosnian Serbs had, like the Croatian Serbs, effectively seceded. Some, on all sides in the conflict, imagined that the only feasible solution to it would be a total redrawing of existing international borders along community lines that would leave Croatian and Bosnian Serbs free to develop stronger links with Serbia, Bosnian Croats free to develop stronger links with Croatia, and a much, much smaller Bosnia somewhere in the middle. Even the peace plans for Bosnia being pushed by the international community were very much focused on identifying separate regions within Bosnia for Croats, Serbs and Bosniaks.

In spring 1993, vicious, open war erupted between the Bosnian Croats and the Bosniaks, and in August 1993, Herceg Bosna declared itself independent. Roughly printed stamps appeared in various denominations (and in two currencies, first in dinars, then in the Croatian currency, the kuna). Some feature strong religious iconography. Another shows the Mostar Bridge, which was later destroyed during Croat attacks on East Mostar.

In Herzegovina itself, where the Bosnian Croats had a military advantage, there was heavy fighting particularly in Mostar, which Herceg Bosna wanted as its capital, but which had a Muslim majority in the east. In the end, despite heavy fighting and heavy shelling, the HVO failed to take east Mostar. In central Bosnia, by contrast, where Croat communities were much more scattered than in Herzegovina, the Bosniak forces often had the military advantage. Bosnian Croats often found themselves trying to defend isolated and surrounded areas, like the Vitez pocket.

The fighting finally spurred the international community into action, and with Washington putting enormous pressure on Croatia, on the Bosnian Croats and on Bosniaks, and with the Bosnian Croats under huge pressure in the fighting in central Bosnia, a peace deal was finally agreed. The Washington Agreement in March 1994 put an end to the fighting, sidelined hardliners on both sides and created the Croat-Bosniak Federation. This would last for the rest of the war and become basically half of post-war Bosnia Herzegovina (the other half being the Serb element, Republika Srpska).

It was, finally, agreed that the Herceg Bosna experiment was going to come to an end. However, even today, there are deep cultural and political divisions inside Bosnia Herzegovina between the Croat and Bosniak communities.

Hyderabad

HYDERABAD IS A booming, buzzing city in the middle of India (it shares a name with a large city in Pakistan, but this piece is about India's Hyderabad). In its centre is the magnificent Charminar, erected as a monument to the end of a plague in 1591 – and later used to spread a new one, as it was the brand name of a popular, strong, unfiltered cigarette (ads used to feature a bare-chested bloke puffing on one, with the slogan 'It takes a Charminar to satisfy a man like me'). The city and its metropolitan area now have a population of around 8 million. In the first part of the last century, Hyderabad was an independent state, the largest and most powerful in India.

The city was founded in 1589 by Sultan Muhammad Quli Qutb Shah. Its name means City of the Brave – though a legend has it that the sultan actually named it after his favourite wife, Bhagmati, a Hindu woman who converted to Islam and was given the name Hyder Mahal. Hyderabad was planned and laid out in a grid, centred on the Charminar, and still has fine parks and gardens. As well as a ruler, the sultan was also a poet, writing in both Persian and the local language, Telegu: his regime was one of cultural and religious tolerance. As such regimes usually are, it was also one of prosperity and peace.

The city flourished. The engine of growth was precious stones: the area was a major source of them, and Hyderabad became the central marketplace in jewellery for the whole of

India and a major hub in global trade. Some of these found their way into the ruler's collection.

The city is surrounded by hills, on one of which sits the Golconda fort, an almost impregnable site that kept it independent from the Mughal emperors for all but a few decades. A tone of fierce independence was set – which persisted once the Mughals had given way to marauding Europeans. The former Mughal Governor of Hyderabad essentially set up his own dynasty in the city, and became its first Nizam. He and his successors played the various contending forces of mid-eighteenth century India against one another. When the British came out top dog, the third Nizam did a deal with them, keeping his independence but allowing them to set up a major military base at Secunderabad, Hyderabad's 'twin city'; the two face each other across the man-made, heart-shaped lake of Hussain Sagar.

Hyderabad was the largest of India's 'princely states', with a population of over 10 million and an area roughly the same as that of the UK. Its Nizams became wealthier and wealthier during the nineteenth and twentieth centuries. When Osman Ali Khan became the seventh Nizam in 1911, he was reputed to be the richest man in the world. This has to be taken in context. There was no government purse; the Nizam was the state and had to finance defence, education, public health, infrastructure and all the things governments spend their money on. Osman Ali Khan fulfilled his expected responsibilities in these departments – but still had a vast personal fortune. Most famous is his collection of jewels, which contained 173 pieces and is estimated to have been worth £2 billion. He is reputed to have used the Jacob Diamond, one of the largest diamonds in the world, as a paperweight (the diamond's name comes from that of its previous owner). The 'Nizam diamond' in his collection was even bigger.

Hyderabad issued its own currency – and, of course, stamps. The first was issued in 1869. A fuller set of definitives, from half an Anna to 12 Annas, followed in 1871. In 1931, pictorials were produced, the 1 Anna featuring the Charminar. The year of 1937 saw a set celebrating the Nizam's Silver Jubilee and featuring public buildings (paid for out of the Nizam's wealth). The ruler himself was not depicted, as strands of Sunni Islam forbid the depiction of living beings.

'Essays' (trial versions) of four stamps exist, which were planned to celebrate the state's independence in 1948. But they were never produced.

With the achievement of Indian independence in 1947, the princely states were expected to sign up to the new Union of India. The Nizam was not convinced. He wanted his substantial, wealthy state to become an independent member of the Commonwealth. He even began negotiating with the Portuguese, who controlled Goa, to see if they would sell the port to him (Hyderabad is landlocked).

The situation between the aspirant state and the new India soon deteriorated. Hyderabad complained of barricades on major routes in and out of its territory. Religion became an ever greater issue: the Hyderabadi elite was Muslim, the majority of the state's citizens Hindu. Under the best rulers, like the first sultan, this had not mattered, but in the fevered atmosphere of India's partition it came to matter terribly. A group of Muslim irregulars, the Razakars, grew ever more powerful – and uncontrollable, killing both Hindus and moderate Muslims. The rising communal violence gave the Indian authorities the reason they needed to invade the state and force it into the Union.

The invasion was officially called a 'Police Action', but it was actually a full-scale military intervention. It had a very British-Raj name: Operation Polo. It was launched on 13 September 1948, and within five days was within 50 miles of the capital. The Nizam dismissed his prime minister, who wanted to fight on, and surrendered to the Indian forces. Thirty-two Indian troops died in the operation, and nearly 2,000 Hyderabadi troops and Razakars. Much more deadly were the reprisals against the Muslim population, by local Hindus and by the invading troops, which mirrored the violence on India's north-west frontier at that time.

The Nizam was made *Rajpramukh*, a kind of formal head of state, of his former kingdom, but this office was abolished in 1956, as part of the erosion of the powers of the old Maharajas. He went into a decline, and in his last days became known for miserliness, knitting his own socks and cadging cigarettes (including, no doubt, Charminars) off visitors. His family squabbled over his wealth when he died in 1967; three decades later, his fabulous jewel collection was sold cheaply to the Indian government, where it is kept in a vault, occasionally emerging for exhibitions. Hyderabad's stamps, by contrast, are easy and relatively inexpensive to collect.

Icaria

ICARIA IS AN island in the south-east of the Aegean, closer to Turkey than Greece geographically but culturally and politically Greek. This is reflected in its name, which comes from Greek mythology. Icarus was the son of Daedalus, who built the labyrinth for the King of Crete but was then imprisoned in it, along with his son. Daedalus built wings out of wax for the two of them to escape, warning his son not to fly too high lest the sun melt the wings. Off they flew; youthful exuberance got the better of Icarus; the sun melted his wings and he crashed into the sea near Icaria. (The legend is a reminder that Greece controlled the Aegean shores of modern Turkey at that time: they would have been making for the modern Turkish city of Izmir, at that time the Greek city of Smyrna.)

Like many Aegean islands, Icaria has been controlled by various powers over the centuries. In the sixth century BC, neighbouring Samos was a major maritime power under the tyrannical Polycrates. A century later, Icaria was under Athenian influence. Fast forward three more centuries and it is part of the Roman Empire – though Strabo, a Roman traveller, visited it in 10 BC and reported that it was largely uninhabited. Into the Christian era and we find Icaria part of the Byzantine Empire. After this, it was Genoese. Genoa had a substantial empire in the thirteenth, fourteenth and fifteenth centuries, including Corsica, northern Sardinia, a number of Mediterranean islands, and colonies in the Crimea (it is believed that the Black Death came to Europe on a Genoese ship from one of these, Kaffa, modern Feodosia). When the Genoese left, Icaria fell under the control of the Knights Hospitaller, based on Rhodes (more on them in the section on Stampalia and the Dodecanese).

However, the notion of 'control' over all this time is relative. Mostly, the islanders were left to get on with their own lives. The most noticed, dominant outside forces were probably pirates, who used Icaria's natural harbours as bases while they preyed on ships entering or leaving the Aegean.

In 1521, Icaria became part of the expanding Ottoman Empire of Suleiman the Magnificent. But in true Icarian tradition, this 'belonging' was not enforced with the brutality that many subjects of empire suffer. A story goes that the first Turkish tax collector disappeared in mysterious circumstances, and that the Turks, unable to find out what had happened, let it pass and told the islanders to collect their own taxes. These were not substantial: a Greek bishop who visited the island in 1677 said that Icaria was the poorest island in the Aegean. But it was free to live its own life at its own pace.

The nineteenth century saw the rise of nationalism; in 1827, Icaria broke away from the Ottomans. However, the newly free Greece was not interested in taking it. The Ottomans returned and life went on.

The island's name was later used for a social experiment in the USA. In 1840, French social theorist Étienne Cabet wrote a book called *Travels in Icaria*, in which he described a model community run on Socialist lines. In 1848, he set off for the USA with 500 followers to set such a place up in reality. They ended up in Iowa; members gradually drifted away and the community was wound up in 1901.

A decade after that, it was the turn of the real Icaria to experiment politically. In 1911, Turkey became embroiled in a war with Italy, and lost. Italy took the Dodecanese; Icaria had a revolution. Armed partisans seized the Turkish garrison of Evidlos, then marched on the other main garrison at Aghios Kyrikos. En route, there was a skirmish with Turkish troops, in which the only fatality of the campaign occurred: an Icarian fighter who had got up late and was riding out to join his colleagues was mistaken by one of them for a Turk and shot. When the rebels reached Aghios Kyrikos they briefly besieged the garrison, which surrendered when it had used up all its ammunition (which it managed to expend without hurting anyone). Some of the warfare in this book takes us to the depths of human cruelty and depravity; by contrast, the Icarian rebellion seems a delightfully civilised affair – one senses neither side wanted to hurt the other, but rather let an inevitable outcome be achieved with minimal loss of face, and life, all round.

The war's one casualty was given a hero's burial, and the Free State of Icaria was declared. Despite the genteel nature of its revolution, there was still some fear that the Turks might return in force. Icaria tried to use expatriate influence to raise funds for defence – there were hopes that the Pan-Icarian Brotherhood of America would buy a second-hand torpedo boat (this sounds absurd, but the Ottoman navy had become so weak that even this might well have proven a sound defence). They didn't, so an old steamer, the *Cleopatra*, became the Free State's navy instead.

The island began to run out of money. One wheeze it came up with to raise funds was to issue stamps to sell to philatelists. A printer in Athens produced 56,000 of a design featuring the image of Penelope, the wife of Odysseus who waited loyally for him to return from Troy, and the inscription *Free State of Icaria*.

Eight values, in different colours, were issued, from a 2 lepta yellow to a 5 drachma grey. They all proved popular with collectors – so much so that forgers soon got in on the act. The value of the stamps collapsed, and the island ended up losing money on the venture.

However, in the end what broke the Free State was its inner division. There had long been a rivalry between north and south. This boiled over into a row about where the new nation's capital should be situated. This in turn nearly turned into a war – it would have been much more vicious than that which liberated the island – but a Greek cruiser, the *Thyella*, put in a timely appearance, visiting both northern and southern ports and insisting the Greek flag be raised in both places, symbolising that the island had become Greek territory. The Free State was free no longer.

Greece had its own civil war after 1945, in which a Communist takeover was narrowly averted. Afterwards, 10,000 Communists, including the composer Mikis Theodorakis, were exiled to Icaria, earning the island the name of the Red Rock. More recently, it has changed colour: Icaria is one of the world's five 'Blue Zones', noted for the longevity of their inhabitants. The key to this seems to be a mixture of family and community engagement, exercise, and natural diet. No doubt the climate helps, too, as does a certain disdain for consumerism and Icaria's independent spirit.

Inini

ININI IS PART of French Guiana, a tropical country on the north-east of South America. It borders Brazil and Surinam. It is also part of the European Union, by dint of it being a region of France.

The first French involvement dates back to 1503, a time when that nation was at war with Spain (in that year, the two nations fought the Battle of Cerignola, which is generally agreed to be the first battle won with superior use of firearms). However, the French did not stick around in Guiana, and it was a hundred years till they had a proper go at creating a settlement there. That didn't last, either; this time, the French were driven out by the Portuguese, eager to enforce the Treaty of Tordesillas, which had, back in 1494, divided everywhere outside Europe between Spain and Portugal.

A second colonisation attempt was driven away by local Amerindians, but finally in 1664, a settlement took root at Cayenne. This then changed hands a number of times – the Dutch had their eye on it, but in the end had to be content with neighbouring Surinam. It ended up back in French control. However, its masters were not sure what to do with it, apart from import hot peppers from it, and in 1854 it became a penal colony. Its most notorious prison was Devil's Island, off the coast, north of the capital.

Devil's Island was actually three islands, ironically known as the Îsles de Salut (Salvation's Islands). Someone had a dark sense of humour. Each island had its own jail. The main one was on Royale, where most ordinary convicts were made to work in timber camps. If they failed to cut a square metre of wood in a day, they would only get a tiny square of bread as rations. Alternative work was building a pointless road through the jungle.

New arrivals were told that the prison had two guardians, the jungle and the sea, and that, if escapees didn't get eaten by sharks or their bones picked clean by ants, they would 'soon beg to return'. Or maybe not beg, as returning meant being sent to a special punishment centre on a second island, St Joseph, where inmates were kept in solitary confinement, usually till they went crazy.

Devil's Island itself was reserved for political prisoners, the most famous of whom was Alfred Dreyfus, a young Jewish artillery captain from Alsace who was sent there in 1893, accused of passing military secrets to the Germans. Rumours soon spread that Dreyfus was innocent and that he had been framed by the actual spy, but the army refused to accept this. Their main reason was probably simple pig-headedness: they had made their judgement and to change it would be dishonourable. But another was anti-Semitism, which was on the rise at that time. Dreyfus was also from a middle-class background, a symbol of aspiration and social change. Old France did not like Alfred Dreyfus.

The affair split the nation. The split has a very modern ring to it, with progressive intellectuals – the term 'intellectual' was used for the first time to describe writers and artists who supported Dreyfus – led by novelist Émile Zola and actress Sarah Bernhardt on one side, and conservative forces on the other.

Even though evidence for Dreyfus's innocence continued to mount, a new court-martial in 1899 found him guilty again. But it was overridden by President Émile Loubet, who gave Dreyfus an official pardon. Dreyfus was only cleared by a court in 1906: he returned to the army, but had picked up too many tropical diseases and was invalided out. He participated in the First World War as a reservist.

Other prisoners on Devil's Island included the 1874 Wimbledon men's finalist, Vere Goold, who was sent there in 1909 for the murder of a woman from whom he and his wife had extorted money in Monte Carlo (leaving the body in a trunk at Marseilles Station didn't exactly help their case in court). Goold committed suicide after less than a year on the island. The prison continued to accrue notoriety thanks to two books, *The Dry Guillotine*, published in 1933, and *Papillon*, published in 1969. Both tell of escapes from the island. They are of course remarkable because so few people managed this feat. The most common form of escape was by death, either by suicide, like Goold, or of natural causes: it is estimated that of the 60,000 people sent to Devil's Island, only 2,000 ever returned.

The 'state' of Inini was founded in 1930. The plan was to develop the interior of the country, which was then (and still is) largely jungle. Roads and railways were to be built – true to local form, by convicts, this time captured rebels from French Indo-China. In theory, this would open up the interior to economic activity such as gold mining.

As often with such ventures, stamps were issued to put a mark of authority on it. The first issue was simply of overprints, with 'Territoire de l'Inini' printed onto the attractive 1924 French Guyana definitives, which featured an archer from the Carib people, three men shooting rapids in a canoe and, celebrating Western civilisation, the government building in Cayenne. In 1939, Inini got its own stamp: for the New York World's Fair of 1939, the French empire issued two standard stamps featuring Indian, Cambodian and Amerindian figures, with different colonies' names on them. Inini was one of these. It had made it into the Stanley Gibbons and Scott catalogues!

The Inini experiment didn't last much longer. The road- and rail-building achieved little, and at great human cost. Inini was reunited with the rest of French Guiana in 1946. Devil's Island joined it in the history books in 1952. French Guiana is now probably best known as the location of the European Space Centre, from which Ariane rockets are sent into space.

Italian Social Republic

THE ITALIAN SOCIAL Republic was a puppet state set up by the Nazis in northern Italy after that nation had formally surrendered in 1943. Its 'leader' was the former Duce and ally of Hitler, Benito Mussolini, though he had no real power at all.

Sicily was invaded on 10 July 1943. It soon became clear that the Axis forces could not hold the island, and they began to retreat to the mainland. On 19 July, Rome was heavily bombed by the Allies. Six days later, the Grand Council, the cabinet that ran Fascist Italy, voted nineteen to eight to depose the Duce. Among the nineteen was Count Ciano, his son-in-law and influential minister for foreign affairs. Mussolini, apparently, thought nothing of this vote – he still reckoned he was the man with the power. The next day, he was summoned to the presence of the Italian king, Victor Emmanuel III, who dismissed him, saying, "My dear Duce, it's no longer any good. Italy has gone to bits … You are now the most hated man in Italy."

The former dictator was arrested, then kept under house arrest in various places to prevent his former subjects from finding him. In August, he was taken to a hotel in a ski resort in the Campo Imperatore, an area about halfway down the spine of mountains that runs down Italy's centre, where he lived a bizarre life as its only guest. On 12 September, he was sprung from it by German commandos in a daring raid. Despite the steepness of the terrain around the hotel, they landed in gliders and surrounded the hotel, upon which the Duce's bodyguards handed him over without a fight. A special aeroplane designed for short take-offs then took him away, almost crashing in the process. It survived, and Mussolini was flown to Germany.

After an audience with Hitler, the Duce was taken back to Italy and set up as head of the puppet Italian Social Republic in the lakeside town of Salò on Lake Garda (the ISR was also known as the Salò Republic). Count Ciano, who had fled to Germany in August, was sent back to join him. Hell hath no fury like a narcissist scorned; Mussolini had Ciano and four other fellow *fascisti* who had voted him out of office tried for treason and executed with maximum dishonour: tied to chairs and shot in the back.

The new republic was given the trappings of legitimacy: a flag, a currency, a motto ('for the honour of Italy') and, of course, stamps. The first ones were old Italian ones overprinted, first with the letters GNR (for Republican National Guard), then later with the fascist symbol, the ancient Roman *fascio littorio*, a bundle of sticks around an axe. In 1944, it issued its own set of definitive stamps, featuring either a drummer boy calling out 'All'armi!' ('To arms!', the first line of a *fascisti* anthem) or classic Italian monuments that had been destroyed by the Allies. There was even a commemorative set, in honour of the Bandiera brothers, two nineteenth-century revolutionaries. Behind this façade, of course, the Italian Social Republic had no power: all decisions had to be run past the German authorities.

Meanwhile, the Allies were battling their way up Italy, fighting not the Italians but the Germans. Churchill had argued that Italy was the 'soft underbelly of Europe', but this was not one of his better military assessments. Winter 1943 saw the Allied advance halted by Field Marshal Albert Kesselring at the heavily defended Gustav Line, a series of fortifications which crossed Italy about 80 miles south of Rome. (These were built by Organisation Todt, the same institution responsible for the defences around Festung Lorient.) The hilltop abbey of Monte Cassino, where some of the fiercest combat of the war took place, lay on this line. The abbey was reduced to rubble in the fighting, and duly featured on a second set of Italian Social Republic 'buildings destroyed by our enemies' stamps.

It took till May 1944 to break the Gustav Line. Rome fell soon afterwards – US General Mark Clark disobeyed orders and marched on the city, which had been declared 'open' and left largely undefended. Elsewhere, however, the Allies continued to encounter stiff resistance from Kesselring, who is generally regarded as one of the most able generals of the Second World War.

Meanwhile, the Italian Social Republic was in a state of civil conflict. It is estimated that by May 1944 there were 80,000 Italian partisans operating in small bands of highly mobile guerrillas, supported by the local populace. Women played a key part in the movement, some as fighters, others as messengers. As the war continued, soldiers from the ISR army began to desert to these bands, bringing military skill and state-of-the-art weaponry. In response to partisan activity, the Nazis attempted vicious reprisals – ten Italians would be executed for every German soldier killed. This, of course, only went to create ever more support for the partisans. There were also bands of Fascist sympathisers, who did not fight the partisans head-on, but informed on them wherever possible, terrorising communities they considered to be partisan-friendly, and hunted down Jews to hand over to the SS.

Mussolini himself had no control over the situation. The former 'Iron Prefect' and Marshal of the Italian Empire probably spent more time listening to the blazing rows between his wife Rachele and his young mistress Clara Petacci than exercising political power. He did keep up the rhetoric, however. As the Allies advanced, he urged Italians to fight to the last man. He himself moved from Salò to Milan, which he felt was safer.

In the end, nowhere was safe. On 25 April 1945, he, Clara – not Rachele – and about fifty associates joined a German column retreating north. His plan was to cross the Swiss border, but two days later, the column was stopped by partisans at the village of Dongo on Lake Como and ordered to hand over any Italians among them. Mussolini hid in a truck disguised as a German soldier, but was recognised and arrested. He and Clara were taken to a remote farmhouse and executed.

Their bodies were then taken to Milan and hung upside-down outside an Esso petrol station in the Piazzale Loreto, a place where his secret police had formerly hung partisans. They were stoned and spat upon by the public. Such was the end of the Italian Social Republic.

Katanga and South Kasai

IN THIS CHAPTER, we'll feature the intertwined stories of two entities – two entities that each had their own stamps.

First, the geography. Katanga is a huge south-eastern region in the even huger country that is now known as the Democratic Republic of the Congo. And South Kasai, a much smaller area, though still about the size of Belgium, was a political entity, situated immediately to the north of Katanga. Both have hugely important mineral resources.

It is interesting that South Kasai is roughly the same size as Belgium, because it too has a very significant part to play in this story. In the nineteenth century, as the European powers rushed to divide up Europe, the little Kingdom of Belgium (which had only come into existence in 1831) lagged behind. Its second king, Leopold II, wasn't happy about this and set out to build himself an African empire. Which he did, and because the Belgian government was less enthusiastic about the whole enterprise, what he ended up with was his own personal colony, the Congo Free State, which issued stamps such as the one shown in the illustrations. The human rights abuses in this, however, became so appalling that in the end the Belgian government was forced to take over, creating the Belgian Congo, an African empire vastly bigger than little Belgium itself.

By the 1950s, though, as elsewhere in Africa, pressure for change and eventual independence increased. One of a new generation of Congolese politicians advocating independence was Patrice Lumumba of the Congolese National Movement (MNC).

Rioting in the capital, then Léopoldville now Kinshasa, in 1959 left many dead and Lumumba was imprisoned accused of inciting a riot after unrest in Stanleyville. However, the MNC did well in local elections and it all led to a conference in Brussels in January 1960 that laid down a timetable for elections and independence. Feeling under pressure to act, and act fast, the Belgians agreed that after elections in May, the country would become independent that same year.

The MNC won the national elections in May and on 30 June 1960, the Republic of the Congo became independent and

Patrice Lumumba became its first prime minister. However, the new country became independent with many questions unresolved, including, could such a large and complex territory with many ethnic and cultural divisions remain united, and how would Belgians both in Belgium and in the new country itself react to the loss of commercial assets such as the diamond mines of South Kasai and the copper and other mines of Katanga?

A major army mutiny occurred on 5 July near Léopoldville, and the Belgians sent in paratroopers to protect Belgian civilians. A significant number of the Belgian troops were despatched to Katanga. On 11 July, Moïse Tshombe, whose party with its allies had won a majority in Katanga's provincial assembly in the May elections, declared mineral-rich Katanga independent, and Belgium was accused of being sympathetic to the secessionist regime. The Congo government appealed for UN assistance and it was agreed a UN force would be sent. In August, Albert Kalonji declared South Kasai to be autonomous. Belgium was also accused of supporting this secession. Lumumba appealed for help to the Soviet Union, which assisted the Congo governments to launch an offensive against the secessionists. However, the involvement of the Soviet Union inevitably produced heavy suspicion and unease in Washington.

The Katangese government, with mercenary assistance, developed an effective little army and even a small air force flown by western pilots. Tshombe's forces managed to see off the initial Congo army offensive but also began to clash with UN forces. A number of pitched battles would eventually occur between Katangese and UN forces, including heavy fighting in Élisabethville and Jadotville which would include action by the Katangese air force. September saw the death of UN Secretary Dag Hammarskjöld when his plane went down while he was trying to broker a ceasefire in Katanga.

In September, Lumumba was also toppled in a coup launched with the assistance of Colonel Joseph-Désiré Mobutu, who would later be the country's long-term ruler. Lumumba was imprisoned, but managed to escape briefly in December. Recaptured, he was eventually handed over to Katangese forces and later killed.

Both Katanga and South Kasai developed the trappings of statehood including, of course, stamps. After early overprints, Katanga produced its own definitives, featuring Katangan art. Commemoratives were also produced, celebrating the 1961 Katanga International Fair, the local gendarmerie and the first anniversary of independence, the last of these featuring a picture of President Tshombe. South Kasai issued two small sets, a rather fine one featuring a leopard, and one of Kalonji. Both bear the proud inscription *Etat Autonome de Sud-Kasai*.

South Kasai's autonomy was not to last for long – even less than Katanga's. Kalonji was toppled in a coup and South Kasai would re-join Congo in 1962.

The UN made repeated efforts to broker a peace deal between the Congolese government and Katanga, but in December 1962, after UN and Katangese forces clashed yet again, the UN decided it had had enough. It launched Operation Grand Slam, a decisive air and land campaign which smashed Tshombe's forces. Within a few weeks, in January 1963 Tshombe accepted defeat and the Katanga secession was finished. At least temporarily.

Tshombe himself was not yet finished. After fleeing into exile in Spain, he made a stunning recovery when in 1964 he returned to Congo as prime minister after a rebellion had erupted in the east of the country. However, he was toppled again in 1965, and when Mobutu launched a second coup and took control of the central government in Kinshasa, Tshombe thought it wise to leave again. He died in exile in Algeria in 1969.

And 1963 was not entirely the end of the road for attempts at Katangese secession either. In 1977, rebel Katangese forces launched an invasion from Angola, and Mobutu had to get French military intervention to repel the invasion. French aircraft airlifted Moroccan troops into Kolwezi and France also supplied additional aircraft and armoured vehicles to assist the operation against the rebels.

Mobutu himself died in exile in 1997, forced out by a rebellion led by Laurent-Désiré Kabila. Bitter years of civil war in the Democratic Republic of Congo would follow, killing vast numbers of people.

Kiautschou

PRETTY MUCH EVERYONE is aware of the British Empire and most people will also be aware that a variety of other European nations, particularly the French and Spanish, but also nations like the Dutch and the Portuguese and the Belgians, acquired extensive foreign empires during the European expansion across the globe. Fewer people, however, maybe know much about Germany's attempts to build an empire around the world to rival those of their European competitors.

Since it was only unified as a country in 1871, Germany rather inevitably entered the race for foreign colonies much later than most of its European competitors. Nevertheless, by the time it entered the First World War in 1914, in an act that would ultimately lead to the dissolution of the German Empire, it had managed to acquire itself quite a lot of colonies in quite a lot of places. It had, for instance, German East Africa, German South-West Africa and German West Africa, and it held a surprising number of islands in the Pacific. And yes, it had Kiautschou, or Kiautschou Bay, a German foothold in China. Or at least, Kiautschou is what it said on the stamps Germany printed, even though now we tend to call it Jiaozhou. At its main centre was Tsingtau or Tsingtao. Again we tend now to call it Qingdao but Tsingtao is what it still says on the beer produced at its world-famous brewery.

Tsingtao had originally been a fishing village and then a commercial Chinese port, and then in the late nineteenth century the situation really began to change. In the 1880s, the Chinese built a small naval station, but China wasn't the naval power that was going to transform Tsingtao and Kiautschou over the next decades – that was Germany.

As early as 1861, Prussian warships in the Eulenberg expedition had turned off the Chinese coast looking to explore the area and make contacts. Among those on the expedition was scientist Ferdinand von Richthofen, whose nephew would be Manfred von Richthofen, the Red Baron. However, in the late nineteenth century the Germans realised even more clearly that if they were to rival Britain globally they would need a global fleet and naval bases around the world for the fleet. Kiautschou/Jiaozhou seemed a good potential base in China. In 1897, two German priests were killed in Shandong and, seeing the opportunity to use this as a pretext for action, German navy ships steamed and seized Tsingtao/Qingdao. In the negotiations that followed, the Germans didn't manage to get the Chinese to accept permanent German control of the port and the surrounding area, but they did get from the Chinese a 99-year lease, which would expire in 1997, the same year that Britain's 99-year lease on Hong Kong's New Territories would also expire.

In 1898, the Germans weren't too worried about what might happen in 1997, so they got to work on turning Tsingtao into a version of a modern European city. They made it a free port and built modern port facilities. They laid out streets like in a European city. They built a rail route to Jinan. And they built a variety of factories and industries. And yes, they built a brewery. Then it was called the rather German-sounding, or, in fact, totally German-sounding Germania Brewery. It was, however, the ancestor of the rather less German-sounding Tsingtao Brewery of today, producing a beer enjoyed by many visitors to Chinese restaurants around the world. And yes, of course,

Kiautschou had stamps, though these were no more Chinese than the name of the brewery: they featured Kaiser Wilhelm's yacht, the SMY *Hohenzollern II* (yachts come in all sizes: the *Hohenzollern II* was nearly 400ft long).

However, unlike British control of Hong Kong's New Territories, German control of Kiautschou was not to last quite until 1997. In fact, not even close to it.

When war broke out in 1914, it would rapidly become clear how vulnerable were Germany's widely dispersed colonies, so far from Germany and so close to territories and colonies held by their enemies. German naval raiders, however, proved themselves a major problem in the Pacific in the early months of the war. For instance, the SMS *Emden* that, along with other ships of Germany's East Asia Squadron, had been based in Tsingtao, left the port in August 1914 and in the next two months captured over twenty ships, bombarded Madras and sank a Russian and a French warship in the Battle of Penang before being defeated by HMAS *Sydney* in the Battle of Cocos Islands.

Seizing Kiautschou, therefore, became a priority for Britain. It was also, however, a priority for Japan. Japan had been since 1902 a British ally and in 1914, it saw the opportunity not only to ally but also to grab some useful real estate. In August, it declared war on Germany. In September, a Japanese naval force started landing troops on the coast near Tsingtao. British forces were also present in the area.

Soon Tsingtao was surrounded and under siege. The siege was militarily notable for, among other events, early use of aircraft by both sides. The Japanese seaplane carrier *Wakamiya*, for instance, launched air raids against targets in the port city.

The Germans in Tsingtao managed to hold out for some time, but in the end, the result was inevitable. In November, the city surrendered. It was the end of German control of Tsingtao. Japan remained in control until 1922, when the port was returned to China. But the Japanese returned to the city in

1938 and occupied it until 1945. Today, Qingdao is a large thriving city with a wide variety of industries and attractions, among them, of course, that brewery.

Kurland

KURLAND, OR COURLAND, is a triangle of Latvia's coastline on the far side of the Gulf of Riga that sticks up into the Baltic, looking a bit like a parrot's head, with a sharp, curved beak. It is low-lying, marshy and prone to fog – not the ideal place to fight a war. So it is perhaps not surprising that it was one of the last parts of Europe to be occupied by the Nazis, a 'pocket' of resistance that only surrendered when Germany as a whole did.

The area's original inhabitants were the Curonians, a warlike people who sometimes allied themselves to, and sometimes fought against, the Vikings. They had a mystical, pagan religion: according to Adam of Bremen, an eleventh-century German chronicler, their 'houses were full of soothsayers, diviners and necromancers'. The horse was sacred to them.

It was only a matter of time before militant Christianity came to what was then known as Curonia. It did so via the Livonian Order, a sub-group of the Teutonic Order, one of those mediaeval international crusading organisations which controlled land as recently as the nineteenth century and which still exists today as a religious body. During the thirteenth century, the Order was in the business of conquest and conversion, which it did successfully in Curonia and its eastern neighbour Semigallia.

Three centuries later, the Reformation was sweeping Europe, and the old mediaeval knightly orders collapsed. Curonia and Semigallia became a non-religious dukedom, with its capital in Mitau (modern Jelgava). In the seventeenth century, under the progressive Duke Jacob, it became wealthy through trade and manufacture. It even indulged in the geopolitical fashion of the day, colonialism. It was the smallest European nation to do this, if one excludes the Knights of Malta, who briefly possessed four Caribbean islands. In 1651, a Curonian fleet sailed to Africa and founded Fort Jacob on the Gambia River. In 1654, a Curonian party landed on Tobago in the West Indies, naming it New Courland (the name had switched from Curonia by then). A fort was built – named, unoriginally, Fort Jacob – and the town of Jacobstadt founded.

The Courland Empire did not last long, as it was soon under attack from rival, bigger colonialists. The duchy went into decline, too. Duke Jacob died in 1682, and his son was more interested in shows of ducal grandeur than the actual business of running a country (let alone an empire). Fort Jacob was seized by the Dutch, and Tobago had to be sold to pay ducal debts.

Between 1710 and 1730, the duchy was ruled by the duchess Anna, daughter of the mad Russian Tsar Ivan IV. She had been married to the then Duke of Courland/Semigallia in St Petersburg, but he died on the way back to Jelgava, probably from alcohol poisoning brought on by the wedding celebrations. She ran the country instead. In 1730, she was summoned back to Russia to become empress. There, she became better known for her size, crude sense of humour and love of hunting than for any leadership skills.

Russian influence remained in Courland, however, and the dukedom was quietly merged into the Russian Empire during the eighteenth century. It became one of the empire's Baltic governorships – though the governors were usually German aristocrats, not Russians.

At the end of the First World War, Germany still occupied Courland. Latvia was declared an independent state, then was invaded by the new Soviet Russia in 1918. It fought this huge adversary off in a brave year-long war (with assistance from the Royal Navy) and became a parliamentary democracy. Sadly, this did not last. In 1940, the Russians came back, then were driven out by the Nazis in 1941, who in turn were expelled by the Red Army.

Or almost. Courland's stamps date from the closing stages of the Second World War. On 9 October 1944, Soviet forces reached the Baltic just above Memel, which lies to the south of Courland, essentially cutting off Germany's Army Group North in the 'parrot's head'. Army Group North consisted of over 200,000 troops. Hitler was advised by General Heinz Guderian to evacuate them, but insisted they stay and fight. Hitler wanted Courland to be the bridgehead for his planned fightback against his bitterest enemy.

He also wanted to protect the submarine bases he had built in Courland. As his forces began losing the war, Hitler placed ever more faith in a technological redemption, whereby amazing new weapons would suddenly turn the tide. His main such weapons were the V1 and V2 rockets, but he also had huge faith in a new class of submarine, the Type XXI. This was a remarkable vessel. It was fast, stealthy and quiet. It could fire and reload torpedoes six times faster than earlier U-boats. Most powerful of all, it could spend much more time underwater. It could, possibly, have turned the Battle of the Atlantic – but like much new technology, there were more glitches in realising the designs than the designers hoped, and the Type XXI saw little active service. Instead, it became the model for post-war submarine design in both Russia and the West.

It is easy to sneer at Hitler's dream of a sudden game-changing technological turnaround, but it is a sobering truth that such a turnaround did happen. Luckily for the world it was at Los Alamos, rather than in Haigerloch and Oranienburg, where Germany's attempts at building a nuclear bomb were centred.

So, in the name of protecting the submarine pens for a vessel that never actually entered them, 200,000 German soldiers spent the rest of the war in what became known as the Courland Pocket. The Russians made six attempts to dislodge them, but none succeeded. And in the meantime, life went on, and part of that life was the sending and receiving of mail. Existing stamps were overprinted with 'Kurland' and with new values. There are essentially two denominations, one of 6 Reichs Pfennig, the standard postcard rate, overprinted on various stamps featuring Hitler, and one of 12, the letter rate, on old parcel stamps featuring a German eagle.

Kurland surrendered only when Germany did, on 8 May 1945. The 200,000 soldiers disappeared into captivity – apart from a few venturesome ones who escaped down the coast and made their way west. Many of the captives never returned.

Latvia became part of the Soviet Union and suffered massive deportations under Stalin. In 1991, it achieved independence; it joined the European Union and NATO in 2004.

League of Nations

WE ALL KNOW the United Nations, with its distinctive blue and white flag, and we all know some of its history. Despite all its well-known faults, it is an organisation that has since 1945 provided an ambitious framework for international cooperation and communications. It hasn't always managed to do what it should have done, but nonetheless, the world would be a poorer and less safe place without it.

But the United Nations did not emerge from nowhere in the ashes of the Second World War. It built on an organisation much less well known today, an organisation that was, in its time, more revolutionary, more ambitious and even more flawed than the United Nations. Unlike the United Nations, the League of Nations was not an institution that had a long and distinguished history of producing stamps. It had overprints created for it, however, by the Swiss government – the league's headquarters were in Geneva. These started in 1922 and were for use by officials working for the league. Switzerland also issued a set of commemorative stamps in 1938, celebrating the league and the International Labour Organization, also based in Geneva. These show the austere headquarters of these bodies (the league's was called the Palace of Nations). The two showing the palace are inscribed SDN, and are sometimes confused with 'League of Nations' stamps – technically they are Swiss ones, unless overprinted.

For a long time before the First World War, various people had discussed the basic concept of international societies of countries that would cooperate to make the world a better and less violent place. The second half of the nineteenth century, for instance, saw the Geneva Conventions, the founding of the Inter-Parliamentary Union and the first Hague Convention. The 1899 Hague Convention failed to achieve a proposed agreement on limiting armaments levels. It did, however, adopt the convention for the Pacific Settlement of International Disputes, which created the Permanent Court of Arbitration. It also agreed a ban on asphyxiating gases, on the use of expanding bullets, and on discharging projectiles or explosives from balloons. All these bans would be violated during the war that was about to engulf the globe.

Inevitably, as the full scale of the carnage that was the First World War became clear, efforts to find a path to preventing such conflicts in the future were given a huge boost. One group that promoted such ideas on both sides of the Atlantic was the Bryce Group, named after Lord Bryce, a Liberal peer and former British ambassador to the United States. Ideas from the group and others got an enthusiastic reception from the President of the United States, Woodrow Wilson.

Wilson had been determined to end the war without actually entering it, but, in the end, German actions had forced him to take the USA into the war on the Allied side. He did not see himself as part of the old imperial European structures that had created the war; instead, he saw himself as part of a new political wave that would sort out the mess left by the war and create a new, more free, more fair world. At the start of 1918,

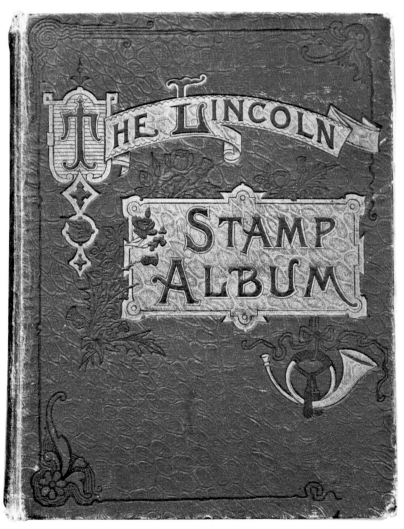

A schoolboy's stamp album from 1901.

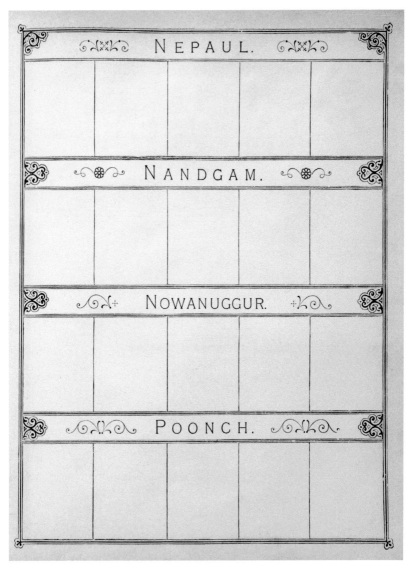

Some places were harder to collect ...

... than others.

Where it all began – the Penny
Black.

Austrian Italy.

Batum.

Niger Coast
Protectorate (later,
part of Biafra).

Cundinamarca (left) and its liberator, Simón Bolívar (right).

Don Republic.

East India Company.

Eastern Rumelia.

Fiume.

French Territory of the Afars and Issas.

Great Barrier Island
Pigeongram Agency.

Heligoland.

Hyderabad.

Inini.

Katanga and South Kasai.

Manchuria
Manchukuo.

North Ingria.

Nyassa Company.

Obock.

Nawanagar.

British South Africa Company.

Czechoslovak Legion
in Russia.

Stellaland.

South African
Republic.

Straits Settlements.

Tibet.

Tuva.

United States of the
Ionian Islands.

the year that would see American forces arrive in France in huge numbers, Wilson enunciated his vision of how the war would end and what would happen afterwards in his famous Fourteen Points. Point Four was that national armaments should be reduced to the lowest point consistent with domestic safety. Point Fourteen was that a general association of nations should be formed which would guarantee the political independence and territorial integrity of both small and large countries.

With the armistice on 11 November 1918, the major fighting finally came to an end, and in 1919, the victorious Allies convened for the Paris Peace Conference to decide how to formalise the peace, punish the losers, and try to ensure that no such war ever took place again. A key element aimed at achieving the last goal was the creation of the League of Nations, which provided for collective security, reduction of armaments, and arbitration over international disputes. The Covenant of the League of Nations established a secretariat under a secretary-general, a council with representatives of the major Allied powers plus others, and a general assembly which would include representatives of all member countries. It also established a Permanent Court of International Justice. Forty-four states initially signed the covenant and Geneva, in neutral Switzerland, was chosen as the venue for the first meeting of the General Assembly in 1920.

From the start, the League of Nations had a major problem. The United States and, in particular Woodrow Wilson, had been instrumental in creating the league (he even got the Nobel Peace Prize in 1919) but the obligations inherent in membership to go to war, if necessary, to counter aggression against a member state, were seen by many US politicians as potentially committing the US to foreign wars it did not want to fight, and, in the end, the US never became a member of the league.

In the early post-war years, the league had some successes in resolving disputes and organising plebiscites to decide peacefully the route of some sections of Europe's new borders. However, the League of Nations mandate system which, for instance, gave the French control of Syria, would help cause problems that still exist today. And in the 1930s, the whole foundation of the League of Nations system came under huge pressure.

The league failed to prevent Japanese aggression in China. It failed to prevent the Chaco War in South America. It failed to prevent Italian aggression in Ethiopia. It failed to prevent the Spanish Civil War and the involvement of foreign states in the war. In 1938, it got itself a splendid new home, the Palace of Nations in Geneva, but the League itself was almost at an end.

In 1939, war once more engulfed the world, and when, yet again, the Allies met to decide how to establish peace and prevent another world war, the discredited League of Nations was no longer their choice. Instead, a few months after the creation of the new United Nations, in early 1946, the league terminated itself, handing the baton on maintaining peace to the new body. Today, the Palace of Nations is the Geneva home of not the League of Nations it was built for but instead the United Nations.

Manchuria Manchukuo

MANCHUKUO WAS A puppet state in China's most northern region, run by the Imperial Japanese Army from 1931 to 1945.

Japan, dragged into the modern era by Commodore Matthew C. Perry in 1853, was determined to prove itself a world power. It won a war with China in 1895, gaining Taiwan and a foothold in Korea. It defeated Russia in 1904/05, the first time that a non-European nation had won a war against a European one. It annexed Korea in 1910. The 1920s saw a debate between those Japanese who felt this was enough, and those, especially in the army, who wanted much more. By 1931, the latter were in the ascendancy.

Manchuria, rich in coal and minerals but underdeveloped and squabbled over by Russia and China, was a perfect target. Its invasion was, as many such invasions are, a put-up job. In September 1931, a small amount of dynamite was exploded under a Japanese-owned railway close to a Chinese army camp near Mukden (modern Shenyang). The explosion caused so little damage that a train passed over it shortly afterwards with no problems. However, the Japanese army accused Chinese saboteurs (the actual saboteur had most likely been one of its own men, a Lieutenant Komoto), and used the event as a pretext to invade. It did this without orders from the civilian authorities or the emperor – but it won a string of quick victories, so any criticism of it soon became politically impossible. This was arguably the moment that the military became the dominant power in 1930s Japan, after which it tightened its grip ever more.

By February 1932, the whole of Manchuria had fallen, and a new state, that of Manchukuo, was announced. The rest of the world tried to protest at this obvious bullying of a weak nation by a strong one, but the Japanese simply ignored this, quitting the League of Nations. Hitler and Mussolini quietly noted the league's total ineffectiveness.

The new state needed a head: enter Pu Yi. The 'Last Emperor' of Qing Dynasty China had ascended to his throne aged 2 and been deposed aged 6. He had grown up as a prisoner in Beijing's Forbidden City – where he studied with a British tutor, Reginald Johnston, and took the name Henry, after Henry VIII. After a warlord seized the capital in 1924, Pu Yi fled to the Japanese-controlled enclave of Tientsin (Tianjin). His new hosts made him welcome, aware of his potential propaganda value. Now, aged 26, he was brought to Manchukuo to be its 'Chief Executive'.

Stamps, as so often, play a key role in a new nation's announcement that it believes it is here to stay. Manchukuo's first definitives appeared four months after its creation, on 26 July 1932 (designed and printed, of course, in Tokyo). Eighteen values were issued, with two designs: one, on lower values, was of the White Pagoda in Liaoyang, the other, on higher values, featured Pu Yi in western dress. He stares owlishly out from the stamp under the Chinese characters for 'Manchukuo Postal Administration'. To reinforce the propaganda point, a special Presentation Album featuring the issue was produced for philatelists, postmasters and foreign dignitaries (it is now particularly prized by collectors).

The puppet state continued to produce stamps. A set from 1934 celebrated Pu Yi's 'promotion' from 'Chief Executive' to emperor, with the reign title 'Kangde'. Propaganda at the time trumpeted that, 'The Emperor and Empress have come home to the throne of their ancestral state.' However, a new set of definitives in 1936 no longer featured the emperor, who was a total figurehead whose job was simply to countersign Japanese orders. Pu Yi was rarely seen outside his palace, where he lived with his empress Wanrong, who had become an opium addict.

Another stamp celebrated the completion of 10,000km of railway. Manchukuo's new masters were turning it into an industrial heartland, where Chinese workers were treated like virtual slaves – watch the film *The Human Condition* to see what it was like. The aim was to supply *matèriel* for the Japanese war machine.

In July 1937, that machine turned its attention to the rest of China. While it never achieved quite the total domination it wanted, Japan conquered large swathes of Chinese territory in the north-east and along the coast. Five years later, its 'Greater East Asia Co-Prosperity Sphere' extended from the north of Manchuria to Guadalcanal Island, almost on the same latitude as northern Australia, and from Burma to the Marshall Islands in the mid-Pacific. It included Singapore, which had fallen in February 1942, an event celebrated on a Manchukuo overprint stamp. At the height of Axis power, the Japanese planned to extend further and share control of Asia with Nazi Germany either side of a line along the meridian of 70 degrees east.

Manchuria was now the industrial heart of this vast empire. It was also the site of the notorious Unit 731, where the Imperial Army experimented with biological and chemical weapons on live prisoners, mainly Chinese.

In the end, the empire overextended itself. Driven back by some of the most brutal fighting of the war, it began to shrink. One of its first components, Manchukuo was also one of the last to fall. Soviet forces built up on the borders of the puppet state. After the atom bomb was dropped on Hiroshima, Stalin's troops poured in from east and west. Like the Japanese army fourteen years before, they met limited resistance. The former state of Manchukuo was handed over to the Chinese Communists the next year.

Pu Yi was captured by the Soviets trying to flee to Japan without Wanrong, whom he left behind. She was captured by Chinese Communists and put in jail, where she soon died, unable to live without opium. When the Communists finally conquered the whole of China, Pu Yi was handed over to them. He fared better than his unfortunate empress, being imprisoned, but pardoned in 1959. The former Kangde Emperor of Manchukuo ended up working as an editor in a government department, married to a Beijing nurse in what seems to have been a genuine love match, and died in 1967.

Memel

MEMEL IS A place you're unlikely to find on any modern map today. However, if you end up hearing or reading the lyrics of the now infamous, banned first verse of the German national anthem that was so popular with the Nazis, there you will find a reference to Germany being united from the Meuse to the Memel. Because the Memel is the old German name of the River

Neman (and it is also the reason it appears in this book), the old German name of the Baltic port at the mouth of the river, now in Lithuania and now known by the Lithuanian name Klaipėda.

Germans have been associated with the city for a long time. When most people think of the Crusades they tend to think of the Middle East, and yet crusading activity took place elsewhere and one of the places it happened was in the Baltic region. People from across Europe would go on crusade in the region. The future Henry IV of England, for instance, did so. But prominent among those conducting crusading activities in this region was one knightly order, the Teutonic Knights. In 1252, they arrived at the mouth of the Memel/Neman and reckoned it was a good place for a castle. So they built Memelberg, the castle on the Memel, which eventually just got shortened to Memel.

Not all the Lithuanians were that keen on having the Teutonic Knights on their doorstep, and the next century would see occasional assaults on the town. However, a peace deal signed at Lake Melno in 1422 established a border between the Teutonic Knights and Lithuania that would last long after the Teutonic Knights had handed over their interest in the region to other Germanic powers. Other powers, however, would not take such a hands-off approach to Memel. During its imperial phase in the seventeenth century, Sweden occupied the city occasionally and in the eighteenth century the new power in the region, the Russian Empire, arrived in the vicinity. Russian troops, for instance, occupied the city during the Seven Years' War and Lithuania became part of the Russian Empire.

Nevertheless, the city remained mainly in the German sphere of influence and it became one of Prussia's key ports. It was a city that did some major international trade. Because of access to good timber, it became a major destination for British ships, and significant parts of the Royal Navy were built from timber that had passed through Memel. The Napoleonic Wars saw assorted armies pass by, and at one stage Memel briefly became the temporary capital of Prussia. Another war would come, though, that would change Memel's situation dramatically.

When the First World War broke out, Memel was very vulnerable to Russian forces and they occupied it in 1914. The Germans then retook it in 1915, then the Russians retook it and then the Germans recaptured it again and advanced into Lithuania. However, in 1917 the revolution shattered any Russian chance of winning the war in the east and the Russian Empire began to fall apart. The Lithuanians declared independence in February 1918 and to appease the occupying Germans decided to choose a German prince as their new king. However, when in autumn 1918 Germany collapsed and lost the war, the Lithuanians ditched the idea of a German king and opted for a republic instead. The new country then ended up in a fight with both newly independent Poland and the new Soviet Union. It did rather better against the Soviets than it did against the Poles.

Meanwhile, the Allies were trying to make up their mind what to do about Memel. While the city itself was mainly German, there were plenty of Lithuanians in the country around the city and Lithuania was desperate to have the major port. They requested it at the Paris Peace Conference in 1919. In the end, though, the conference established a special separate Memel territory and sent in French troops and French administrators. Memel's first stamps are overprints on French definitives but, oddly, also on German ones (this was done to use up existing stocks of stamps at a time when resources of all kinds were scarce). In 1922, a commission was established to review the final status of Memel. Then, when the commission started to show some interest in the idea of an independent Memel state somewhat similar to the Danzig Free State, the Lithuanians decided to act.

In the Klaipėda Revolt of January 1923, Lithuanian forces crossed the border into Memel territory and linked up with local

Lithuanian volunteers. Brief fighting took place in Memel itself, but within a few days Lithuanian forces were in total control. France wasn't happy, but the Allies were divided on how to react and had plenty going on elsewhere to occupy their attention. In the end, the Klaipėda Convention allowed the Lithuanians to keep the port city.

The new bosses issued original stamps to show their ownership, in three designs, one showing a liner steaming out of the port of Memel, a second the arms of the city and the third, for the highest denominations, the Memel lighthouse. The biggest of the higher denominations was 3,000 Marks. This was a time of hyperinflation. Memel switched to a new currency, and overprints in Centu and Litas followed. Used examples of some of these are rare.

The Klaipėda Convention could have settled Memel/Klaipėda's status forever. Except it didn't. Many people will be aware of the gradual process in which, in the run-up to the Second World War, the international community accepted Hitler sending troops into assorted territories he fancied. Many will also be aware of the German occupation of Czechoslovakia. Few are aware, outside the region, of Germany's reoccupation of Memel/Klaipėda. In March 1939, under threat of violence, the Lithuanian government agreed to hand the Memel/Klaipėda region over to Germany, and Hitler arrived on the cruiser *Deutschland* to see his new conquest.

In the summer of 1940, the Soviet Union invaded and annexed Lithuania. In the summer of 1941, Germany invaded the Soviet Union. By Autumn 1944, however, Soviet forces were pushing retreating German forces into a pocket around Memel. A three-month siege followed before the city was finally taken by the Red Army in January 1945. Klaipėda became part of Lithuania again and Lithuania became part of the Soviet Union. Then finally, in 1990 Lithuania declared independence and in 1991 it joined the United Nations, with Klaipėda as its main port.

Moldavia and Wallachia

MOLDAVIA IS A name that will look familiar to some, and indeed, the name of one of Europe's smaller (and admittedly not hugely widely known in the UK) countries is Moldova, sandwiched between Romania and the Ukraine. And the name Moldova is basically the same as Moldavia, though the country doesn't cover all the Moldavian territory we will be looking at in this chapter. Wallachia, however, is one of those names that if people are aware of it at all, they may know it from old O-Level courses on Victorian and nineteenth-century history.

Since we have already chucked two great names into this chapter, we might as well add a third – Bessarabia. This, rather confusingly, has nothing to do with Arabia, or indeed Bess, but seems to have been named after a local Wallachian Basarab dynasty. Bessarabia itself was part of Moldavia and is now divided between Moldova and Ukraine.

At the heart of all this is a people known in English as the Vlachs. Not the Vlads. We're not onto Vlad the Impaler just yet. It tends to be used to refer to speakers of a language group ultimately derived from Latin (as is modern Romanian) in parts of Eastern Europe.

Wallachia is, yes, a name that basically means the country of the Vlachs. Its borders obviously changed at times, but basically it occupied what is now south-central Romania. It traditionally came into being in the late thirteenth century under Radu the Black, though Basarab I (he of the dynasty) also had a lot to do with it. This lot of Vlachs had only ended up where they were because they were trying to distance themselves from the power of the Hungarian monarchy. The Hungarian monarchy itself wasn't hugely keen on being thus distanced, but defeat in battle in 1330 by Basarab changed Hungarian minds for a while. Independent Wallachia stood tall and victorious.

Though not for long. The Hungarians still weren't entirely reconciled to being distanced, and a new power was soon making itself felt in the region. Yes, the Ottomans had arrived. Prince Mircea the Old had to pay tribute to the Turks in 1391 and by 1417 Mircea the Old was definitely feeling his age and accepted Turkish suzerainty. The next year he gave up entirely and died. He was 63. It doesn't seem that old, but then his name was basically given to distinguish him from Mircea the Young rather than as commentary on how many birthdays he'd had.

Wallachia did not give in meekly to Turkish control. There would be much more fighting and resisting and indeed some impaling. Yes, Vlad III Dracula, is also known as 'the Impaler', a somewhat less friendly nickname than 'the Old'. In 1462, Vlad managed to shock even the not-easily-shocked Ottoman forces by impaling thousands of victims in a field to put off (or at least distract) any pursuers. Vlad has, of course, become linked with the global Dracula industry and tends to be much better known now, outside Romania, for potential vampire connections than as a Wallachian resistance fighter against the Ottomans.

Vlad himself was born in Transylvania and Michael the Brave even managed to unite (somewhat briefly) Wallachia, Transylvania and Moldavia in the late sixteenth century. Generally, however, the Turks would over time manage to impose their control increasingly over Wallachia.

Meanwhile, to the north of Wallachia was Moldavia. This was founded by Vlachs too and was independent by the mid-fourteenth century under Bogdan. Unlike early Wallachia, which mainly had the Hungarians to worry about, Moldavia had to worry about the Hungarians and the Poles as well. And then, like Wallachia, it had the Turks to worry about, too. Prince Stephen IV, also known as the Great, fought the Turks in the fifteenth century. But his son, Bogdan III, also known as the One-Eyed, was forced in the end to pay tribute to the Turks.

As with Wallachia, however, such a tribute did not mean the end of resistance. For instance, John III, known as the Terrible and also as the Brave (maybe it depends which side you were on), fought both his own Moldavian nobles and the Turks. From the north, the Poles also intervened, occasionally, in a sign of future developments.

However, in the eighteenth century, the Turks imposed on both Wallachia and Moldova Phanariote rule. Phanariote, not a word we hear on TV much, means an Ottoman-appointed Greek administrator, named after Phanar, the Greek quarter of Constantinople. The Phanariotes became unpopular in Moldavia and Wallachia, and this at a time when European powers were starting to nibble away at Ottoman-held territory in Europe. The forces of the Habsburg monarchy made occasional advances into the area and, for example, in 1774 Austria seized a chunk of Moldavia, but it was Russia which would really transform the situation in Moldavia and Wallachia.

Russia's forces were beginning to make regular incursions into the region. In 1812, for instance, Russia got Bessarabia. Turkish defeat in the Russo-Turkish War of 1828–29 saw Russia occupy Moldavia and Wallachia, still technically part of the Ottoman Empire, and introduce a new constitution. Russia's defeat in the Crimean War saw it ejected from Moldavia and Wallachia, but the two places were already firmly set on a more European and less Ottoman path. Moldavia even got its own stamps, in 1858: a set of four highly distinctive ones, with a star, the head of a bull and a post horn in a round frame (in denominations of 27, 54, 81 and 108 parale). Genuine 'Moldavian Bull's Heads' are now extremely valuable. There are fewer than 100 of these stamps in mint condition known still to exist, and around 600 used ones. Fakes, of course, abound. A second series, with the same motifs but in a square frame (and with less eccentric denominations), followed later the same year. These are less rare but still valuable.

In 1859, Moldavia and Wallachia voted to unite under Prince Alexandru Ioan Cuza as the basis of what would become Romania. Moldavia-Wallachia got stamps, too, with the Wallachian eagle squeezed in next to the ox of Moldavia. After the 1877–78 Romanian War of Independence, Romania got fully recognised independence.

There would, however, be many other border changes in the area before today's borders were finally reached. For instance, after the First World War, Romania got Transylvania off Hungary – for a while, Hungarian stamps overprinted with a Romanian monogram were used there. The slice of old Moldavia and Bessarabia that had become the Moldavian Soviet Socialist Republic in the USSR became, after the collapse of the Soviet Union, the independent country of Moldova.

North Ingria

INGRIA IS A town in Piedmont, Italy. It is also, and of rather more importance for this chapter, the name of the region around where St Petersburg is now located.

For many, many centuries it was something of a border region. Early Russians expanding their area of control north-wards eventually reached the region and chunks of it came into the possession of first Novgorod and then the grand princes of Moscow. But while they were trying to enter the area from the south, another power was also trying to enter the area from the north. The Swedes then were not the militarily neutral nation they later became. On the contrary, they had a long history of empire-building. Other groups, like Danes and the Teutonic Knights, would intermittently get involved, but for centuries the main competition for control of the region would be between Russia and Sweden.

Control of parts of the region had already see-sawed to and fro between Sweden and Russia when in 1610 the Ingrian War broke out between, yes, Sweden and Russia. The Swedes attempted to put a Swede on the Russian throne, something which if they'd have managed it could have changed history forever. They didn't manage it. Instead a certain Michael Romanov would end up as the first tsar of a dynasty that would still have a tsar on the throne at the start of 1917. The Swedes did manage, however, to seize Ingria in the war and this time they were determined to take rather more extensive measures in an effort to keep it, including building a number of fortresses on the Neva River. Swedish Ingria was not, however, to remain Swedish forever.

In 1700, the Second Northern War broke out. It's also called the Great Northern War. This has nothing to do with any British rail company. It was not so great for Sweden since in the war, Russia, along with a bunch of others, fought Sweden, and at the end of it Sweden was in decline and Russia was ascendant. An energetic new tsar, Peter I (now called with hindsight Peter the Great), was on the throne and on the attack. He built a fleet on the Svir River and used it to attack the fortress of Nöteborg. It fell in 1702, and shortly afterwards Peter's forces took the Swedish fortress at Nienshants as well. Soon after that Peter started the construction of a splendid new city – yes, St Petersburg – which would consolidate Russian power in the region.

Not only had Sweden lost Ingria, it would eventually lose a whole lot more in the area. Russia started to eat into Swedish-controlled Finland. The Finnish War of 1808–09 was, well, pretty much the finish of Swedish power in Finland. Finland became a Grand Duchy within the Russian Empire. And it was still under Russian control in March 1917 when the revolution broke out in Russia. Under the new regime, Finland got autonomy and the last tsar of the dynasty launched by Michael Romanov, Nicholas II, was forced to abdicate. After the Bolshevik Revolution later the same year, Finland declared independence and Lenin accepted the declaration.

But it was not only Russia where revolutionary reds would be active. In January 1918, red Finns seized Helsinki. Unlike the Russian Civil War, the Finnish Civil War was short. The Whites won it and the Reds lost it. General Carl Gustaf Mannerheim decisively defeated the Red forces at the Battle of Tampere in April and German troops were sent to aid his forces.

And with Russia still in chaos, Finns in Russian territory on the south-eastern part of the Karelian Isthmus saw an opportunity to take their land out of Russian control and attach it to Finland. In June 1919, they grandly declared the freedom of the Republic of North Ingria. Santeri Termonen became the first chairman of the governing council of the republic and the North Ingrian forces prepared themselves to defend their new state against Red attack. It was not a big republic. It consisted of five parishes, with about 400 people in it, and it had as its capital the village of Kirjasalo. The area did, however, also contain refugees from elsewhere in Ingria and volunteers did come across the border from Finland to help. It also produced its own stamps – very impressive ones, given the lack of resources available. The first set, seven definitives, feature the area's eighteenth-century coat of arms in various colours. A pictorial set soon followed, showing local life (and, in one stamp, a burning church). These stamps, though not hugely valuable, have been much forged.

It also had its own army, even though it, like the republic itself, was very small. The Finns didn't want to alienate the new Russian regime too much, so finance and arms were taken discreetly from Finland into the North Ingrian separatists rather than openly. It was, however, always going to be a somewhat unequal battle. They might perhaps have had more luck if they had made their bid for freedom somewhat earlier, while the Russian Bolshevik forces were under more pressure.

The North Ingrian forces were unable to hold off advancing Russian forces. And in the end, in October 1920 at Tartu, Finland accepted that Northern Ingria would remain part of Russia. In December 1920, as refugees and North Ingrian fighters fled across the border into Finland, the Republic of North Ingria collapsed.

It would not be the last fighting in the region between Finns and Russians, not by any means. There were minor and major conflicts still to come, including the so-called Winter War of 1939–40 and the Continuation War of 1941–44, when Finland took the opportunity represented by the German invasion of the Soviet Union to invade it as well, seeking to regain lost territory. However, the Republic of North Ingria would not be part of it.

Nossi-Bé

NOSSI-BÉ SOUNDS endearing and exotic, but these days the location tends to go by the name Nosy Be which is still endearing but to the British ear sounds quite nosy. However, in reality Nossi-Bé or Nosy Be apparently just means 'big island' in the Malagasy language. 'Big island' itself doesn't sound massively exciting so it's probably best we keep it in its Malagasy original. It also makes more sense, because Nossi-Bé or Nosy Be is, in fact, a rather small island situated just off the fourth-biggest island in the world, Madagascar. However, presumably it is called Nosy Be because it is a big island compared to the other little islands around it. These are also Nosy, for instance Nosy Komba and Nosy Sakatia.

In recent decades, it has become one of Madagascar's best-known tourist destinations, but prior to that it had a long history, part of which included having stamps with its name on.

Not long after the Portuguese rounded the Cape of Good Hope and arrived in the Indian Ocean, Europeans started exploring the area around Nossi-Bé. Already in the seventeenth century some of them were making plans (unsuccessful as it turned out) to colonise the island.

In the seventeenth and eighteenth centuries, European pirates took to operating in the seas around Madagascar.

In the early nineteenth century, King Radama, with British support, started a campaign trying to unite a big chunk of Madagascar under the Merina monarchy. Merina success in this campaign inevitably, though, meant other local dynasties would lose out. In 1837, Merina forces won a major victory over the forces of the Sakalava Boina kingdom and Queen Tsiomeko. To be fair, Tsiomeko was only 8 years old. After the defeat, Tsiomeko needed somewhere safe to escape and a powerful friend to help her against the Merina. She retreated to Nossi-Bé and ceded her rights in both it and Nosy Komba to the French. In the end it didn't help her much. Her kingdom was annexed by the Merina monarchy and she died in 1843.

The French, however, had a nice new territory to try to control. The French admiral who signed the deal with Tsiomeko was called Admiral de Hell, so the French created on the island the settlement of Hell-Ville, not the sort of name favoured these days by English-speaking estate agents.

In 1849, the French abolished slavery, causing a revolt by slave-owning Sakalava. It was the start of a somewhat uneasy few decades for the French as they battled to impose control on the island. However, even if the French wouldn't let the locals have slaves, they would let them have stamps.

The first overprints were issued in 1889 on the standard French colonial stamp of the time. Genuine examples of these are rare. In 1893, Nossi-Bé got its own stamps, or at least another standard colonial issue with space for its name to be inscribed on it.

In the early twentieth century, Nossi-Bé was to play a crucial and little-known role in one of the decisive battles of the period.

In February 1904, war broke out between Russia and Japan as the two imperial powers competed for territory and control in Manchuria and Korea. It soon became clear that control of the seas in the region would be crucial and it also soon became clear that with the limited naval forces at its disposal in the area, Russia was at a disadvantage. So the decision was made to send a Russian fleet from the Baltic on a journey across half the globe in an attempt to defeat the Japanese navy decisively. The voyage of the Russian fleet got off to a bad start when, in the Dogger Bank incident, it fired on British trawlers in the North Sea thinking they were Japanese torpedo boats. The Russians managed to kill some fishermen as well as some of their own men, and would probably have killed more Britons if the accuracy of their fire hadn't been so poor.

Due to this, the Russian fleet in question was banned from using the Suez Canal and forced to travel the long route around the Cape of Good Hope rather than taking the short-cut. And Nossi-Bé became a key stop on that route. Here the Russian fleet met up with another Russian naval detachment and spent two months coaling and getting resupplied before heading east to the planned decisive battle. The Battle of Tsushima was indeed decisive, but it was a decisive victory for the Japanese, not for the Russians. It led to the Russians accepting defeat in the war and a long-term change in the balance of power in the region.

Later in the twentieth century, war would come to Nossi-Bé itself. And fascinatingly again, there was a Japanese connection.

In December 1941, a Japanese fleet led by Isoroku Yamamoto, who had served at Tsushima, attacked Pearl Harbor. By early 1942, Britain was becoming increasingly concerned that collaboration between Vichy French forces on Madagascar and Japanese submarines could severely threaten Allied supply lines across the Indian Ocean.

In May 1942, in Operation Ironclad, British and Commonwealth forces captured the key strategic port of Diego Suarez (or Antsiranana) to the north of Nossi-Bé. They then followed this up with Operation Streamline and by 6 November it was all over as Vichy French forces on Madagascar surrendered.

During the invasion, a South African Beaufort airplane spotted a ship and two submarines at Nossi-Bé. The aircraft dived to attack but the submarines submerged. When the Royal Navy arrived on the scene it captured the ship, which turned out to be the French supply vessel *Duchesne* that had been resupplying

Japanese submarines during their operations in the Indian Ocean. Eventually an amphibious force was sent in to take control of the island, which it did after having suffered some casualties.

Nyassa Company

AT THE VAST conference that gathered in Berlin in 1884 to carve Africa up among European nations, Portugal was made master of Mozambique. Portugal had been the European nation of influence in the area since Vasco da Gama first ventured there in 1494 (more about him in the section on Quelimane). However, the Iberian nation didn't have the funds to administer the territories of which it now found itself formally in charge, so farmed the running of large chunks of its colonies out to commercial enterprises. If you thought 'privatisation' of the business of government was a purely modern affair, think again …

One of the successful bidders was the Nyassa Company, established by Bernard Daupais, a Lisbon businessman, though its main shareholders were British and French (later German, too), with the Portuguese government holding a 10 per cent stake. It was given a thirty-five-year charter and the brief of furthering agricultural and infrastructure development in Nyasa District, the northern part of Mozambique between the River Lurio and the border with what was then German East Africa. It was also expected to build lighthouses along the coast and a railway from Lake Nyasa to the area's capital, Porto Amelia (modern Pemba), on the coast. It was given administrative powers, including the right to tax the local inhabitants – and to issue stamps – and military support from the Portuguese army.

The company initially concentrated on the coastal area, though didn't seem in a great hurry to build the lighthouses.

Its interest seemed to be more in raising money from customs duties. It began to extend its influence inland, towards Lake Nyasa, but again seemed more interested in taxing local people than railway-building. A 'hut tax', similar to the modern poll tax, was unsurprisingly unpopular – though, sadly, it was common in Africa at that time (the British had been experimenting with it in Cape Colony since 1870). On a more positive note, the company, with one eye on the healthy philatelic market, began to issue attractive stamps featuring giraffes, dromedaries, zebras and, rather oddly amid these zoological delights, Vasco da Gama.

The company was taken over by South African interests in 1908, after which it had a new purpose – to ensure a supply of cheap labour for the gold and diamond mines of that country. At the same time, it kept taxing huts and not doing anything about the lighthouses or the railway.

In 1910, the Portuguese monarchy was toppled in a republican revolution. Nyassa Company stamps now had 'REPUBLICA' overprinted on them, but otherwise the inhabitants of northern Mozambique saw little difference. Hopes that the new rulers would take a more liberal view were ill-founded. If anything, they were more determined colonialists than the monarchs, hoping to redirect any old emotional identification with the monarchy into new dreams of empire.

In 1914, the company's northern border became a potential war zone, as north of it was German East Africa. Initially, Portugal was neutral in the First World War, but it found itself being drawn in on the side of Britain. Germany declared war on Portugal in 1916, upon which Portuguese forces occupied a small, disputed corner of German East Africa, around modern Quionga. In 1917, the tables were turned. German General Paul Emil von Lettow-Vorbeck invaded northern Mozambique.

Lettow-Vorbeck's main purpose was to harass his enemy rather than acquire territory, and he was remarkably successful, tying up Allied troops as he marched round Nyasa District for the best part of a year. Unlike most European military men of the era, he had no racial prejudice; he became a fluent Swahili speaker and promoted local troops to officers. After the war, he returned to Germany a hero – he was the only German general to have successfully invaded British territory (as well as harassing Mozambique, he occupied parts of British East Africa). He later became an opponent of Hitler, and was lucky to survive the Nazi era, living to his 90s and dying in 1964.

After the war, the Nyassa Company bumbled on. No railway, no lighthouses, but new systems for getting more work and tax out of local inhabitants. The company's charter was allowed to expire in 1929, after which Nyasa District became centrally administered from the capital Lourenço Marques (modern Maputo), a thousand miles south. Despite its eagerness to raise taxes from the local inhabitants and its reticence to spend money to meet its charter promises, the Nyassa Company wasn't even a successful business. It never paid a dividend and when it was wound up, it was virtually bankrupt.

The other big charter company in the country was the Mozambique Company. This had been set up at the same time as the Nyassa Company to administer the central 'slice' of the country, the modern provinces of Manica and Sofala (and the northern parts of Gaza and Imhambane). It lasted longer than the Nyassa Company, but only because it had initially been given a fifty-year charter. It was no more successful (though it also produced nice stamps). It did not have its charter renewed either. The odd experiment of colonial government by charter company was abandoned in 1942.

Obock

OBOCK STILL EXISTS and can still be found (or one of its slightly different spellings can be) on maps today, but it is one of those names where, unless you actually know where it is, it's hard to guess. In fact, Obock is situated in what is now the country of Djibouti in the Horn of Africa and just across the Red Sea from Yemen. It is a little port and it has an airstrip.

At first glance, it might not seem like a hugely important place, but it does have quite a lot of strategic importance and has been of major interest to the militaries of a surprising number of nations. The reason, of course, is shipping lanes. Obock is situated close to the Bab-el-Mandeb, the narrow strait at the southern mouth of the Red Sea. To the east of Obock, shipping lanes run along the Arabian Peninsula out into the Indian Ocean. To the south of Obock, shipping lanes run along the East African coast. To the north of Obock, shipping lanes run up the Red Sea towards the Suez Canal and eventually the Mediterranean.

Already in antiquity, ships were making the journey down the Red Sea coast from Egyptian ports into the seas around Obock. The area known in ancient Egyptian texts as the Land of Punt was probably located in roughly this region. And already in antiquity ships were heading further east out towards the riches of the east and south, too, on trading missions along the East African coast.

Frenchman Ferdinand de Lesseps started the process of building the Suez Canal in the 1850s and it would be completed in 1869. The French no longer wanted to be in a position of having to rely on British-held Aden for coaling facilities in the region. On 11 March 1862, they signed a deal with local rulers to take control of the anchorage at Obock. French facilities at Obock didn't expand hugely fast, but French traders soon settled there, hopeful, for instance, of developing trade with Ethiopia. In the 1880s, the French got a bit more ambitious. French colonial administrator Léonce Lagarde was appointed governor of the region and he expanded the area of French control in the Gulf of Tadjoura as Egyptian forces were withdrawing.

Then in 1889, the Russians arrived. Yes, it does seem somewhat unlikely but one Russian, Nikolay Ivanovitch Achinov, had decided that what Russia needed in the late nineteenth century was an African empire, if only a small one. He decided that the old Egyptian fort at Sagallo was a good place to start one. It wasn't. Shortly after he arrived with a bunch of Cossacks, news of the arrival reached Obock, and French warships turned up to evict him. After a brief bombardment, the Russians surrendered and Achinov was deported ingloriously to Odessa.

Obock got its first stamps in 1892 – or at least overprinted versions of what was then the standard stamp for French colonies. In the next two years, it got its own distinctive definitives. Two designs were used. One featured Somali warriors; for higher denominations from 2 to 50 francs, a distinctive triangular one depicted camel herders.

However, in 1888 Lagarde had founded Djibouti City to the south, and in 1894 the French colonial administration of the region moved there. Though it continued to use its own stamps till 1902, Obock became somewhat quieter.

The late nineteenth century was not the last time that Obock would be a base of strategic importance, however. During the British blockade of Vichy French-held Djibouti during the Second World War, Obock became a port for blockade runners trying to take supplies into Djibouti. On one occasion Vichy French submarine *Le Vengeur* made a blockade-running attempt from Diego Suarez in Madagascar into Djibouti. Off Obock, it found the Free French gunboat *Savorgnan de Brazza* trying to enforce the blockade. *Le Vengeur* fired two torpedoes at it and missed.

In the period after the Second World War, Obock was still used as a base by the French military. And even after Djibouti became independent in 1977, the French military still made some use of facilities at Obock for a time.

In the 1990s, Obock got caught up in the Djiboutian Civil War. The fighting erupted in November 1991 when an Afar rebel group, FRUD, the Front for the Restoration of Unity and Democracy, took up arms. The rebels quickly seized much of the north and made attempts to seize Obock, where there was heavy fighting. Most of the fighting ended in 1994.

In the period after the 9/11 attacks, America looked to expand its presence in strategic areas like the Horn of Africa. It constructed the huge US military base of Camp Lemonnier near Djibouti, but its military also took an interest in Obock, conducting live-fire amphibious landing exercises there. America even financed the construction of a pier there. The area of Djibouti has recently attracted attention from another major twenty-first-century military power – China – which is now taking an interest in that part of the world as well.

Patiala and Nawanagar

INDIA WAS ONCE a mass of states, many of them ruled by princes who became known for fabulous wealth. Patiala and Nawanagar are two examples.

Patiala is located in the south-east of Punjab, about halfway between Delhi and Amritsar. It was founded in 1763 by Sikh warlord Baba Ala Singh, but soon had to fight hard for its survival, with the Afghan Durrani Empire on one side of it and the Maratha Confederacy (a Hindu empire that had supplanted the Mughals in North India) on the other. In 1808, its ruler decided his best option was to throw his lot in with a third imperialist force in the subcontinent, the British. It proved a wise strategic move.

Patiala became one of the 'princely states', which were protected by the British but had a measure of autonomy. They could not go to war or negotiate directly with foreign governments, and the British monarch had 'paramountcy' (a term that was never clearly defined), but Britain was not supposed to meddle in their internal affairs. There were over 550 of these when the British finally left, and they covered about 40 per cent of the country. The rest of India, technically known as 'British India', was under direct British rule.

True to Raj form, the princely states were ranked according to carefully nuanced and rigidly adhered-to protocols, which manifested themselves in numerous ways, including the number of guns that would be fired to honour their ruler on formal occasions. The heads of the most powerful of these states – Hyderabad, Baroda, Gwalior, Mysore, and Jammu and Kashmir – would receive a twenty-one-gun salute. The Maharajah of Patiala merited a seventeen-gun salute. A scale then led down to nine guns. Three quarters of the states, known as 'non-salute states', didn't get any guns at all. The titles by which rulers were known were also linked to this ranking: if your state merited eleven guns or more, you were allowed the title 'Highness'.

To our modern eyes, these distinctions look rather comical, but they mattered at the time. One gets a strong sense of a meeting of minds here: the Victorian British, with their fascination with the minutiae of class, found genuine soulmates among the rulers of these principalities and, more widely, in a culture where a complex caste system had been in operation for millennia. No doubt some of our cherished values will look rather silly in 150 years' time.

The rulers of these states embraced other aspects of upper-class British life, too. The Maharajah of Patiala from 1900 to 1938, Bhupinder Singh, was particularly keen on cricket, captaining the Indian team that came to Britain in 1911 and playing a number of first-class games after the First World War. He bought a fleet of Rolls-Royce cars and was the first man in India to own an aeroplane. His energy extended to the bedroom – he had five wives, a number of 'consorts' and is reputed to have fathered eighty-eight children. This is more than his highest score in first class cricket, which was 83.

Other princely rulers graced the cricket fields of England around the same time, finest of whom was the Maharajah of Nawanagar, a smaller state on the Gulf of Kutch in modern Gujarat (its ruler was only entitled to thirteen guns). Prince Ranjitsinhji, or 'Ranji', played for Sussex from 1895 to 1920, made fifteen appearances for England and was regarded as one of the finest batsmen in the Edwardian 'Golden Age' of the game. He had a career average of over 55, which ranks him among the top twenty all-time greats, and a highest score of 285 (he had many fewer children). Ranji became a byword for aristocratic elegance – the writer Neville Cardus described him as 'the Midsummer Night's Dream of cricket' – and a powerful symbol of the cultural symbiosis between Edwardian Britain and India. The Maharajah of Patiala understood this: when he (Patiala) sponsored a trophy for Indian inter-state cricket, he named it after Ranjitsinhji rather than himself. The Ranji Trophy is still contested – though the highly commercial Indian Premier League limited-overs competition is what draws the crowds on the sub-continent today (the name is, of course, a twenty-first-century Anglo-Indian cross-cultural reference: old links die hard).

Different princely states had different postal systems. 'Convention' states used stamps from British India with overprinting done at the government printers in what was then Bombay. These stamps were valid around India, and using them was a sign of the issuer's close administrative link to the British. Patiala was the first state to sign up to the convention, in 1884. Its earliest stamp features the words 'Puttialla State' over Queen Victoria – if you want a picture of Bhupinder Singh, he appears on Patiala's Revenue stamps.

However, most states preferred to issue its own stamps with its own designs, for use only within its boundaries. Nawanagar was one of these: its first stamp, the 1 Docra (there were six of these to the Anna) of 1877, features a curved dagger and the state's name in Hindi and English. The 1893 issue, showing the Nawanagar coat of arms, has no English on it at all. This is a nice illustration of the flexible nature of 'paramountcy'. The princely states might have played the British game when it suited them, but were proud of their independence, too.

Their independence did not last. India was given its freedom 'at the stroke of the midnight hour' on 15 August 1947. Both the British, for whom Lord Mountbatten oversaw the transition as governor general, and the new rulers of India, especially the staunch republican, Pandit Nehru, sought to bring the princely states into the new 'Union of India' (an entity that lasted till 1950, when it was formally replaced by modern republic). Some of the states were more accepting of this than others. Patiala and Nawanagar were both early adopters of the new system, quickly taking their places in the Constituent Assembly, the forerunner of the modern Indian parliament. Others needed a mixture of threat and diplomacy to join it (see the section on Hyderabad).

By 1950, 'Instruments of Accession' had been signed by almost all princely states. These seemed to give the princes a measure of autonomy, but over time this was whittled away – much to the disgust of, amongst others, Winston Churchill. In 1956, many of the old state privileges were removed, and in 1971 this was extended by India's new prime minister, Nehru's daughter Indira Gandhi, to the princes themselves. Their titles lost official status; they lost their 'privy purse' (a payment from the Indian government in return for signing the Instruments twenty years earlier); they were no longer entitled to their numbered gun salutes.

Historians still argue about the inevitability of the disappearance of the princely states: most of their subjects seemed to want to be part of a united India, and except for in some remote areas it made little geographical or economic sense to buck the trend. They had probably become anachronisms. They live on in old stamp albums, however.

Quelimane

QUELIMANE IS A port in Mozambique, with a population of around a quarter of a million. Modern visitors describe it as sleepy and run-down, though its current mayor, Manuel de Araújo, is trying to revitalise both its cultural life and its decayed infrastructure with an energetic public works programme. He has a lot to do: the city was a busy port in the 1960s, but since then, war has dragged it down – as has geography. Quelimane is not on the sea but 16 miles inland on the once-large Rio dos Bons Sinais, and has an exhausting, hot, damp climate.

The city, on high ground overlooking the river, was founded by Arab traders in the Middle Ages. In 1498, the area was visited by Vasco da Gama – he gave the river its name, which means 'River of Good Signs', the 'good signs' being the Arab traders, who showed he was on his way to India, the goal of his expedition. Da Gama was not the first European to sail round the Cape of Good Hope – his countryman Bartolomeu Dias had achieved that feat a decade earlier – but by the time he reached Quelimane, he was breaking new ground: no westerner had ever sailed that far up the eastern coast of Africa. A Portuguese trading post was established there in 1530, dealing largely in gold and ivory.

The surrounding area was parcelled out – in large chunks – to Portuguese settler families in the seventeenth century, in a system known as *prazo*. These became plantations, places that seem to have their own slow, harsh pace, wherever they are. Quelimane itself was described by a visitor in 1766, Antonio Pinto Miranda, as a sprawl of wooden, straw-covered houses, and 'a wasteland where tigers and hippopotamuses roam'. However, Quelimane's first stone buildings were begun later that century, including the old cathedral (sadly, now a ruin and a home for street children).

By that time, slavery had become one of Quelimane's main businesses. The East African slave trade, run by Arabs, dates back over a thousand years – there was a huge slave rebellion in the Euphrates valley between the years 869 and 883. Historians disagree on the size of the East African trade, but the consensus seems to be that it was almost as big as its gruesome cousin in the west of the continent, though the latter was more intense, being concentrated in a shorter period of time.

Quelimane's heyday as a slave port came in the early nineteenth century: the Eastern trade continued unaffected by British abolitionism. Quelimane lost its dominance in it, not thanks to any moral effort by the Portuguese or any other locals but by the silting of the river. The trade moved north to Zanzibar, where it was only abolished in 1898, under British pressure.

In the middle of the nineteenth century, Quelimane became famous as the end-point of David Livingstone's walk across Africa. Livingstone was an archetypal Victorian hero: devout, adventurous and self-made, the stuff of Samuel Smiles and *John Halifax, Gentleman*. He was born to a large, poor family in Blantyre, near Glasgow, and worked in the local mill to earn money to educate himself in medicine, a skill he was determined to use as part of his missionary work. In 1841, this work began when he arrived in Cape Town. Spreading the Gospel and pure exploring went hand-in-hand with Livingstone. In 1854, he set out from Luanda on the West coast to walk across Africa. On his way he 'discovered' the great waterfall known locally as 'The Smoke that Thunders': more prosaically, he renamed it after Queen Victoria. He arrived in Quelimane on 20 May 1856.

Livingstone returned to the UK, but Africa remained his passion. He returned in 1858 and based himself in Quelimane, from which he launched an expedition up the nearby Zambezi River. He hoped this would create a trade route into the heart of Africa – Livingstone was convinced that ordinary commerce would drive out the slavers, whom he detested. His discovery of the Cahora Bassa rapids, 400 miles upstream, ended these hopes, and the expedition fell into disarray. Tragically, his wife came out to join him, and became a victim of malaria, one of the many tropical diseases rife in the area.

Around this time, the Portuguese government tried to replace the sclerotic *prazo* system with one where smaller holdings could be taken on by energetic young colonists from the motherland (not, of course, by local Africans). The *prazeros* (and the area's climate and mosquitoes) saw this attempted reform off with ease.

The 1880s saw the bizarre 'scramble for Africa', when European nations began formally dividing the continent into colonies (in 1870, only 10 per cent of Africa belonged to outside nations: by 1914, that figure was 90 per cent). Portugal formally became master of Mozambique in 1884. It divided the country into 'districts'. Quelimane became the capital of Zambezia District, which issued its first stamp (or at least overprint) in 1894. This long, thin district was split in two in 1902, one half being Quelimane (the other being Tete, which also issued stamps).

Quelimane's first stamps came out in 1913, appropriately celebrating Vasco da Gama. Next year, Constantino Álvaro Sobral Fernandes' attractive issue featuring Ceres, the Roman goddess of agriculture, which was used in a range of Portuguese colonies, appeared in a Quelimane version. In 1920, these were superseded by stamps of Mozambique.

Mozambique has now moved on from colonial times. In the late 1950s and early 1960s, Africa's main colonial powers, Britain and France, divested themselves of (almost) all their possessions. Portugal, however, was under a right-wing dictatorship, the *Estado Novo*, which saw the colonies as symbols of traditional power and had no intention of letting them go. In reply, exiles set up the Mozambique Liberation Front (FRELIMO) in Dar es Salaam, up the coast, in 1962. Attempts to negotiate decolonisation failed; a ten-year campaign of violence began in 1964.

FRELIMO was armed and supported by the Soviet bloc. The Portuguese fought back with western anti-insurgency tactics, and the conflict – a proxy Cold War – turned into a vicious stalemate, though one which cost Portugal, an already poor country, ever more money. Only when Portugal itself underwent a revolution in 1974 did power change hands. The new Mozambique lurched to the Marxist-Leninist left – the Soviet fleet was welcomed to Quelimane in 1976 – and a civil war broke out, continuing the proxy Cold War. This dragged on till 1992, was even bloodier than the anti-colonial struggle – it is estimated that a million people died either in the fighting or as a result of it – and left the country littered with landmines.

Modern Quelimane is still recovering from this legacy. One wishes it well.

Rhodesia

HISTORIANS ARE STILL arguing about who built the great city of Zimbabwe, or when it was built. Evidence seems to favour the ancestors of the modern Shona people, and that work began around 1200. It was probably abandoned around 1450, though nobody is really sure why. It was certainly a ruin by the time a Portuguese soldier/explorer, Vicente Pegado, visited them in 1531. In the eighteenth century, the area around Zimbabwe was part of the Shona Rozwi Empire; in the nineteenth, this was supplanted by the Ndebele, under their warrior leader Mzlilikazi. And in 1890 the British came, with Martini–Henry rifles and the Maxim machine gun.

It wasn't just 'the British' who came, but one particular Briton, Cecil Rhodes. Rhodes is currently the centre of controversy as students try to have traces of him removed from Oxford, where he studied as a young man. Track back a hundred years or so, and he was a national hero. When he died in 1902, Rhodes was lauded as 'the greatest of modern Englishmen'. People wept at his massive funeral procession in Cape Town (after the procession, his body was taken and buried in the Mapotos Hills, in modern Zimbabwe).

This diversity of opinion says much about how values have changed, but also that Rhodes was a complex character. He had qualities we admire today. He had boundless energy – his last words were 'So much to do' – and a roving, curious intelligence. On first arriving in Africa in 1870, to grow cotton with his brother, he took a then-unfashionable interest in African life, living for a while in the kraal. He was a decent employer, paying his workers in advance if they needed it. What seems to have destroyed him morally was the discovery of diamonds in Natal. He became ever more ruthless, living by the motto 'Every man has his price', and his views on race changed to conform with the worst prejudices of the era.

By 1889, Rhodes was chairman of the British South Africa Company, a charter company like the East India Company or the Nyassa Company. By 1890, this company was issuing stamps – a full set from ½d to £10 – and playing power politics. Having negotiated mining concessions with local rulers, the BSAC convinced the authorities in Cape Town that trade was under threat from other colonial powers, especially the Boers, and that military occupation was the only way to prevent this. The Pioneer Column, a group of settlers protected by what were effectively paramilitary police, marched up into the territories of first the Shona, then the Ndebele. A series of wars, known in Shona as *Chimurenga*, was fought in the 1890s, ending in 1897. By then, the territory had already been renamed Rhodesia, though the new names did not appear on stamps until 1909 (as overprints) or 1910 as fully fledged stamps.

The BSAC continued to rule over the territory until 1923. It was then split into Southern Rhodesia (modern Zimbabwe) and Northern Rhodesia (modern Zambia). After the Second World War, pressure grew for the decolonisation of Africa, and in 1964, Northern Rhodesia became the independent nation of Zambia.

Southern Rhodesia had other ideas, however. Its largely white government did not want majority (97 per cent of the population) black rule. On 11 November 1965, its prime minister, former spitfire pilot Ian Smith, made a Unilateral Declaration of Independence. A 2/6 stamp was issued to celebrate.

Britain was unwilling to use force against the secessionists, and imposed sanctions instead. These were only partially effective

– South Africa was happy to send forbidden goods across the Limpopo River, and other nations, including the Soviet Bloc, traded with Rhodesia, too. A series of talks between Smith and UK Prime Minister Harold Wilson, on various vessels moored in the Mediterranean, got nowhere. Meanwhile war – known by some as the 'bush war' and by others as the 'second *Chimurenga*' – began to escalate between the government and two guerrilla forces, ZANU led by Shona Robert Mugabe, and ZAPU led by Ndebele Joshua Nkomo (the Shona are the majority people in the country, with over 70 per cent of the population; the Ndebele constitute about 20 per cent.)

For a while, the government was able to contain the rebellion – the rebels seemed to dislike each other as much as the whites. Visitors to Salisbury, Rhodesia's capital, found life prosperous and 'normal'. However, the situation could not last. In the mid-1970s, the Cold War ramped up. America began to worry that Southern Africa would 'go Communist', and felt that Rhodesia's white rule was exacerbating tension. Rhodesia's great ally, South Africa, began to feel the same. The country was becoming an anachronism.

In 1975, the Portuguese colony of Mozambique became independent and started actively supporting the rebels. Rhodesia has a 1,200-km border with Mozambique – longer than with any other country – and suddenly the insurgents were welcome to operate across it.

The bush war/second *Chimurenga* grew ever more violent. ZANU and ZAPU finally overcame their differences and formed the Patriotic Front. Smith realised the need for compromise. In June 1979, a black churchman, Bishop Abel Muzorewa, became prime minister of a Government of National Unity. However, this was a misnomer, as the Patriotic Front had boycotted the changes and was not represented. The changes had been too little, too late. After more talks, this time in the elegant surroundings of Lancaster House overlooking London's Green Park, it was agreed to hold proper, full suffrage elections in 1980.

These were won by Robert Mugabe. The now legally independent country was renamed Zimbabwe.

The new nation got off to a good start. In his inaugural speech, Mugabe said, 'The wrongs of the past must now stand forgiven and forgotten.' Sadly, this did not last. Joshua Nkomo was thrown out of the cabinet in 1982. Protests broke out in the Ndebele north of the country, and these were viciously put down by the Fifth Brigade, a kind of private army, trained by North Koreans and directly answerable to Mugabe. Estimates of deaths in this campaign, known as the *Gukurahundi,* vary from 4,000 to 20,000.

There have been some steps forward – especially in the early years, spending on education and health rose sharply. But overall, the story of independent Zimbabwe has been a tragic one. The country has been ravaged by hyperinflation, corruption, state violence, epidemics and poverty. Mugabe, once seen as the saviour of his country, has turned into a cruel, narcissistic tyrant – 'a caricature of an African dictator' according to Desmond Tutu. Bizarrely, his story points to the same moral as that of Cecil Rhodes, of the corrupting nature of power.

Río Muni

RÍO MUNI ACTUALLY still exists as a region of a stamp-producing country today. You just have to know where on the map to look. Many people might note the Rio element and start looking at South America or Central America, but if so, they'd be wrong by several thousand miles, because Río Muni is, in fact, the mainland section of Equatorial Guinea which in colonial days used to be known as Spanish Guinea. Rio means river and Muni refers to the town called Mbini in the local language, which is at the mouth of what is now called the River

Benito. (Although, to be fair, that's also called Mbini in the local language.)

Somewhat confusingly, Equatorial Guinea itself does not, as you might guess from the name, actually straddle the equator. It's all to the north of it, except a little island. It is, however, closer to the equator than other Guineas, like Guinea and Guinea-Bissau, so that's probably fair enough.

As everybody knows, Spain, thanks to Christopher Columbus, got off to a flying start in colonising America. However, in terms of colonising sub-Saharan Africa it had a much slower start. Due to the 1494 Tordesillas deal between Castile/Spain and Portugal which divided the world into areas of influence for each country, it was their Iberian neighbours, the Portuguese, who led many of the early European attempts to explore Africa's west coast, leading to Vasco da Gama sailing round the Cape of Good Hope in late 1497.

Already in the fifteenth century, a Portuguese explorer had encountered Bioko island, now Equatorial Guinea's main island, and it had been named after him. He was Fernão do Pó and the island became known as (among other variants) Fernando Poo. European exploration of the Río Muni mainland, however, progressed rather more slowly. The Portuguese were active in the area and in 1641 the Dutch made a brief attempt to muscle in on the action.

By the eighteenth century, the Spanish were starting to have some regrets about giving the Portuguese a free hand in Africa in return for the Portuguese giving Spain a free hand in almost all of the Americas. Mainly because the sliver of Portuguese territory in South America envisaged by the Tordesillas deal had begun to bulge as Portuguese settlers pushed far inland, ultimately creating Portuguese-speaking Brazil, South America's largest country.

In the end, in order to compensate for Portuguese expansion in South America, Portugal agreed at El Pardo in 1778 to cede to Spain its claims to African territory, including what is now Equatorial Guinea.

The Spanish had high hopes for Río Muni. They reckoned they could use it as a source for slaves in their American colonies, and from 1778 to 1810 it was administered, somewhat bizarrely, by Spanish South American colonial authorities as an element of the Viceroyalty of the Río de la Plata, which was based in Buenos Aires. However, disease and other difficulties hampered Spanish exploitation of Río Muni for a long time. Not only that, but increasingly French colonial efforts were expanding into areas the Spanish had originally envisaged as theirs under the 1778 deal with Portugal. In the end, at Paris in 1900, Spain accepted a deal with France which left Spain with just Río Muni on the mainland in that part of Africa. It was a humiliating end to Spanish hopes of carving out a huge African empire for itself.

Despite Spanish neutrality in the conflict, Río Muni got briefly involved (sort of) in the First World War, when in 1916 German troops from their colony in Cameroon fled into it to avoid surrendering to Allied forces.

The twentieth century would see more determined attempts by Spain to exert control over more and more of Río Muni. At first they had only controlled the coast and rivers, but gradually campaigns against the indigenous Fang people expanded Spanish control.

In 1936, the Spanish Civil War came to Río Muni. It was the most excitement there had been in the territory for some time. Fernando Po fairly quickly went over to Franco, but the sub-governor of Río Muni, Miguel Hernández Porcel, remained loyal to the republic and defeated armed attempts by timber barons and their followers to topple him. Rebels from Kogo clashed with Republican forces. A ship sent by Franco-supporters in the Canaries arrived on 14 October in Bata, the capital of Río Muni. The ship was the *Cuidad de Mahón*, recently equipped with two cannons, and on board were two companies of infantry, machine gunners, an artillery battery and snipers from Spanish Sahara. They launched a bombardment which managed to sink the mail ship *Fernando Poo*, which allegedly had militiamen and prisoners seized by the Republicans on it. Republican fighters briefly tried to hold off the rebel column but were forced to withdraw. Then Bata and the rest of Río Muni too rapidly fell under Franco's control. Some Republicans were captured and some were shot. Many escaped into nearby French colonies.

In 1926, the Spanish had combined Río Muni with Bioko to form Spanish Guinea. However, in 1959 the two areas were administratively separated again and Río Muni got stamps printed for it with Río Muni on. The first set, nine definitives, show a smiling African boy reading a book, with a missionary looking on in the background. Another set depicts flowers, then the stamps change, no longer just saying Río Muni but 'Espana' (in big letters) and 'Río Muni' in smaller ones. Like many colonial stamps, some of these reflect local life: African art or a girl in an attractive traditional headdress, for example. Others have nothing to do with Río Muni at all – one series was in aid of flood relief in Seville. Religion also features in some of the stamps. As we get into the mid-1960s, new designs look more like identikit 'stamps for collectors' than stamps from anywhere distinctive.

Río Muni's time as a stamp-issuing entity was coming to an end anyway. In 1968, despite assorted Spanish attempts to delay or restrict autonomy, Río Muni became part of the now independent Republic of Equatorial Guinea. This nation, it would be fair to say, has had a controversial history (see, again, the section on Fernando Poo).

Ryukyu Islands

NEVER HEARD OF the Ryukyu Islands? There's a good chance you'll have heard of at least one of them, Okinawa, the site of bitter fighting as US forces seized the island from Japanese forces in 1945. But Okinawa is just one of the chain of Ryukyu Islands that stretch south from the main islands of Japan to Taiwan between the East China Sea and the Philippine Sea, and the battle in 1945 is one incident in a long and fascinating history that eventually led to the islands earning their place in stamp albums and stamp catalogues around the world.

Because of their location, the Ryukyu Islands have long been something of a bridge between China and Japan, but they are also a part of the world that has developed its own special identity. The Ryukyuan language, for instance, has links to Japanese but it is very different. And that sense of an area sandwiched between two competing giants continues even to this day. The small chain of islands known to the Japanese as the Senkaku Islands and administered by Japan as part of the Ryukyu Islands are also claimed by a China keen to assert its authority over wider stretches of ocean.

Early history, perhaps inevitably, shows China trying to exert influence over the Ryukyu Islands from one end and with Japan trying to exert influence from the other, and with each having the most success in the areas of the chain closest to them. Gradually, however, there emerged in the Ryukus a force that for a while could to some extent hold its own against both China and Japan, a kingdom that is known, not surprisingly, as the Ryukyu Kingdom.

The first ruler of the kingdom was one Shō Hashi. When he started out, little Okinawa was divided into three separate, even littler kingdoms. By the time he'd finished, it was all one kingdom. Shō Hashi's successors would gradually expand the control of their dynasty across other parts of the Ryukyu chain and the Ryukyu kingdom would become a major player in maritime trade across the region. This early Ryukyu kingdom had close links to China, but that situation was about to get more complicated, as Japan began efforts to assert itself in the area.

In 1609, the Ryukyu Kingdom suffered a Satsuma invasion. This invasion had very little to do with delicious orange citrus fruit. Instead it was a much less tasty onslaught by the ferocious army and fleet of the Japanese Shimazu family, lords of the Satsuma domain. The Ryukyu forces resisted stubbornly but the Amami Islands, closer to Japan than Okinawa is, fell to the invaders and eventually Shuri Castle fell too. The Ryukyuan king Shō Nei was also captured and then taken to Japan. Satsuma kept the Amami Islands but Shō Nei was eventually allowed to return and from then on the Kings of Ryuku would both be tributaries of China and Japan. And when Japan closed itself off virtually entirely to the outside world, the Ryukyu Kingdom became one of the few loopholes in the trade barrier.

When, in 1853, Matthew C. Perry headed for Japan determined to open it up to international trade with a display of US naval might, he did so going via the Ryukyu Islands. Before visiting Japan, he went to meet the Ryukyuan king Shō Tai at Shuri Castle. The opening up of Japan was, however, going to have long-term effects that the US government that had sent Perry to Japan would never have expected.

The collapse of the Tokugawa Shogunate and the Meiji Restoration would eventually lead to an increasingly self-confident and assertive Japan enthusiastic for modern western technology and keen to use it at a time when China, by contrast, was a weakened power.

In the so-called Mudan Incident of 1871, fifty-four shipwrecked sailors from the Ryukyus were murdered on Taiwan. Japan, newly equipped with western weapons and keen to show itself as some kind of defender of Ryukyans, sent a military expedition to attack Taiwan in retaliation. Leading the expedition was the ironclad warship named *Ryūjō* but designed by Thomas Blake Glover and built at Alexander Hall and Company, in Aberdeen. The attack was successful (from the Japanese point of view) and the force withdrew after the Chinese government agreed to pay compensation. To many in Japan it seemed to demonstrate the strength of Japan and the weakness of China. In 1879, Japan annexed the Ryukyu Kingdom and Shō Tai was forced to move to Tokyo.

The 1874 Taiwan attack was the first foreign expedition by the new Japanese Imperial Navy and Japanese Imperial Army. It would not be the last. However, not all subsequent Japanese foreign military adventures would have the quick, easy success of that early attack.

In February and March 1945, as US forces advanced towards Japan, fighting raged on the small island of Iwo Jima. When that island finally fell to the Americans, their next major target in the island-hopping campaign was Okinawa.

US forces landed on Okinawa and various nearby islands on 1 April 1945. With the battle taking place so close to the main Japanese islands, the fighting was expected to be fierce, and it was. The battle went on for over eighty days and by the time it was finished and the US forces were victorious, somewhere near 100,000 combatants were dead and very many civilians as well. The viciousness of the fighting and the high casualties were two of the factors that contributed to the decision to use atomic bombs against Japan rather than launch a conventional invasion.

After the end of the war, the islands came under the United States Military Government of the Ryukyu Islands. This was followed in 1950 by the United States Civil Administration of the Ryukyu Islands. In 1952, US forces withdrew from Japan as a whole, but the United States kept control of the Ryukyus and established a local civilian government of the Ryukyu Islands to work under the US administration. Okinawa became the site of assorted major long-term US military bases.

The first stamps were actually issued in 1948. A flow of stamps followed – so much so that in 1958, the islands were able to issue a commemorative celebrating the stamps they had issued over the decades. Like the US, the islands tended to issue single stamps rather than commemorative sets. The stamps are attractive, even if the items commemorated tend to be rather dull: Afforestation Week, the tenth anniversary of Ryukyu Book Week, a meeting of the Junior International Chamber in Naha, the completion of the government museum in 1966, the 22nd All-Japan Formative Education Study Conference in Naha.

In 1972, the United States allowed the Japanese government to resume control of the Ryukyu Islands. However, the US military retained bases there. And still today, many of the people of the Ryukyu Islands regard themselves as different from the Japanese, and some still think the islands should be independent again.

Saar

NOTHING TO DO with czar or tsar, the Saar is a river that runs through the border regions where France and Germany meet. Saarland (meaning, not surprisingly, the land of the Saar) is one of the federal states of modern Germany. It is a small state and has its capital at Saarbrücken. This means 'the bridges over the Saar', though not everybody is actually convinced that bridges were the origin of the name.

A Frankish royal castle by the name of Sarrabrucca is recorded on the spot. The area has a Celtic and Roman past so various suggestions have been made for the origin of the actual name, ranging from an old Roman bridge to Celtic words for rock etc.

In 999, the castle of Sarrabrucca was given to the Bishop of Metz. And in 1168, the Emperor Barbarossa ordered the castle to be slighted. This does not mean people being rude to it, or refusing to greet it properly, but instead is a technical term for destroying a castle's defensive capabilities. Nevertheless, in 1321 Saarbrücken was chartered and the counts of Nassau-Saarbrücken basically ruled it and the region around it from the fourteenth century until 1793. We include the word basically here because during the period it became increasingly apparent that there was another power with its sights set on the area, and that area was France.

In 1677, Saarbrücken had a visit from a large body of French. They weren't tourists as they might be today, but in fact forces of Louis XIV, and instead of enjoying Saarbrücken's historical and cultural sights, they burned them down and nicked the surrounding region for France. At least temporarily. In 1697, they were forced to give it all up again. Nevertheless, something of a precedent had been set, and the French weren't going to be easily dissuaded from the idea that one day they might permanently get their hands on the region.

The Saar region was about to get even more attractive – if not in a scenic sense, then definitely in a commercial sense. During the eighteenth century, rich coal deposits in the region were systematically exploited and gave rise to a little industrial revolution in the area. In 1793, French revolutionary troops seized the now even more strategic area, and it was incorporated into France. Temporarily. In 1815, Napoleon's future lay on St Helena and the Saar region's future lay with Prussia's Rhine Province.

The early nineteenth century saw increasing industrialisation of the area and, perhaps unwisely considering France's past and future history in the area, some integration of local rail and canal networks with their French counterparts. Indeed, in 1870, the French were to return.

The Franco-Prussian War is these days largely known for the French getting clobbered by the Prussians. However, when the French emperor declared war on the Prussians on 19 July 1870, the French had no intention of getting clobbered and indeed their generals were confident that their newly re-armed and re-organised forces would be victorious. On 2 August 1870, a French invasion force swept aside Prussian defenders and boldly advanced into Alt-Saarbrücken. The French were not to be in Saarbrücken a long time on this occasion. Long weekends have lasted longer. After drinking thousands of litres of beer and requisitioning sausages and bread, they had left by 4 August and on 6 August they suffered a serious defeat at the Battle of Spicheren and were forced to retreat towards Metz. There was plenty more clobbering of the French to come before the war was finally over.

If 1871 was a bad year for the French, then 1918 was a pretty bad year for Germany. Saarbrücken had been bombed occasionally during the war, but after the German collapse in 1918, the French had other plans for it.

In the Versailles peace negotiations of 1919, the French were determined that the defeated Germans would pay for the damage they had caused to France. And they got a lot of what they wanted. As part of the peace deal, it was agreed that for fifteen years the French would take control of the Saar coal mines, that the Territory of the Saar Basin would be jointly administered by the French and British under the League of Nations, and that at the end of the fifteen years a plebiscite would be held on the territory's future.

The inhabitants of the Territory of the Saar Basin obviously still needed stamps, so they got them. Overprints first, on old German stamps, with the words 'Deutsches Reich' obliterated and the word Sarre (its French name) printed instead. In 1920, a series of rough but expressive pictorial definitives followed. They gave a broad picture of the region, showing both old monuments and mines and factories. A smoother set was issued in 1926. Saar also specialised in charity stamps, where purchasers paid a premium above the postage rate, which was given to good causes. In the run-up to the plebiscite, stamps were issued overprinted with 'Volksabstimmung 1935'.

France hoped that the inhabitants of the Saar would at the end of the fifteen years vote to join France, and indeed 0.4 per cent of them did. Unfortunately for the French, over 90 per cent voted to rejoin Germany.

But another world war was not far off, and nor was another German defeat. And after that, yes, the French were in the Saar again. After the German defeat, the French established a Saar Protectorate. The Saar sent a team to the Helsinki Olympics in 1952, and, naturally, it issued its own stamps. As before, the area's industrial nature was reflected in many of them. The charity stamps were issued regularly, too. All the stamps were inscribed in German – so it is little surprise that when a second referendum was held, asking the people which nation they wished to belong to, the result didn't turn out quite how the French wanted. In the end, the French gave up and accepted defeat. They allowed the Saar to rejoin Germany, which it did as of January 1957. After this, Saar still had its own stamps for two years, now inscribed 'Deutsche Bundespost' (German Federal Post) and 'Saarland'. This was because the Franc had been the currency in the old Protectorate. In 1959, Saar started using the Deutschmark, and at the same time switched to ordinary German stamps.

Sedang

THIS CHAPTER TAKES us into the surreal world of what are called Cinderella stamps – stamp issues that do not come from a proper issuing authority or which are official but none of which has ever been used for sending anything through the post. Most serious philatelists look down on these, but other people collect them and enjoy the experience.

We have, actually, already peeked into this world. Icaria does not make it into the Stanley Gibbons catalogue. It declared itself a republic and attempted to make a go of this, so it qualifies as a proper issuing authority. However, its stamps were never used to post anything. The Great Barrier Island Pigeongram stamps were genuinely used for sending mail, but were not issued by a government.

Cinderella status can be a grey area. The stamps of Sedang would seem to be obvious Cinderellas, proudly stepping into their coach and heading for the ball, eager for romance. But they have found their way into some catalogues. This chapter will later mention some even more bizarre Cinderella issues, who never met this handsome prince of partial philatelic acceptance, and are unlikely ever to do so.

The Sedang are a people living in the inaccessible central highlands of Vietnam. In 1888, they received a visit from Marie-Charles David de Mayréna. De Mayréna was there in an official capacity: the French governor of Cochin-China had sent him to negotiate a treaty with them. De Mayréna had other ideas, however. When he met the chiefs of the Sedang and of two other local peoples, the Rengao and the Bahnar, he convinced them that they should recognise him as their king. The Kingdom of Sedang came into being, with King Marie I of The Sedang as its ruler. His Majesty returned to the port city of Haiphong and had the nation's constitution published in the French press.

De Mayréna's motive in all this became apparent when he opened negotiations with the French authorities: he would relinquish his title, but only if he were granted mineral exploration rights to the area. The authorities ignored him, after which he tried to interest Britain in a deal. To further these negotiations, he went to Hong Kong, where he had various trappings of nationhood made – including, of course, stamps: seven denominations, in a made-up currency consisting of the math, the mouk and the Sedang dollar. All feature the kingdom's made-up coat of arms.

Eventually, de Mayréna returned to Europe, where he had another set of stamps printed and managed to raise finance for another trip East. This time he bought a posse and some weapons with him. On arrival, they were denied entry and the weapons were seized. Like many unsuccessful wheeler-dealers, de Mayréna was an odd mixture of deviousness and naïveté. Unable to return to his kingdom, he took himself off to Tioman, a small island off the Malaysian Peninsula, where he died shortly afterwards. Different stories have his death as the result of a snake bite or a duel.

In 1996, a set of stamps appeared in Canada, courtesy of the Sedang Nobility in Exile. De Mayréna had showered orders of merit on anyone who helped him with his ventures, and some of these people's descendants decided to recreate the nation. Stamps have been issued (the new philatelic authorities of Sedang seem very keen on cats). Attempts were made to trace the family of de Mayréna, who left no direct descendants – finally some were found, but sadly, they were not interested in taking on the mantle of kingship. As a result, the kingdom is currently ruled by a regent, the Comtesse Capucine Plourde de Kasara.

Sedang was what is now called a 'micronation', an entity that claims nationhood but does not have that claim officially recognised. Since 1889, many mirconations appeared – the Principality of Sealand, for example. This was declared on an abandoned Second World War fort in the North Sea in 1967. The fort was outside UK territorial waters: a court ruled in 1968 that as a result, UK law did not cover it. In 1969, Sealand issued its first stamps, featuring great seafaring explorers. A 1977 issue celebrated International Women's Year and featured women from Africa, Australia, Europe, Asia and America – plus Princess Joan, the wife of Sealand's founder. In 1978, a rival claimant to the fort tried to muscle his way onto it: a fight broke out and one man was kept prisoner. The man was German, and the German embassy had to send a diplomat to the fort to secure his release.

In 1987, the UK extended its territorial envelope from 3 to 12 miles, removing any claims Sealand might have had to legitimacy. However, Sealand continues to inspire good-natured eccentricity around the world. There is a 'national' football team, which competes against other micronations with varying degrees of success: it lost 8–0 to Occitania, which comprises people who speak Occitan, an ancient language from Southern France. More impressively, British mountaineer Kenton Cool placed a Sealand flag on the top of Mount Everest in 2003.

Perhaps the most bizarre source of Cinderallas is the lost kingdom of Atlantis. This was mentioned by the Greek philosopher Plato in two of his works, the *Timaeus* and *Critias*, where he says it lies 'beyond the pillars of Hercules', in other words in the Atlantic, and that it sank beneath the waves around 9,000 years ago. Since then, many people have believed in its existence. The Theosophists, a late-nineteenth century philosophical movement, believed that the Atlanteans were one of the 'root races' of humanity.

As such, it surely deserves stamps, and it had some made for it by a 1930s Scandinavian expedition that went to the West Indies in search of it. In 1964, Leicester Hemingway, brother of Ernest, founded the micronation of New Atlantis on a barge off the coast of Jamaica. Again, stamps were issued: two celebrated the Democratic Party candidates in the 1964 US Presidential Election, Lyndon Johnson and Hubert Humphrey, hailing them as 'protectors of the entire free world'. Sadly, the micronation was rendered unusable in a tropical storm in 1966.

More seriously, micronations can play a role in political activism. The Gay Kingdom of the Coral Sea was declared on Cato Island off the coast of Australia in 2004 as a protest against the refusal (at that time) of the Australian government to recognise gay marriage. A sheet of nine stamps was issued in 2006.

Cinderella stamps can also have a criminal side – Ugly Sister stamps, perhaps. Nobody seriously believes that Sedang, Sealand or Altantis are worthy of a seat at the UN, but in the past, illegal stamps have been issued from real places without the permission of the issuing authorities. Tuva (a place discussed in its own section below) has suffered this fate. Collectors, and by extension the hobby of philately, have been the losers.

Modern technology makes it ever easier to print one's own stamps. It also makes it easier for virtual nations to form over the Internet. One can expect ever more Cinderella stamps to appear.

The best policy for the stamp lover seems to be to stay sceptical about their financial value but curious about their varying stories, and for the historian to see them as signs of an increasingly individualistic, post-national world.

Senegambia

CATCHY NAME FOR a country isn't it? And you won't be surprised to know that Senegambia is a name for a combination of Senegal and the Gambia. It could have been Gambegal, perhaps, but somehow Senegambia sounds better.

Senegal is named after the Senegal River, and Gambia, or indeed the Gambia (since it is apparently still correct to call the country the Gambia, like the Netherlands or the Bahamas, though what used to be the Ukraine is now just Ukraine) is named after the Gambia River. Senegambia has often been used as a name for the geographical area encompassing the two rivers.

The period after the arrival of Europeans in the region would see a battle for control in the area between two great powers, France and Britain. Yes, the Portuguese reached there first and when the English reached there in the late sixteenth century they ended up paying the Portuguese for rights in the area, and yes, some other Europeans were occasionally involved, like the now somewhat surprising presence of Courlanders from the Baltic region at various stages, but fundamentally for a lot of the colonial period it was going to be Britain vs France, and the history of Senegambia, Senegal and the Gambia would be greatly affected by it.

In the 1660s, the English seized an island in what is now the Gambia with a fort on it. They called the island James Island, after the then James, Duke of York (the future, though only briefly, James II), and the fort Fort James. Well why bother to go to the effort of coming up with two different names? But in

1681, the French established a fort at nearby Albreda. It could only mean trouble. Meanwhile, to the north, in what is now Senegal, the English had seized a key trading post called Gorée, only to have it seized from them by the French in 1677. That could only mean trouble, too. And it did.

For instance, the French managed to capture Fort James a few times, although Britain always managed to retake it. And equally, during the times Britain was at war with France, which tended to be quite a lot, it tended to seize from the French places like Gorée and St Louis, their settlement at the mouth of the Senegal River. Finally, after 1758 and a successful surprise attack, Britain decided it was in a strong enough position to consolidate the territory it held in current-day Gambia and Senegal into a big Senegambia colony. It turned out that it wasn't in a strong enough position. British merchants weren't really doing enough trade in the region to make such an ambitious scheme feasible, and by 1779, with British attention focused on the Revolutionary War in America, the French were in control again. Not only there, in fact, but in Fort James as well, which they'd seized yet again, though Britain had control of that returned to it at a peace deal in 1783.

Britain did temporarily seize Gorée and St Louis again during the Napoleonic Wars. And the French managed to hold onto Albreda until 1857. At times in the nineteenth century, Britain did consider handing over the Gambia to the French in exchange for territory elsewhere in Africa. With little Gambia surrounded by Senegal, it could have made some strategic sense for both countries, but a deal was never actually done. Eventually, with the long traditional hostility between Britain and France gone, the borders in the region of Gambia and Senegal stabilised. An agreement between the two nations in 1889 agreed the borders.

As the European race to divide up the interior of Africa developed and the colonial map of Africa became more defined, the French began to develop and rearrange their colonies. Which is how we come to Senegambia stamps or, being more accurate, stamps for Sénégambie et Niger, or Senegambia and Niger as it tends to be known in English.

This was the name of a short-lived French colonial territory in West Africa. Very short-lived, in fact, because it only existed from 1902–04. Nevertheless, it existed long enough for the French to produce some stamps for it, thirteen definitives using the colony's name inscribed on the standard French colonial issue of the time, before they decided to change names and reorganise again. Somewhat confusingly, this Senegambia didn't include territory in British-controlled Gambia, but then, the Gambia River didn't just run inside the borders of British-controlled territory either.

Senegal would eventually become independent in 1960 and the Gambia became independent in 1965. Nevertheless, the idea of Senegambia as a political entity had not gone forever.

By 1981, security fears were making governments in both Senegal and the Gambia think that a combination of two countries that had such strong cultural and geographic links might make sense. For example, that year Senegalese troops had helped defeat an attempt to take power in the Gambia. So, late in 1981, both countries signed a deal establishing the Senegambia Confederation. Under the deal, the two countries were supposed to establish economic and monetary union, join security forces, establish a common foreign policy and come up with a series of confederal institutions. There was some logic to the idea and the process did commence. For instance, they set up a Senegambian executive and legislature.

In the end, though, Gambia felt it wasn't getting enough out of the confederation concept to press ahead with it and the Senegambian Confederation was terminated in 1989.

Serbian Krajina

MOST PEOPLE WILL be aware that Serb forces controlled big chunks of Croatia for much of the war there in the 1990s. What a lot of people may not be aware of, though, is that those areas were organised as a little separate mini-state, with its own name – the Republic of Serbian Krajina – its own army and, yes, its own stamps.

The word Krajina basically means borderland. It's a similar Slavonic word that is also the basis of the name Ukraine. However, along Croatia's border with Bosnia in the area that once formed territory of the Republic of Serbia Krajina, the word has a huge additional historical and cultural significance which to some extent helped shape the tragic events of the 1990s, because this was the heartland of the Military Krajina, the Military Frontier that for centuries formed the tense, and sometimes violent, border between the Habsburg Empire to the west and north, in what is now Croatia, and the Ottoman Empire, to the east and south, in what is now Bosnia.

Much of the territory is rugged and beautiful, including stunning scenery like that at the Plitvice Lakes. In the seventeenth century, the Habsburg monarchs decided to improve the security of their southern frontiers by organising the Military Frontier. It was directly controlled by the Habsburgs and it became a place where people, particularly Serbs fleeing the Ottoman Empire, were encouraged to settle in return for service defending the area. It became an area that had its own distinct character, somewhat different from the other Habsburg territories situated further west and further north. And when, in 1878, Turkey ceded control of Bosnia to Austria-Hungary, and the Military Frontier was no longer needed, that separate identity persisted, aided by a concentration of Serbs in some parts of Bosnia neighbouring Croatia.

At the end of the First World War, as the Austro-Hungarian Empire split up, both Croatia and Bosnia became part of the new Kingdom of the Serbs, Croats and Slovenes which would soon become known by a more familiar name, as the Kingdom of Yugoslavia, meaning the Kingdom of the South Slavs. But while the First World War created the situation in which Yugoslavia could be born, the Second World War added some history that would eventually help destroy the country.

In 1941, Hitler invaded Yugoslavia. He found allies in Croatian nationalists who saw the opportunity to establish an independent Croatia like they had been agitating for some time. And so was born the Independent State of Croatia, under the dictatorial Ustasha leader, Ante Pavelić. For some Croatian nationalists, it was a dream come true. For many others, including communists, Jews and Serbs, it was the start of a nightmare. The Ustasha regime was brutal in eliminating those elements that did not fit with its vision of a new Croatia. Everybody has heard of the Nazi concentration camps. Far fewer have heard of the Ustasha regime's camps, but the camp at Jasenovac, situated near Croatia's border with Bosnia, for instance, saw appalling atrocities.

In 1945, the Ustasha regime fell and Croatia was reincorporated into Yugoslavia, but into a Yugoslavia that was no longer a kingdom but Tito's Socialist Federal Republic of Yugoslavia. Under Tito, great efforts were made to suppress nationalism and instead emphasise unity between the different communities within the country. The main road linking Croatia and Serbia was, for instance, known as the Road of Brotherhood and Unity. However, when in 1990 Yugoslavia started to fall apart, the history of the region in the Second World War started to re-emerge to help poison the atmosphere. There was genuine fear from the past but it was also a rich source of convenient propaganda. Some Croatian nationalists would start using symbols and language from the Ustasha era. Some Croatian Serb nationalists would start using the symbols of the Chetniks, Serbian nationalist guerrillas in the Second World War. With the Croatian nationalist HDZ in power in Zagreb, with Serb nationalist politicians organising in the Krajina region, and with Milosevic prepared to offer support to Serbs unenthusiastic about becoming a minority in an independent Croatia led by the HDZ, the scene was set for war.

Clashes started breaking out between armed Serbs and Croatian security forces. In June 1991, Croatia declared independence. The now Serb-dominated Yugoslav government and army rejected the move and launched a widespread military campaign in coordination with local Croatian Serb forces. The campaign originally had wider goals, but with the new Croatian security forces putting up often stiff resistance, for instance, in the brave, determined and prolonged defence of Vukovar before its final fall, the campaign eventually settled for taking control of areas in and around the territory where Croatia's Serb community was concentrated. In December 1991, the Serbs declared the territory they held along Croatia's border with Bosnia and a separate enclave they held in the east along Croatia's border with Serbia as jointly the Republic of Serbian Krajina, and in January 1992 a ceasefire agreement led Yugoslav army forces to start to withdraw from RSK territory.

The new state needed stamps, and it got them. The first, basic definitives were issued in March 1993 (overprinted Yugoslav stamps served for higher values). By 1994, it was producing glossy flower commemoratives and new definitives showing local scenery (in new denominations, following currency reform). Later definitives all show places of worship.

Serbian Krajina also needed peace and international recognition, but it would get neither.

After the shock of the initial onslaught by the well-equipped Yugoslav army, the Croatian army began to re-train, re-equip and quickly nibble at the edges of the Republic of Serbian Krajina. For instance, in January 1993, a Croatian offensive in the Maslenica area drove RSK forces away from the coast and re-opened the main coastal route. But far worse was to come for the Republic of Serbian Krajina. For much of the international community, the war in Croatia had by now become just a sideshow to the Bosnian War. But not to the Croatian government. Inside Bosnia, Croat forces began to advance north, isolating southern areas of the RSK from Bosnian Serb areas. Then in May 1995, Operation Flash seized control of a finger of RSK territory that had cut the main road between Zagreb and the east of Croatia. In July, Croat forces inside Bosnia cut the main supply route between the Croatian Serb capital of Knin and the main Bosnian Serb city, Banja Luka. Then, in August, the Croatian army's Operation Storm crashed into the remaining part of the RSK situated along Bosnia's borders. It was a decisive victory achieved in just a few days of fighting, but it sent a stream of refugees fleeing eastwards.

In November 1995, with the war in Bosnia almost at an end as well, the Erdut Agreement provided for the peaceful reintegration into Croatia of RSK territory along the Serbian border. The process happened under international supervision and by 1998 the process was finished.

Shan States

THE MODERN SHAN State is on the eastern side of Burma (also known as Myanmar), a kind of bump sticking out from that tall, thin country. Its northern border is with China, its eastern border with Laos and its southern one with Thailand. Its terrain is mountainous and overgrown by jungle, and it is home to an estimated 1.5 million Shan people, as well as a range of minorities: nothing is simple in the demographics or politics of this area.

It never has been simple. For most of history, Shan State has really been a collection of smaller states, traditionally ruled over by *saophas* (princes) who often feuded with one another. One list has sixty-one such princedoms. In the early sixteenth century, a number of them formed a confederation and managed to conquer the entire north of Burma. In the 1550s, this was reconquered by the great Burmese emperor Bayinnaung, who built a large empire. This empire did not outlive him very long, however: by 1600 it was another piece of history.

Since then, the power of Burma over the Shan States has ebbed and flowed. In addition, China and Thailand have both attempted to nibble away at parts of the territory.

In the late 1880s, it was the turn of the British, who occupied most of Burma in 1886, but took four more years to subdue all the warlike Shan peoples. Burma became a province of India (writer George Orwell joined the Indian Imperial Police, but ended up serving in Burma, an experience that inspired his bitter novel *Burmese Days*). The new rulers treated the Shan *saophas* in the same way they treated the Indian Maharajas, letting them rule their 'princely states' as long as they accepted ultimate British power. In 1922, however, they were amalgamated into a federation – still ruled, of course, by the British.

As war threatened, the British pulled their forces out of the Shan States, effectively leaving a power vacuum that was filled by the Nationalist Chinese. They, in turn, were ejected by the Japanese and the Thais in 1942.

Thailand's role in the Second World War has been compared to that of Italy, as the sidekick to the big Axis Power. Thailand's prime minister from 1938, General Plaek Phibunsongkhram, was an admirer of fascism. He courted the Japanese, especially wanting their help to take back former Thai territory that had been occupied by the French – a brief war was fought with the colonial power in 1940–41. However, the Japanese had their own agenda and offered little help. Suddenly realising that Japan had designs on his country, the general turned his attention to the West. He appealed to Britain and America to treat Thailand like Poland, and regard an invasion of its territory as something that would initiate a war. America was not prepared to do that at the time, and Britain would not 'go it alone'.

On 8 December 1941, the day after Pearl Harbor, Japanese forces landed at points along the Gulf of Thailand and took the south of the country. Bangkok was bombed. The government conceded at 1 p.m. that day, and a few days later signed an alliance with Japan. Thailand formally declared war on Britain and the United States in January 1942.

Burma was next in Japan's sights. In March 1942, Rangoon (Yangon) fell, and by May most of the country was effectively occupied. Japanese and Thai forces then invaded the Shan States, reaching their biggest city, Kengtung, in July. The Thais were given control over part of the Shan area, which was named Saharat Thai Doem. The Japanese kept the rest, which became part of an 'independent' state of Burma in 1943. This independence was in name only; it was a puppet Japanese state.

Stamps for the Shan States were issued by the Japanese in 1943, showing a bullock cart and a woman in traditional headgear. When the states formally became part of 'independent' Burma, overprints were issued.

On the Axis's defeat, the British took the Shan States from them and the Thais, and reintegrated them back into Burma. Burma itself became independent on 4 January 1948 at 4.20 a.m. (a time chosen by an astrologer).

In 1950, the Shan States were invaded by Chinese Nationalist forces driven out of China by the Communists. These soon became de facto rulers of the area. After diplomatic and military pressure, they signed a deal in 1953 whereby they would leave and be flown to Taiwan, where their leader Chiang Kai-shek had taken refuge. However, not all the Nationalists complied, and the rest of the 1950s saw continuing unrest. The Burmese army tried to root out the stragglers – and did so with such fierceness that the local populace became ever more determined to reassert their ancient independence.

As part of its drive to assert control over the Shan areas, Rangoon clipped the wings of the *saophas* in 1959. They received similar treatment to the Maharajahs in India, losing their titles and privileges in return for a pension.

In 1962, there was a military coup in Rangoon. The new rulers sought to increase control of the Shan States even further. This fuelled guerrilla resistance; the area is currently a conflict zone.

More recently, another political force has entered its life; the rising power of drug barons. Part of the Shan States lies in the 'Golden Triangle', where a substantial part of modern illegal opiate-based drugs are grown and produced. Attempts were made in the 1990s to eradicate the trade, but they only had short-term success. The area is still estimated to be the second-largest producer of opium in the world.

Burma (the name was changed to Myanmar in 1989, with the first Myanmar stamp appearing in 1990, but the position of the current government is that either name can be used) was under an increasingly brutal and inept military dictatorship until a few years ago. A more democratic age is dawning, but much still needs to be done, including deciding the exact status of the Shan States.

Siberia, Far Eastern Republic and Priamur

THIS PIECE COVERS a number of mysterious empty spaces in our stamp album: the Government of Admiral Kolchak, the Czechoslovak army in Siberia, the Far Eastern Republic, and 'Priamur and Maritime Provinces'. All relate to the Russian Civil War and how it played out in the east of that vast nation.

Back in 1918, the east was White, not Red: Siberia was controlled by anti-Bolshevik forces under former polar explorer Admiral Alexander Vasilyevich Kolchak. By July 1918, the admiral was advancing on Yekaterinburg, which is often seen as the gateway to 'European Russia' from its (larger) Asian part. Yekaterinburg was also where Tsar Nicholas, Alexandra and their children were kept prisoner. Lenin feared they would fall into Kolchak's hands and prove a rallying point for White forces. They were murdered on 17 July (there is no paper trail leading to

Lenin, but most historians agree that the ultimate decision was his). Yekaterinburg fell into White hands a week after the killing. Kolchak was so confident of further victories that he ordered a handsome series of new stamps to be designed and printed.

The stamps never got beyond the design stage. Sadly, the murder of the tsar was good realpolitik; without Nicholas II, there was no real figurehead for the Whites to fight for, just competing military bigshots who commanded no heartfelt loyalty. The year 1919 saw fortunes change. The Red Army became ever better organised, and morale in the White forces began to crumble.

By the winter of 1919/20, the Whites had been pushed back to Irkutsk, on Lake Baikal, deep in Siberia. Kolchak fell into the hands of another force in the area, the 'Czech Legion'. This was an army of over 50,000 men that had been fighting against the Germans to secure the freedom of their homeland from the Austro-Hungarian Empire. With the Bolshevik withdrawal from the war, they found themselves marooned in Russia; their only way out was east, down the Trans-Siberian Railway to Vladivostok. On this journey, they found themselves having to fight both Reds and Whites, neither of whom trusted them. By late 1919, they were more afraid of the Reds than the Whites, and when Kolchak's train, containing both the admiral and the former Russian Imperial gold reserve, ended up on a section of the line that they controlled, they handed it over to the Bolsheviks, who shot Kolchak and helped themselves to the gold. (The Czech Legion also did what every self-respecting participant in the Russian Civil War did: issue stamps, some of the finest from the era.)

Under a new leader, General Vladimir Kappel, the retreating White Army tried to head east from Irkutsk by the only way available to it, across the frozen lake (the Reds had by then taken control of the main route east, the railway). Baikal is 50 miles wide – it is virtually an inland sea. Part of the way across it, a blizzard overcame the Whites. Many froze to death, their bodies remaining on the ice as a kind of giant sculpture until they disappeared into the depths of the lake with the spring thaw. Kappel made it to the other side, but died soon after from the effects of frostbite. Others survived and headed east towards the coast – following the Czechs, who made it to Vladivostok in 1920 (the last of them left Russian soil in September of that year).

While all this had been going on, the Japanese had taken control of Vladivostok and the surrounding area. This had been conquest by accident. The Japanese had sent a naval force to the port to forestall other nations' attempts to seize it. Anti-Japanese riots followed; they found themselves having to protect Japanese nationals; they ended up controlling the city and its hinterland.

With this powerful former enemy of Russia on Russian soil, Lenin decided that he wanted a buffer state between himself and it, so he created one. The Far Eastern Republic covered a large chunk of south-eastern Siberia – in essence, draw a line from the top end of Lake Baikal to the top end of Sakhalin Island, and the territory lies between this and the Chinese border. It had a national assembly, which promised elections. A constitution, based on that of the USA, was drawn up. And, of course, it issued stamps. The first of these were overprints on standard tsarist stamps. However, the republic wanted its own postal identity, and an issue was designed and printed in Vladivostok. They kept it simple, taking the tsarist stamps and working 'Far Eastern Republic' around the old double-headed eagle. This was probably the cheapest option, but it was also a gesture of defiance to the Bolsheviks.

Despite this gesture, the Japanese did not trust the Far Eastern Republic, which they saw not as an independent buffer state but as a puppet of the regime in Moscow. They wanted a buffer state of their own, and when the remnant of the White Army reached Vladivostok, this gave them the chance to set one up.

On 27 May 1921, the Provisional Priamur Government seceded from the Far Eastern Republic. Its territory was essentially Vladivostok and the area around it. The nominal heads of this government were two brothers, who had been part of the Kerensky government in mid-1917, Spiridon and Nikolai Merkulov. They, however, were soon deposed, and a soldier took over, General Mikhail Diterikhs. Diterikhs was a passionate traditionalist. He summoned a *Zemsky Sobor*, an old-style feudal parliament that dated back to Ivan the Terrible. This proclaimed the tsar's first cousin once removed, Grand Duke Nicholas, as Emperor of all Russia. (Nicholas was safely in exile in France at the time.) Diterikhs' government also issued stamps, or at least printed 'Priamur Rural Province' ('Province' because it was the general's intention to restore the new tsar to the throne of all Russia) onto existing issues, first onto those of the Far Eastern Republic, then, appropriately, onto old tsarist Russian ones.

The dream did not last. Two months after the *Zemsky Sobor*, the Japanese pulled out. The occupation of Vladivostok and the surrounding area had proven unpopular at home; it was expensive and did not seem to bring Japan any real benefits. (A decade later, that nation would be planning an empire.) The Red Army advanced on Vladivostok, and it fell on 25 October 1922, the date that is normally given for the end of the Russian Civil War, though small pockets of resistance fought on.

Vladivostok was technically part of the Far Eastern Republic again – but Moscow's commitment to the independence of this state did not last long. Three weeks later, the republic dissolved itself and became part of the 'Russian Soviet Federative Socialist Republic', which in turn soon became part of the USSR. A small set of overprints was issued in 1923 to celebrate this change – no longer onto decorative, traditional-looking tsarist stamps, but Soviet ones featuring a craggy soldier and an equally craggy worker. The flurry of Siberian philately was over, as were the brief experiments of the democratic Far Eastern Republic and of Priamur's new Romanov Empire.

Silesia

IT'S ONE OF those places that sounds deeply historical and people may think doesn't actually exist anymore. Well it is deeply historical but it does still exist, even though it is now split between the countries of Poland, Germany and the Czech Republic. And yes, it does have a place in stamp history as well.

Silesia had a Celtic period and then a Germanic period, and eventually Slavs arrived as well. The tenth century saw the Czech Přemyslid (no we don't know how to pronounce it either) dynasty competing with the (slightly easier to pronounce) Piast dynasty from Poland for control of the territory. In the end, Mieszko I of Poland managed to take the area of Boleslav of Bohemia (a Přemyslid) in around 990. Then the Polish king (also called, somewhat confusingly, Boleslaw) established a bishopric in the region in the year 1000 which eventually settled at Wrocław (German name Breslau). In 1163, an argument over succession led to a split in Lower Silesia and Upper Silesia, each with its own Piast. And the Piasts kept on growing in number and so did the sub-divisions of Silesia. By 1500, there were sixteen sub-divisions. Piasts spent a lot of time fighting each other and occasionally other people as well. In 1241, Henry II led an army against a Mongolian invasion force that had been devastating the country in the Battle of Legnica. He won but was killed in the process.

As assorted Piasts assaulted assorted other Piasts, Bohemia managed to get in on the act again, taking sides in the internal fighting. And in the end, in 1335 Charles I of Hungary put Silesia under the Bohemian crown and consequently made it part of the Holy Roman Empire. Thus, in the early fifteenth century, it got dragged into the Hussite Wars. And got devastated again. A period under Hungary followed and then it ended up with the Habsburgs. The area had seen an influx of German immigrants and when the Reformation arrived, Silesia enthusiastically embraced it, which meant that when the Thirty Years'

War arrived, Silesia was on the same side as Bohemia and Saxony against the Catholic Habsburgs. It got devastated again. Poland also took a renewed interest in Upper Silesia.

Nevertheless, in the decades after the war, Silesia, with its mining and textile industries, became increasingly wealthy. This was on one level good news for the Habsburgs and on another bad news. Because it prompted Frederick II of Prussia to take an (from the Habsburgs' point of view) unhealthy interest in the area. So much so, in fact, that after he defeated Maria Teresa (she of the dollars) in the War of Austrian Succession, he seized most of Silesia for Prussia. Austria then tried to retake the lost territory during the Seven Years' War and managed to recapture Breslau (Wrocław) temporarily, before eventually being forced to retreat again.

During the Napoleonic Wars, Napoleon's allies in the Confederation of the Rhine seized Breslau but eventually the city became the centre of the German and Prussian resistance to Napoleon. The Iron Cross award was first instituted here and the campaign that led to Napoleon's decisive defeat at the Battle of Leipzig in 1813 started here.

And so, after some revolutionary activities in the 1840s, in the nineteenth century Silesia became one of Germany's most important industrial areas. Lower Silesia's population had become almost all German while Upper Silesia's population was part German and part Polish. But another war was coming.

By the end of 1918, Germany was defeated and its ally the Austro-Hungarian Empire was being dissected. As borders changed, Czechoslovakia was born and Poland was reborn. After the war, the parts of Silesia that Austria had retained would be divided between the two new states.

Lower Silesia with its large German majority was less a matter of controversy, but Poland wanted industrialised Upper Silesia with its mixed Polish and German population for itself. In the end, the peace negotiations at Versailles agreed that there would be a plebiscite. In preparation for this, the area was occupied by British, French and Italian troops.

Stamps were issued at this time. The first issue is a simple abstract design with the denomination and the area's names in German and Polish. A smarter stamp followed, showing a dove of peace flying over a landscape that features a power station on one side and a farm on the other. Between them, a road winds off into the distance – into the nation's future? Inflation was beginning to kick in; the 'landscape' stamps were re-issued later in the year, in larger sizes and with larger denominations. There are also overprints, with 'Plebiscite, 20 March 1921' on them.

The Poles were, however, impatient with the process and unsure of the outcome. They decided not to wait. In August 1919, Poles in Upper Silesia rebelled against German rule, but the rebellion failed. The Poles tried again with a second rebellion in August 1920. That failed, too, and the plebiscite went ahead in March 1921. Over 700,000 votes were cast for Germany. Under 500,000 were cast for Poland. Soon after, the Poles, unhappy with the details of Allied plans to partition the area, resorted to arms again and the spring and summer saw heavy fighting as Poles clashed with German forces before the Allies stepped in to restore order. In the end, Poland got much of what it wanted when it was allowed to keep the south-eastern part of Upper Silesia where most of the region's coal mines and steelworks were located.

But the status of Silesia was not finally settled yet. In 1939, when Germany conquered Poland, it took Upper Silesia off the Poles again and sent in German settlers, forcing some of the Poles out. However, after the war against the Soviet Union turned against Germany, the war came in full force to Silesia. Hitler declared Breslau a fortress city and ordered that it be held to the end. It virtually was. Though surrounded by Soviet forces since mid-February, German forces held out until 6 May, after Hitler was dead, and only two days before the surrender of all German forces everywhere.

In the border shifts that established the post-war frontiers in the region, Poland was given almost all of Silesia. This time it was Germans who were forced to leave; over 3 million left and the area was repopulated with Poles.

Today Silesia remains part of Poland and Wrocław is the capital of the Lower Silesian Voivodeship. Poland has accepted the existence of Silesian as an ethnicity, and significant numbers have identified themselves as Silesian.

Slesvig

NOT THAT MANY people outside Denmark are going to have heard of Slesvig. If you change the Danish version to the German version 'Schleswig' and tack 'Holstein' on the end, as in Schleswig-Holstein, then the place becomes recognisable as one of Europe's great political fracture points. Actually, today Schleswig-Holstein is innocently enough the name of the northernmost of Germany's sixteen constituent states, but there's a whole lot of history that has gone on in the region.

Slesvig or Schleswig is the lower bit of the Jutland peninsula and today it straddles the border between Germany and Denmark.

It's a very important area from the point of view of the history of early England because, from territory in the region, assorted peoples would cross the North Sea in the fifth century to Britain and create communities that would form the basis of England.

The area has been a sort of frontier zone for a very long time, as demonstrated by the Danevirke, an impressive linear defensive work, first constructed as a sort of earthwork Hadrian's Wall probably sometime in the early mediaeval period. The Vikings got in on the act, obviously, and in the twelfth century Slesvig became a Danish duchy. That didn't mean it always got on well with the Danish crown (because it didn't), but it did have some basic influence on the orientation, and future, of

Slesvig. Meanwhile, to the south, Holstein, by contrast, was in 1111 (not a typing error, that's the actual date) made a County of the Holy Roman Empire, which again had some basic influence on its orientation.

It did not, however, stop the dynastic futures of the two territories becoming intertwined, with the same duke taking charge of Slesvig/Schleswig and Holstein around the end of the fourteenth century. And by 1474, the King of Denmark was duke of both Slesvig, which was in Denmark, and Holstein, which still wasn't. Holstein remained part of the Holy Roman Empire. Nevertheless, there was some resentment among the German-speaking majority of their new Danish master.

Plenty more complex dynastic history was to follow in the area in the seventeenth and eighteenth centuries, including Sweden, a regional superpower at times getting involved and even, somewhat confusingly, with a member of the Holstein-Gottorp family ending up as Tsar Peter III of Russia. Nevertheless, the basic competition between Danish and German influence in the area would continue, and in the nineteenth century have a dramatic impact both on the future of Germany and indeed of the world.

The Holy Roman Empire ceased to exist during the Napoleonic Wars, but by 1815, Holstein, despite its Danish links, was a member of the German Federation alongside Austria, which played a dominant role in the Federation.

The early nineteenth century saw moves towards greater clarification of national identities across Europe. This happened in Denmark, where pressure grew to incorporate Slesvig/Schleswig into Denmark fully. However, at the very same time there was a developing awareness of a German identity that was building across a Germany that at that stage was still divided into different states. And Prussia was increasingly looking to compete with Austria for leadership of the German-speaking world.

In 1848, the Year of Revolutions, Germans in Schleswig-Holstein rose in rebellion against the Danes, and the Prussians joined in to help the rebels. The war saw both victories and defeats for the Danes, but in the end, under pressure from other European powers who didn't want a major war over this, Prussia accepted the London Protocol of 1852 which restored the Danish crown's control of Slesvig/Schleswig and Holstein but with some measures designed to reassure the German-speaking population that there were limits to integration with Denmark.

However, the aging Danish King Frederick VII's lack of an heir provided something of a succession crisis and in 1863 the new king, Christian IX, was persuaded despite reservations to sign a new joint constitution for Denmark and Slesvig. In December 1863, the German Federation led by Prussia and Austria marched into Schleswig-Holstein. The war did not last long. The Danish strategy had centred on defending the Danevirke, still there after all those centuries, but it was no match for the brutally efficient Prussian military. The Danish military collapse in Jutland left Prussia and Austria in October 1864 in a position to decide the future of Schleswig-Holstein. But to Prussia there was an even more important question at stake, deciding the future leadership of the German-speaking world. An original deal, to give Prussia control of Schleswig and Austria control of Holstein, collapsed, and soon Prussia and Austria were fighting each other. The short war is known as the Seven Weeks' War. It was short and disastrous for Austria and short and victorious for Prussia. The peace deal that ended it gave Schleswig-Holstein to Prussia, signalled Prussia as leader of the German-speaking world and prepared the path for Prussia's declaration of the German Empire in 1871 and all that followed on from that for Europe and the world.

However, fifty years after Denmark was decisively defeated by Prussia, the German Empire was at war with the Allies. And four years later it too had been decisively defeated. Denmark itself had remained neutral during the conflict but it saw in Germany's defeat an opportunity to regain lost territory. The Allies agreed to hold a plebiscite in Slesvig/Schleswig on whether the inhabitants wanted to be Danish or German. Or, more specifically, two plebiscites were to be held on the question in northern Slesvig/Schleswig and central Slesvig/ Schleswig. A small international administration went in to prepare for the plebiscites.

Amongst other things, it had stamps designed and printed. A series of fourteen definitives was printed, using two designs, one showing the arms of Slesvig, and the other, a longer, rectangular stamp for higher denominations, the (rather bleak) local landscape. Two versions were prepared, one denominated in German Marks, the other in Danish Ore and Krone (the latter also has '1 Zone' overprinted on it). The German denomination stamps also exist, overprinted 'C.I.S.', for use by the administrators. These are by far the most valuable of the Slesvig stamps.

In the plebiscite in the northern region, over 70 per cent voted to be Danish, while in the plebiscite in the central region 80 per cent voted to be German, and so Slesvig/Schleswig came to be divided by the border between Denmark and Germany.

Sopron

SOPRON WAS NEVER a country, but issued overprints which tell a sad story, of youthful idealism soon to be trampled underfoot. The underlying stamps date from 1956, and are definitives of the Hungarian People's Republic: at the time, Hungary was part of the Soviet Empire. The stamps belong to a series issued in 1951 (seventeen stamps) and 1953 (nine more), celebrating its rebuilding plan. The plan was certainly needed – Eastern Europe's infrastructure had been devastated by the Second World War. However, the stamps show the style of the rebuilding to have been grimly cold – though the liberal democratic West was not without its architectural monstrosities at this time.

The 60 fillér stamp in this series shows the Mátyás Rákozi Cultural Institute. Rákozi was Hungary's de facto leader from 1949 to 1956. An admirer of Stalin, Rákozi used secret police, the AVH, to launch a purge of the party and send thousands of the capital's inhabitants to work on collective farms, where many died due to the farms' inability to grow enough food. He attempted to build a personality cult around himself – as well as having a Cultural Institute named after himself, Rákozi had three stamps issued for his 60th birthday in 1952. American journalist John Gunther described him in his 1949 book *Behind the Curtain* as 'the most malevolent character I ever met'.

However, by 1956 change was in the air. Stalin had died in March 1953; in February 1956, his excesses were denounced by Russia's new leader, Nikita Khrushchev, in a 'secret speech' to the party elite. The secret soon got out. Did this mean the end of repressive rule in Eastern Europe?

Hope that this might be the case grew in Hungary when Rákozi was removed from office in June. He was taken to the Soviet Union 'for medical reasons', and then exiled into what is now Kyrgyzstan. That autumn, students returning from vacation began to form protest groups, calling for more liberalisation. In several universities, including that in Sopron, a city near the Austrian border, they refused to join the official Communist student union and formed their own.

The overprint stamps were made by Sopron students on 22 October 1956. That date is printed on them, along with the words *Hazàdnak rendületlenül..!*, which mean 'Yield Not Your Country'. They are taken from *Szózat* (Appeal), a poem by romantic writer Mihály Vörösmarty, which dates from Hungary's attempt to break free from the Habsburg Empire in the 1830s and 1840s (Hungary eventually became independent in 1849). Set to music, the poem became an unofficial national anthem for the rest of the nineteenth century.

Some of the Sopron overprint stamps were used in the post, though unused examples are more common.

The day after the overprinting, a huge rally took place in Budapest. It began with 20,000 people, but as they marched on the parliament building, the numbers swelled. People cut the Communist emblem out of the Hungarian flag and waved it. A statue of Stalin was toppled – the new flags were placed in his boots, the only part of the statue left. Crowds also gathered outside the Radio Budapest building; here, things turned nasty, as the AVH fired on them. Rioting broke out. That evening, Soviet troops were called in by Rákozi's successor, Ernő Gerő.

The troops met with fierce resistance and, after several days of vicious fighting, made a tactical retreat. On 28 October, reformist Imre Nagy was made leader, a gesture that Moscow hoped would calm things. However, Nagy proved a radical choice, and started talking about leaving the Warsaw Pact (the Soviet version of NATO). This was too much for Moscow. In the early morning of 4 November, Soviet tanks rolled into Budapest. This time, the Red Army left nothing to chance: led by Second World War hero Ivan Konev, seventeen divisions took part in this invasion, rather than the five that had entered the country in October. Fighting between the Red Army and both the Hungarian army and groups of rebel irregulars was bitter, but within a few days the capital was in Soviet hands, and the rest of the country soon followed. Nagy and his minister of defence Pál Maléter were arrested, and executed in 1958.

Many Hungarians fled across the border – including students from Sopron University. Money was raised around the free world to support them (Elvis Presley made an appeal on American TV for funds), and many were resettled. Sopron's Forestry Department relocated to the University of British Columbia, where lectures were given in Hungarian till 1961.

The long-term consequence of the uprising and its quelling were to heighten the tension of the Cold War, but at the same time to kill off Communism as a political force in Western Europe. Before 1956, a number of serious public European intellectuals had been supporters of Moscow. After 1956, very few were.

Sopron later played its part in the ultimate ending of Soviet rule. In August 1989, a 'Pan-European picnic' was organised on the Hungarian side of the border with Austria, a few miles from the town. Beer, sausages and music were provided, speeches made – and then, unexpectedly, the Iron Curtain was opened. This last part seems largely to have been an on-the-spot decision rather than one passed down from Budapest: the picnic was originally just planned as a gesture of cross-border friendship. About 600 East Germans walked across to the West, some leaving their Trabant cars parked near the picnic site. Three months later, the Iron Curtain had fallen, and the dreams of the young men and women who had made the Sopron overprints finally became reality.

Spitsbergen

SPITSBERGEN IS ONE of those places that sounds like it probably doesn't actually exist, like somewhere found in a 1960s Cold War submarine thriller or an ancient Viking saga, a remote island so far north that few people actually know where it is. But it does exist and not only that, there are stamps with its name on.

Spitsbergen, which means pointy peaks (seems fair enough), is the largest island of the Svalbard (meaning cold coast, which again seems fair enough) archipelago situated in the remote Arctic Ocean north of Norway. The archipelago belongs to Norway and Spitsbergen was originally the name of the entire archipelago.

Nobody is entirely sure when humans first made it to this remote spot. A reference in the Icelandic Annals refers to Svalbard in 1194, but it seems rather unclear whether this Svalbard is what we now call Svalbard or some other 'cold coast'. There are plenty to choose from in the region. If the Vikings did find Spitsbergen, the place was so remote and distant that humans lost it again, and didn't find it again until June 1596, when Dutch explorers William Barents and Jacob van Heemskerck gave it its not hugely imaginative name.

Remote it may be, and dark for chunks of the year, but somebody could still quickly see a profit in it. Only a few years after Barents and van Heemskerck arrived, so too did Dutch and English whalers, and French, Scandinavian and Hanseatic League whalers arrived soon after. Nobody's entirely sure when the Russians first arrived, but certainly some of them were there in the early eighteenth century.

Being quite so far north, Spitsbergen became something of a useful jumping-off point for polar expeditions, including the very first, led by Britain's Captain C.J. Phipps in 1773. And hard, in a sense, though it is to believe that people would come to such a cold and inhospitable place to mine coal, they did that as well. Again, different groups from different nations, including Americans, Dutch, Swedish and Russians, wanted a piece of the commercial action.

Not only that, but it became a tourist destination with cruise ships taking tourists north to see the dramatic scenery and wild-life. Today, as a tourist, you haven't been somewhere unless you've got a selfie taken there. At the end of the nineteenth century, as a tourist you hadn't been there unless you'd sent a postcard home with a local stamp. Since at the time the inter-national community hadn't actually agreed who Spitsbergen belonged to, assorted bodies including cruise-line authorities printed Spitsbergen stamps so that the tourists could say they'd been there even if they also had to use official stamps from an actual country as well.

The heyday of Spitsbergen stamps was between 1896 and 1913. The best-known ones were issued by the Norwegian Vesteraalen Dampskibsselskap shipping company, and show a hunter shooting a polar bear. Polar bears, at this time unthreatened by humanity, also feature on the attractive 1913 issue from the Hamburg American Line.

Spitsbergen was a neutral condominium from 1913 to 1920, but in that year an international agreement accepted Norway as the sovereign power in Svalbard. The countries signing the deal were allowed to continue mining. So a situation developed where Soviet miners shared this bleak home with Western companies. Spitsbergen's biggest settlement is Norwegian Longyearbyen (named after American miner John Munro Longyear, not because a year there seems a long time, though it may), but its second biggest is a Russian mining settlement called Barentsburg, named after, yes, Willem Barents.

Spitsbergen is remote, but even it wasn't remote enough to escape the Second World War. After Germany occupied mainland Norway in 1940, and particularly after Germany invaded the Soviet Union, Spitsbergen and its valuable coal mines seemed to the Allies to be vulnerable to a German invasion. Svalbard was also a good location for weather stations. In August 1941, in Operation Gauntlet, British and Canadian troops landed on Spitsbergen, evacuated Norwegians and Russians, and destroyed the coal mines and valuable stores.

In 1942, in Operation Fritham, despite German bombing, Norwegian troops from Scotland managed to reach Berentsburg and after being supplied with anti-aircraft guns, managed to establish a stable presence there.

But the Germans could mount operations in Svalbard as well. During the war, parts of the archipelago were at times home to small German weather stations and, in September 1943, the Germans decided to attack Barentsburg in Operation Zitronella. They sent in a formidable naval force including the *Tirpitz* (on the only occasion it fired its main armament at a hostile surface target), the *Scharnhorst* and a number of other ships. A number of settlements were attacked and a battalion was landed and destroyed much of Barentsburg before withdrawing.

Actions like Zitronella could not, however, significantly change the course of the war. Germany surrendered in May 1945, leaving a German weather station crew at Haudegen in Nordaustlandet on their own. They were only rescued in September, months after the surrender.

Mining has declined on Spitsbergen but its unique international ambience remains and these days it is possible to fly there, so the archipelago isn't quite as remote as it used to be and it's never liable to be lost again.

Stampalia and the Dodecanese

STAMPS FROM SOMEWHERE called Stampalia? It sounds too good to be true, but there it is, in the Stanley Gibbons catalogue.

Stampalia is one of the Dodecanese islands, which were once under Ottoman rule but which were wrested from the Turks by Italy in 1912. Overprints of pre-war Italian stamps were then issued for each of the twelve main islands of the archipelago. After the Second World War, the islands were occupied by the British, during which time their stamps were British ones overprinted with 'M.E.F.' (Middle East Forces). In 1947, the islands were handed over to Greece, since then it has simply used ordinary Greek stamps, and Stampalia has reverted to its Greek name – Astypalaia.

The Dodecanese islands have seen conquerors come and go since the Minoans in the sixteenth century BC. Mycenean Greeks followed, then Dorians, Persians, Athenians, more Persians, Alexander the Great …

Rhodes is the biggest of the islands. It was famous for its Colossus, one of the Seven Wonders of the Ancient World. Records tell of a giant bronze statue of the Greek sun god,

Helios, built over twelve years between 292 and 280 BC at the mouth of Rhodes harbour. Some antiquaries say that the statue straddled the entrance to the harbour, but modern engineers consider this unlikely. More probably, it stood on one side. It seems to have been about 100 feet high. It, or at least an imagined version of it, was an inspiration for New York's seafarer-welcoming Statue of Liberty; other statues of Helios show the god with one hand held up high, and with a kind of crown on his head. The Colossus lasted fifty-four years, till an earthquake hit the islands and the mighty statue snapped at the knees, collapsing onto the shore. Its ruins remained a tourist attraction for 800 years, until the Arab Caliph Muawiyah I joined the list of the islands' invaders in 654. He had what was left of it melted down.

Kos, or Cos, the third-biggest island in the archipelago, was home to Hippocrates, the father of modern medicine, who lived from 460 to 377 BC. Patmos, a much smaller island, is known as the place where the Book of Revelation was written. Nobody knows exactly who the author was, except for his first name, John, which was as common then as it is now. He had been sent to Patmos by the Roman Emperor Domitian – the islands had become part of the Roman Empire in 164 BC – for his preaching activities, probably as part of a sentence that included hard labour.

Stampalia itself is another small island, further from the Turkish coast than any other of the islands. It has a quieter history: it was bought in 1207 by Zuanne Querini, a member of a wealthy Venetian family, and became a family stronghold, especially after members were banished from Venice after attempting a coup in 1310.

In the same year as that coup, Rhodes fell to the Knights Hospitaller, a Catholic order initially founded around 1100 to care for pilgrims to the Holy Land. The Hospitallers' service soon extended to providing armed protection, and they became a formidable military power, though one without a national base: they were a kind of early mediaeval multinational. The Knights made the islands their centre for 200 years, becoming 'the Knights of Rhodes' and building the massive castle that dominates the town. In 1522, they were besieged and driven away by the Ottoman Sultan, Suleiman the Magnificent, who soon extended his rule to the rest of the islands. Stampalia held out for longest – the Querini were skilled diplomats – but in 1540 Suleiman took possession of it. The family retained links with the island, however, even ruling it again briefly in the seventeenth century.

At the start of the twentieth century, the Dodecanese were still part of the Ottoman Empire. In 1912, Italy fought a war with Turkey (see the sections on Fezzan and Cyrenaica) for control of Libya, but ended up with the islands as well; Italy was supposed to give them back at some time in the future, but events soon overtook this requirement. Stamps – or at least overprints – appeared very soon after the change of ruler. Each main Dodecanese island had its own: as well as 'Rodi', Cos, Patmos and Stampalia, one can collect Calimno, Caso, Karki, Leros, Lipso, Nisiros, Piscopi, Scarpanto and Simi. In 1929, Rhodes got its own stamps to celebrate the visit of Victor Emmanuel III, King of Italy.

Under Mussolini, attempts were made to 'Italianise' the islands, whose population is mainly Greek. This was ignored, though the Italians did improve the infrastructure of the islands, including repairing the Knights' castle, which had fallen into disrepair.

In the Second World War, the Dodecanese were used by the Axis as a jumping-off point for its invasion of Crete. When Italy changed sides in 1943, the Germans invaded Rhodes. British troops fought back, invading other islands, but were driven off, largely due to superior German air power in the region. The Stuka dive-bomber was particularly effective.

After the war, the islands were briefly occupied by the British, then given to Greece in 1947. Recently they have been in the news because of the Syrian refugee crisis, with thousands trying to make the crossing from Turkey: Kos is only 4km off the Turkish coast. This is still too far for some people crowded onto unsafe boats by traffickers. Aylan Kurdi, the drowned boy washed up on a beach near Bodrum, whose photograph alerted the world to the full horror of the situation, had been trying to reach Kos.

Stampalia, being furthest from Turkey, has not seen such tragedy. Instead, perhaps it is now best known for the fine art gallery in Venice that bears its name. The last of the Querini died there in 1869 – they'd been forgiven their treachery of 1310 – and left his mansion and art collection to the city. The Querini Stampalia Gallery contains works by masters such as Tiepolo, Longhi and Giovanni Bellini. Residents of Venice still get free admission.

Stellaland

STELLALAND WAS NAMED after a comet that was blazing across the sky at the time it was founded. The name proved appropriate: the 'Great Comet of 1882' subsequently broke into five pieces and disappeared (though the pieces will be back in a few hundred years' time). Stellaland was soon gone, too.

It was founded on 6,000 square miles of land granted to a group of around 400 Boer settlers by Mosweu, a Kora Chief, in return for their having helped him defeat a local rival, Mankuroane. The settlers decided they should turn this grant into an independent nation. Legend has it that while camped out on land that would soon become their capital Vryburg, a group of them looked up at the autumn night sky, saw the comet and decided on the name.

Stellaland soon acquired the trappings of nationhood: a coat of arms, a flag, an emblem (a lone star), a belligerent motto ('Armed and Justified') and, of course, stamps. These simple, attractive items featured a korhaan, a type of bustard and the symbol of Mosweu; the star emblem; the scales of justice (for the white settlers, anyway) and a skewered fish – the symbol of the defeated Mankuroane.

In 1883, Stellaland merged with a neighbouring mini-country, Goshen, which had also been set up by mercenaries rewarded for intervening in a local dispute (but which had never issued stamps). The new entity became the United States of Stellaland. This mighty-sounding country had a population of around 25,000.

Its independence was doomed by geography, however. The United States of Stellaland lay on the main route between Central Africa/the Rift Valley and Cape Colony. Cecil Rhodes (more about him in the section on Rhodesia) was already dreaming of his red line of uninterrupted British territory from the Cape to Cairo, and wasn't going to let Stellaland stand in its way.

Rhodes travelled to Stellaland in 1884 with the aim of persuading its inhabitants to accept British rule. Their land titles would be respected, he said. They just had to give up their nationhood. After an initially frosty reception, Rhodes talked the leaders of the original Stellaland round. He had less luck in the original Goschen, however. He sent his representative Frank Thompson to negotiate on his behalf. The first question Thompson was asked was 'Who the hell is Rhodes?', after which Thompson was arrested, only to be released after complex negotiations between Rhodes and the settlers. The empire-builder left empty-handed.

The British began to hatch plans for taking the area by force, but were pre-empted by the Boers in the neighbouring South African Republic (modern Transvaal). On 10 September, the republic's president, Paul Kruger, announced that the area was 'under his protection'. On 3 October, the Reverend Stephanus du Toit, an SAR official, travelled to the old Goschen capital Rooigrond, raised the four-coloured SAR flag and announced that the town would be renamed Heliopolis – the sun outshone any comet.

This was the final straw for Britain. In November, parliament voted that £675,000 (around £35 million in modern money) be set aside for military action. A force of 4,000 British and African troops under Sir Charles Warren marched north in December. As well as the usual armaments, Warren took with him three giant hydrogen reconnaissance balloons, the first time British forces had used this technology (attempts at military balloon-ing had been made in the American Civil War, but had not proven workable).

The balloons were not necessary. The force, vastly superior to the local militia, met with no resistance, entering Vryburg on 7 February 1885. Even Goshen surrendered without a fight. In August 1885, the United States of Stellaland was abolished. Most of it became part of a new colony, British Bechuanaland, while small parts were ceded to Transvaal, to keep the peace.

Britain's road to central Africa was now open. Five years later, Rhodes's 'Pioneer Column' would march up through what had once been Stellaland to invade the lands of the Shona and the Ndebele.

In 1899, war broke out between the Boers and the British. The former United States of Stellaland was the scene of one of its most iconic events. The British, under their commander Robert Baden-Powell, were besieged in the small fortified town of Mafeking for 217 days, during which, amongst other things, they produced their own stamps – a 1*d* featuring a messenger boy on a bicycle and a 3*d* featuring Baden-Powell in his trade-mark hat. The relief of the siege, by Lord Roberts, was a cause for national rejoicing in Britain: the word 'mafficking' was coined, meaning wild celebration. While of limited strategic importance – the core battles of the Boer War were fought else-where – the Relief of Mafeking was a boost for British morale and arguably turned the conflict, which up to that point had not gone well for the British. Baden-Powell returned to Britain a national hero and, inspired by the messenger boys on the 1*d* stamp, founded the Boy Scout movement.

British Bechuanaland had become part of Cape Colony in 1895. Confusingly, north of it lay a larger territory, also controlled by the British, which was named the Bechuanaland Protectorate. This remained in existence – and issued stamps – till 1966, when it became the Republic of Botswana.

The old United States of Stellaland is now part of the Republic of South Africa. The name has recently resurfaced in political debate thanks to far-right groups who want to establish a white-dominated state there. There seems to be little support for this locally: in recent elections, almost everybody in the area voted for the ANC or their centrist rivals the Democratic Alliance. Vryburg is now a town of 50,000 people. A centre for the cattle industry, it is nicknamed the Texas of South Africa, because of the cattle but also because of the old one-star emblem of Stellaland.

Straits Settlements

THE NAME STRAITS Settlements seems particularly bland for an entity, giving as it does so few clues to where it was and what it was. As it turns out, the Straits in question were the Malacca Straits, and the settlements were part of the British Empire, and though some of the names won't be familiar to many, one at least will be familiar to almost all, one that on its own is now a country in its own right – Singapore.

Originally it was the British East India Company which came up with the idea of administratively uniting a bunch of separate settlements spread across the Malay Peninsula, roughly along, or at least somewhere near, the Malacca Straits. Then, in 1867, it became a Crown Colony and in the end it included Malacca, Dinding, Penang, Labuan, Singapore and some small islands in the Indian Ocean, of which more later. Apart from being roughly located in the same area, the separate elements had not that much in common. They weren't geographically contiguous and there were huge differences in their origins and in what happened to them.

Penang, an island in the north of what is now Malaysia, was Britain's first settlement in the region. In 1786, Captain Francis Light landed and took control of the island in the name of the king and of the East India Company. Arthur Wellesley, later the Duke of Wellington, was an early visitor to Penang, and in 1800 the settlement was expanded to include a chunk of land on the mainland which was then called Province Wellesley. Penang thrived as a trading centre under British control, but lost some of its administrative power with the rise of Singapore.

South from Penang, along the Malay Peninsula, lay Dingding, where Britain took full control in 1874 as part of a deal to sort out some local disputes. And further south is Malacca. Malacca had a long colonial history even before Britain got involved. The Portuguese had already taken Malacca in 1511, less than fifteen years after Vasco da Gama first rounded the Cape of Good Hope. Eventually, however, after several attempts the Dutch managed to seize Malacca from the Portuguese. British forces interrupted Dutch control in 1795 and eventually the Dutch agreed to swap Malacca with the British in 1824 in exchange for another bit of territory in Sumatra which they rather fancied.

British involvement with Singapore started in January 1819 when Sir Stamford Raffles, working for the East India Company and looking for a handy trading spot, landed and managed to buy some land there. The Dutch weren't too happy, but again in 1824 accepted British control of the area, and the same year Britain paid to take control of the whole of Singapore Island.

And then we come to Labuan. In 1846, James Brooke – an interesting character, an adventurer who became the first White Rajah of Sarawak – gave Labuan island to Britain as a present. And HMS *Iris* turned up in a show of force to accept the present. Hopes that Labuan would be the new Singapore never quite came true, and in 1907, despite the fact that Labuan is a long distance from the Straits of Malacca, it became part of the Straits Settlements.

The Straits Settlements saw occasional internal strife, for instance convict rebellions in Penang and Singapore in the 1850s. And in the Battle of Penang in October 1914, a German warship, the SMS *Emden*, sank two Allied warships. However, much greater violence would eventually come to the settlements. After the Japanese attack on Pearl Harbor, Malaya became a major target for the Japanese. Penang fell to the Japanese on 19 December 1941, less than two weeks after the Pearl Harbor attack. To the east, Labuan was captured the same month. Malacca was captured on 15 January 1942. Singapore fell to the Japanese on 15 February 1942. The Japanese had taken all the Straits Settlements. Except they hadn't because at the beginning of March 1942, somewhere out in the Indian Ocean, the British flag still flew over two small groups of islands that, like Labuan, were not close to the Straits of Malacca but were part of the Crown Colony despite that.

The Cocos or Keeling Islands were first permanently settled by a British man Alexander Hare and a group of Malay women he took with him in the early nineteenth century. In 1857, the islands were annexed to the British Empire. The Battle of the Cocos Islands in November 1914 saw German forces from the SMS *Emden* invade the islands to destroy a radio and cable centre and then saw HMAS *Sydney* damage the German ship and subsequently, when it beached itself, accept its surrender. During the Second World War a Japanese submarine shelled the islands, but they remained in British hands throughout the war.

Not quite so lucky was Christmas Island, the other Indian Ocean island element of the Straits Settlements. This originally uninhabited island got its name from a passing East India Company ship commanded by Captain William Mynors which sighted it on Christmas Day 1643, and it was annexed to the British Empire in 1888. After it had been bombed and shelled by the Japanese, at the end of March 1942, Japanese forces landed on the island and seized control.

The Second World War was pretty much the end for the Straits Settlements colony. In 1946, after the war's end, the colony was split up. Singapore would eventually become a country in its own right. Penang, Dingding, Malacca and Labuan would become part of Malaysia. And as for Christmas Island and the Cocos Islands, well they would become a little part of Australian territory that few people are now aware of, far from Australia, far out in the Indian Ocean.

Straits Settlements had a long philatelic history. The first stamps were overprints on issues from British India. In 1867, it got its own stamps, featuring, of course, Queen Victoria. For decades, there was little on the stamp to indicate the locality, apart from the inscription. Its stamps in celebration of George V's silver jubilee feature Windsor Castle. Finally, in 1936 we see George V, then his son George VI, framed by palm trees – but these are the last two sets of stamps that the area would issue. With their new, Australian identity, Christmas Island and the Cocos Islands have loosened up and issued a number of colourful issues. From the former, inevitably, come special Christmas ones (the 40c from 1999 shows Santa Claus relaxing on a beach in a hammock, not the image we associate with him in Europe!)

Thurn und Taxis

STARTING IN 1852, stamps were being printed with the name Thurn und Taxis on them. The period of Thurn und Taxis stamps didn't last very long and, even at the time, if you'd gone looking for a state of Thurn und Taxis you'd have ended up disappointed. Because Thurn und Taxis isn't a where, it's a who, a family which grew rich and famous by organising the post of one of Europe's greatest empires. And their story is such an interesting one that they've earned a place in this book.

Somewhat disappointingly for a family whose name sounds a bit like 'Turn a Taxi', taxis don't feature largely in the family story. Instead, the Taxi part of the name seems originally to have come from northern Italy and been Tasso and then Tassis. The origin of the name may be the Italian for 'badger', which is fun in itself, though taxis would probably still have been more fun. The original Italian name then acquired its present form when the family became more prominent in German-speaking territories.

And the name of the empire served by this family? The Holy Roman Empire. Voltaire famously quipped that the Holy Roman Empire was neither holy nor Roman nor an empire. All of which is arguably true, but at least Thurn und Taxis made sure it had a decent postal system.

The Taxis family developed their mail and courier skills originally in imperial territories of northern Italy, but soon they began to branch out, reaching out to the other key Habsburg territories of the time. Soon they were running post into Austria and then further afield, with postal routes, for instance, running up to Brussels. A letter could be delivered in just five and a half days from Innsbruck to Brussels, which at the time was quite an achievement.

And their triumphs in this early international communications revolution would not go unnoticed or unrewarded. In 1615, the Holy Roman Emperor Matthias made the family hereditary imperial postmaster generals, with the title passing through the male line. And the family were getting ever more noble, too. In 1608, they had the status 'imperial free barons'. In 1624, that became 'hereditary imperial count'. And in 1695, the Emperor Leopold I upped that to 'imperial prince'. Today's courier and postal companies may make profits but they don't get those kind of rewards.

Then, in 1748, the family made yet another step up. The Emperor Franz I made Prince Alexander Ferdinand of Thurn und Taxis principal commissioner, imperial representative at the Perpetual Diet at Regensberg. This was more fun than it sounds, since the Perpetual Diet was not anything to do with long-term healthy eating but was instead the sort of parliament of the Holy Roman Empire. Heavyweight feasting was permitted as part of Prince Alexander Ferdinand's new job and, indeed, pretty much obligatory. And the family acquired themselves an impressive place to do their feasting. They'd had to move from Frankfurt to Regensberg to get the job, and in Regensberg they moved into St Emmeram Palace, still their home today.

But the days of Thurn and Taxis' imperial postal glory would not last forever. And nor for that matter would the Holy Roman Empire.

Voltaire had mocked the Holy Roman Empire and it was another Frenchman (or Corsican) who, in the end, would pretty much kill it. It's hardly his best-known achievement today, but Napoleon's rampage across Europe was going to bring about the final death of an empire that lived on, at times slightly improbably, over many centuries and through many crises.

In November 1805, Vienna fell to Napoleon's forces, but the Holy Roman Emperor and Austrian Emperor Francis did not despair. He knew that huge Russian reinforcements under Tsar Alexander I were rushing to support him against the French. In December, the armies finally met at Austerlitz, now in the Czech Republic. Between them Francis and Alexander had more men than Napoleon, and when an Allied assault was launched on the French right, Russians and Austrians were optimistic. However, Napoleon's battle plan saw the French smash the Allied centre and after that the Allied efforts collapsed. The French took huge numbers of prisoners and Napoleon achieved one of his most significant victories. Such a defeat was too much for Francis. He made peace with Napoleon. Napoleon formed the Confederation of the Rhine, a confederation of states previously part of the Holy Roman Empire. Francis abdicated from his position as Holy Roman Emperor. He was to be the last Holy Roman Emperor ever.

The end of the Holy Roman Empire meant the end of the Thurn und Taxis position as hereditary imperial postmaster generals. However, even without an empire, people still needed access to postal services and Thurn und Taxis could still provide them for a while. The now privatised family operation managed to secure for itself the role of running postal services for a number of the German states. And in 1852, they started printing stamps for it. Thurn and Taxis served two distinct geographical areas, one in the north, one in the south. These had different currencies, so two sets of stamps were printed. The northern ones, featuring a square frame, are denominated in 'Silbergroschen'; the southern, in a circular one, are denominated in 'Kreuzer'. The 1852 stamps were 'imperforate', meaning that they had to be cut out by hand from a sheet by the postal clerk. Perforations were added in 1865.

However, as the Battle of Austerlitz had brought one era of the Thurn und Taxis family's postal operations to an end, so another Austrian military defeat was about to do the same again. In 1866, in the Austro-Prussian War, Prussia and its German allies swiftly defeated Austria. As a result, Prussia became the foremost power in the German-speaking world and, in October 1866, it annexed the Free City of Frankfurt. It also took control of something else. Frankfurt was the centre of the Thurn und Taxis postal operation, and in January 1867 Prussia bought the service.

It was the end of centuries of Thurn und Taxis post, but far from the end of the Thurn und Taxis family. They live on today, as one of Europe's leading aristocratic families.

Tibet

AROUND 780 AD, Tibet was an imperial power, extending from Afghanistan to China's modern borders with Burma and Vietnam. Like all empires, it then began to crumble, with a full civil war breaking out between rival claimants to the throne in 841. For the next four centuries, there was little central power until the Mongols invaded in 1240. They held sway there for a century, until their own dynasty in China began to weaken (it collapsed in 1368). After that, there was a period of calm, during which Lhasa's great monasteries – the Ganden, Drepung and Sera – were built by the Gelugpa ('Yellow Hat') Buddhists. From 1450 onwards, there were struggles between the Gelugpa and a series of rivals, often lumped together as 'Red Hat'. The hats in question were the ones worn by monks at certain ceremonies: the differences in Tibetan society at this time were between branches of Buddhism.

The first Dalai Lama was Gendun Drup, who died in 1474 – but he was only given this title posthumously. The first living person to have the title was the third Dalai Lama, Sonam Gyatso, who had it bestowed on him in 1578. The Dalai Lamas belong to the Yellow Hat sect and are supposed to be reincarnations of the Buddha of Compassion, Avalokiteshvara. The current Dalai Lama is the fourteenth.

During the eighteenth century, the powerful Qing Dynasty in China increased its power over Tibet, taking a chunk of the country and making it part of China (modern Qinghai Province) and exercising ever more control over the government in Lhasa. A few Europeans visited at this time, including George Bogle, a Scotsman who had an audience with the second most important religious figure in the country, the Panchen Lama. In 1785, however, Tibet's Chinese rulers banned foreigners.

The British, concerned about potential Russian incursion, began mapping the country in secret in 1865. The cartographers were known as pundits; Nain Singh, a particularly intrepid one, was celebrated on an Indian stamp in 2004. In 1903, this knowledge was put to use by Francis Younghusband, who led a military expedition to Lhasa, ostensibly to sign a trade deal but in practice to show who was boss in the new century's world order. Ironically, this servant of imperial *realpolitik* had a mystical experience on his march back from the capital, and spent much of the rest of his life developing and writing about a philosophy that would grace any modern 'New Age' enthusiast. Amongst other things, he believed the star Altair was a planet inhabited by aliens with translucent skin.

Meanwhile, back on Earth, China responded to Young-husband's expedition by launching one of its own. This didn't bother with niceties about trade; it was a simple exercise in conquest. The Dalai Lama fled the Potala Palace; the Chinese took over – and then, in 1911, the Qing Dynasty collapsed and the Chinese pulled out. The Lama returned and declared that Tibet was independent again. Tibet's first stamps – so often an early symbol of a nation's claim to freedom and international identity – appeared next year. Even the denominations of these stamps are exotic, the smallest being one-sixth of a Trangka (six and two-thirds Trangka make one Sang).

The Chinese denied that Tibet was free, but were so embroiled in their own problems that they did nothing about this. Tibet was left to its traditional ways. In the inter-war years, it is estimated that only ninety foreigners visited Lhasa. Thus cut off, Tibet slowly gathered a reputation as a remote, mysterious paradise. The stamps help, but a much bigger influence was James Hilton's 1933 novel, *Lost Horizon*, whose kingdom of Shangri La was based on his (second-hand) knowledge of the country. During the war, Heinrich Harrer, a German mountaineer who had escaped British internment in India, sought refuge there. His post-war book *Seven Years in Tibet* added to the myth.

As with many Lost Countries, global power politics crushed the aspirations of an economically weak nation. In October 1949, the Communists finally won the civil war that had effectively been raging in China since the collapse of the Qing. In 1950, the People's Liberation Army marched into Chamdo, the easternmost part of Tibet, which borders on Sichuan. They overcame any opposition, but rather than having them march on to Lhasa, the Chinese government summoned Tibetan diplomats to Beijing and made them sign a Seventeen-Point Agreement. While this handed over national independence, the agreement did promise non-interference in Tibetan life. The fourth point reads: 'The central authorities will not alter the existing political system in Tibet. The central authorities also will not alter the established status, functions and powers of the Dalai Lama. Officials of various ranks shall hold office as usual.' The eleventh says: 'In matters relating to various reforms in Tibet, there will be no compulsion on the part of the central authorities.'

For a while, this agreement was adhered to, but it slowly broke down. Exactly how this happened is complex. A theme of this book is the corrupting influence of power: China's leader, Mao Zedong, became ever more psychopathic, and started inflicting bizarre and vicious policies on his own people. His 'Great Leap Forward', which began in 1958, is estimated to have caused the deaths of 30 million people through famine. The effects of this rippled into nominally autonomous Tibet. Add to this stirring from the CIA and the lingering dislike of the Chinese among many Tibetans ...

The Tibetan uprising began on 10 March 1959, when an attempt was made to arrest the Dalai Lama. Barricades went up in the streets of Lhasa, and the Lama was spirited out of his palace and began a dramatic escape across the mountains, travelling only at night to escape Chinese patrols. He reached northern India on 31 March. By this time, the Chinese had overcome all resistance in Lhasa. Many monks were executed and temples were destroyed – estimates of the death toll of the subsequent crackdown vary wildly, but 87,000 is a figure often quoted.

Since then, the Dalai Lama has carried on a government in exile in Dharamsala – a few stamps were issued by this government, but they are regarded as 'Cinderellas'. The Dalai Lama was awarded the Nobel Peace Prize in 1989. Tibet is now an 'autonomous region' of China, though how much autonomy it has is a matter of some debate.

Transcaucasian Socialist Federative Soviet Republic

NOT THE SNAPPIEST of names, it has to be said. Bit of a tongue twister, in fact. Try it. So not surprisingly it tends to get shortened to either TSFSR or Transcaucasian SFSR. The latter is fair enough because in some senses, it's that first bit, Transcaucasian, that's the most interesting.

Transcaucasia literally means 'on the other side of the Caucasus', and it's a somewhat Eurocentric word because when it says 'on the other side of the Caucasus' it actually means south of the Caucasus. If you were looking at the Caucasus, from a Turkish or Iranian perspective, then the other side of the Caucasus would be north. Also it's slightly confusing because Transcaucasia and Ciscaucasia (this side of the Caucasus) actually divide the Caucasus mountains between them. Also confusing is that in early times, the area included parts that were called Iberia and Albania, even though the Caucasus is a huge distance from either Spain or Albania.

It's a region that has produced a huge amount of history and is still producing plenty more today. A key element in the historical mix in modern times has been Russian involvement in the area.

Already by the seventeenth century, Russia was getting involved in disputes in the Caucasus, and in the eighteenth century Peter the Great took it a bit further. He took control on the Caspian in 1722 and seized Baku in 1723. In 1770, Russian forces moved south of the Caucasus for the first time on a major venture, seizing Kutaisi in Georgia.

The nineteenth century would see Russia gradually extending its control over the entire area. It was a messy and complex process. For instance, in 1801, the Russian tsar incorporated a big chunk of Georgia into Russia, then the Ossetes accepted Russian control and in 1803 they incorporated Lezgian. Russia took Mingrelia the following year and the Imereti Kingdom fell in 1810. Russian victory in the Russo-Persian War of 1804–13 forced Persia to cede its claims on another big chunk of territory to Russia. They took Armenia and more of what is now Azerbaijan from Persia after victory in another Russo-Persian War in 1826–28, and more land in the region from Turkey in 1829. And Russian victory in the Russo-Turkish War of 1877–78 gave Russia yet more land. The place in the region where the Russians experienced the toughest struggle to take control was mountainous parts like bits of Dagestan. But even here, eventually, Russian military might managed to impose the tsar's control. In 1864, hundreds of thousands of Circassians moved to Ottoman-controlled lands to avoid Russian rule.

The territory of Armenia, Georgia and Azerbaijan ended up united under one administrative control within the Russian Empire. Revolutionary and nationalist movements did develop in the region in the late nineteenth and early twentieth centuries, for instance, the Armenian Revolutionary Federation, but still, the Russian Empire's grip on the region might have remained secure in the long term, until that is, the First World War came along.

There was heavy fighting in the region between Ottoman and Russian forces, in which Russian troops eventually made substantial advances, capturing cities like Trebizond and Erzurum. The revolution of 1917, however, changed the situation entirely. The Russian armies in the area collapsed and so did the Russian Empire. Turkish troops advanced.

In April 1918, from the ashes of the Russian Empire in Transcaucasia emerged the Transcaucasian Democratic Federative Republic, incorporating Georgia, Armenia and Azerbaijan. If the Russians weren't prepared to continue fighting Turkey in the Caucasus, then the Transcaucasian Democratic Federative Republic was. For a bit. Armenian forces scored a number of victories over the advancing Turkish troops and in May the Transcaucasian Democratic Federative Republic split up. First Georgia declared independence, then Armenia and Azerbaijan.

After this the situation started to get even messier. Both German and British troops started to arrive in the area. Georgia had allied itself with Germany and a British unit called Dunsterforce was advancing towards Baku. Both sides wanted the oil of the region. And the Turks were advancing again as well. In September, after heavy fighting, the Turks seized Baku.

In the end, though, just as Russian forces in the Caucasus had been beaten mainly by distant events on other fronts, so would the Turkish forces be. Less than two months after Turkish forces seized Baku, the Armistice of Mudros was signed on 30 October, taking Turkey out of the war. A few days later, Germany agreed to an armistice, too.

There would, however, be little peace in the Caucasus. Georgians fought Armenians, Armenians fought Azerbaijanis, Turks fought Armenians. And to the north, the Russian Civil War was raging. In the end, the British gave up in despair and went home. Soon Russian forces were advancing south in the Caucasus, though this time they weren't forces of the Russian Empire, but were instead forces of the Red Army. The collapse of Denikin's White Russian Army allowed the Red Army to advance into the area and link up with local Communists. Azerbaijan and Armenia went Soviet in 1920. Georgia followed in 1921.

In 1922, however, Lenin reunited the three countries in not the Transcaucasian Democratic Federative Republic, but now the Transcaucasian Socialist Federative Soviet Republic. And it got its own stamps. For a year, anyway. Stamps showing Mount Ararat (minus ark), oil derricks and the inevitable Communist symbols were issued in 1923. They tell an interesting story. The first issue was denominated in old roubles, and show hyperinflation reaching its peak: the series runs from 40,000 to 500,000 roubles. A second set shows that a new monetary order had been established, with values ranging from one to eighteen new 'gold kopeks'.

However, just as the Transcaucasian Democratic Federative Republic wasn't to last, neither was the Transcaucasian Socialist Federative Soviet Republic. In 1936, under Stalin – himself a Georgian – the Transcaucasian Socialist Federative Soviet Republic was split to form separate Georgian, Armenian and Azerbaijani Soviet Socialist Republics all within the USSR. And that's how it remained until the end of the USSR. Armenia, Georgia and Azerbaijan all became independent again in 1991. More wars would follow and even today a number of the disputes in the region remain unresolved.

Trans-Juba

IT ACTUALLY SAYS Oltre Giuba on the Italian stamps printed for this place, which could, in some sense, literally, be translated as Ultra Juba. Both names sound interesting.

The Juba, or Jubba, in question here is Somalia's main river and both Trans-Juba and Oltre Giuba in this context mean 'on the other side of the Juba'. This was being looked at from the point of view of the rest of Somalia, so, in fact, Trans-Juba was the bit of territory sandwiched between the Juba River and the Kenyan border.

Like Germany, Italy only having been unified in the nineteenth century came somewhat late to the European scramble for colonies in Africa. But late though it was, once it got started it pursued its goal with some enthusiasm, and in the late nineteenth century and early twentieth century it set about establishing itself in Mogadishu and along the Somali coast. Meanwhile, to the south, Britain had long been involved with the Sultan of Zanzibar, a ruler with extensive interests along the African coast. One of these interests was the port city of Kismayu, now the major city of southern Somalia, and capital of the Jubaland region. In the 1870s, the sultan established a garrison in the port. Britain became extensively interested in getting more control over the sultan's extensive interests in the region (and also in ending the slave trade there). In 1887, it seized Kismayu. And in 1890, it did a deal with Germany, which had also been extensively interested in Zanzibar, sort of swapping German interests there for the then British island of Heligoland in the North Sea. Zanzibar became a British protectorate and when, in 1896, a sultan took power who seemed not very keen on British protection, Britain launched one of the shortest wars in history, which deposed the sultan and replaced him with someone more to the British liking. In 1895, the East Africa Protectorate was established, most of which would go on to become Kenya and Uganda.

Italy had, however, already started taking an open interest in the Kismayu area in the late nineteenth century, at the same time as it was establishing itself on the coast to the north. The Italians wanted to buy Kismayu off the sultan and Italy thought it had a deal with Britain that would result in joint occupation of Kismayu. It didn't get that, though they did get special access to the port, and after the First World War the situation would change, to Italy's advantage.

Many people will be aware of the bitter fighting between British and Italian forces during the Second World War (more of which later in this chapter). However, in the First World War, of course, Britain and Italy were allies, which meant that in the early 1920s, Britain was generally feeling quite benevolent towards Italy. And it was in this atmosphere of victorious bonhomie that Britain agreed on 15 July 1924 to hand over to an enthusiastic Italy the territory around Kismayu. On 30 June 1925, it actually did hand over control of the area to the Italians and the Italian colonial territory of Trans-Juba was established and stamps printed. The first ones were overprints, with 'Oltre

Giuba' on standard Italian stamps. In 1926, the colony had its own issue of seven commemoratives to celebrate the first anniversary of its founding. These show a map of its part of Africa. Standard Italian colonial stamps, inscribed 'Oltre Giuba', followed in the same year.

Italian Trans-Juba did not, however, have ahead of it a long and bright future. It didn't, in fact, have a long future of any description ahead of it, because on 30 June 1926, the Italians united Trans-Juba with the rest of Italian-controlled Somalia in the colony of Italian Somaliland.

Though nobody knew it at the time, as it turned out, Italian-controlled Somalia didn't have a bright future ahead of it either. Mussolini's Italy used military force to establish its control of its Somali territory internally. And Italy's brutal invasion of Ethiopia in 1935, and subsequent occupation of the country, helped solidify a major block of Italian colonial territory in the region, Italian East Africa. However, just fourteen years after Trans-Juba joined Italian Somaliland, the former allies Britain and Italy were at war, and the border between British East Africa and Italian Somaliland was a front line.

Italy initially declared war on Britain as German panzers were racing through France. Mussolini saw the opportunity for adding some easy acquisitions to his colonial empire and the Italians made some early gains in East Africa. In the north, they managed to capture British Somaliland and Italian troops advanced across the border into British-held Kenya. However, it would not be long before the tables were dramatically turned across the East African war zone, and the borderland between Kenya and Italian Somaliland was no exception.

In January 1941, General Cunningham's forces thrust across the border between Kenya and Italian Somaliland. The Italians made little effort to defend Trans-Juba, but instead tried to establish something of a defensive line along the Juba River. In February, Cunningham launched Operation Canvas against the Italian forces in the Juba region. Kismayu fell within a few days and the Italians suffered a major defeat at Jelib. The route to Mogadishu, the Somali capital, was now open and it was captured a few days later.

After the Allies invaded Italy in 1943, it signed an armistice with the Allies and in the final stages of the war Italian forces would fight against both Germans and those Italian forces in the north of the country still loyal to Mussolini. After the war, Italy was allowed to regain control of Italian Somaliland, but only under UN mandate and only on the condition that independence would soon follow. British Somaliland and Italian Somaliland became independent as Somalia in 1960.

Transskei, Bophuthatswana, Venda, Ciskei

WE'RE GOING TO examine these four locations in the same chapter because they are all part of the same phenomenon. The apartheid-era South Africa wanted the world to see these four 'homelands' as independent countries. The world didn't and they weren't.

The homelands policy came about as an attempt to solve one of the many dilemmas presented by a white minority trying to rule over a black majority in South Africa. The basic concept was that small areas mostly rural and poor would be set aside as homelands for a number of the main black ethnic groups in South Africa. The concept developed gradually but the end goal was to deprive black South Africans from these ethnic groups of their South African citizenship and instead gave them citizenship of the homeland that had been reserved for their ethnic group. From the point of view of the South African apartheid government this was an excellent idea, since it meant that the people involved would then have even fewer rights in South Africa than they had had before. It would also enable the South African government to expel people into the homeland allotted to the ethnic group to which they belonged to.

The international community was not impressed at the idea and it was equally unimpressed when South Africa began a process of declaring some of the homelands independent countries under black regimes cooperating with the South African government.

The first homeland to become 'independent' like this was Transkei in 1976. Transkei consisted of three separate land parcels in the south-east of South Africa with a long coastline on the Indian Ocean and a capital at Umtata. It was reserved for part of the Xhosa-speaking community. The Xhosas had fought numerous wars against both Boers and British during the colonisation of the region but had eventually been subdued. Transkei means 'beyond the Kei' and refers to the Great Kei River and designated Xhosa lands to the east of the Great Kei River. Chief Kaiser Matanzima became Transkei's first prime minister and then its president. Transkei became a not hugely successful democracy under Matanzima and eventually General Bantu Holomisa of the Transkei Defence Force took over control of the government in 1987. Transkei produced many stamps, some of which initially featured local life, but which slowly became a series of 'collectors only' issues (dogs, birds etc.). For some reason, it issued numerous stamps in a long-running series 'Celebrities of Medicine'. In the end, in 1994, as South Africa abolished apartheid, Transkei was reincorporated into South Africa.

The next homeland to go 'independent' after Transkei was Bophuthatswana, not a name everyone finds that easy to pronounce after a few beers. Or even before them. Boputha means 'that which binds' and the homeland was designated for Tswana-speaking people. Whereas Transkei had three separate parts, Bophuthatswana had seven, located in central-north-ern South Africa, much of the land close to the border with Botswana (a name meaning 'country of the Tswana'). Its capital was Mmabatho, but it did also eventually acquire Mafeking, a name known to many Brits because of the Boer War, the Relief of Mafeking and, of course, none other than Colonel Robert Baden-Powell (later of Scouts fame), who became famous while active in the defence of the town. It also, of course, played host to the leisure resort of Sun City. This tried with some success to lure international singing stars to perform there, but also prompted anti-apartheid campaigners to attack the idea of stars playing at Sun City. Bophuthatswana did, of course, have stamps. As with Transkei, there was quite a flow of them. The country is best known for issuing Easter stamps, which it did every year from 1981 to 1993. Rather bizarrely, it also produced several sets documenting the history of the telephone.

Lucas Mangope became president in 1977 and man-aged to remain in power with South African help, despite two coup attempts. He was ousted from power in 1994 and Bophuthatswana was reintegrated into South Africa.

Venda was the next homeland after Bophuthatswana to try 'independence'. Venda was at least one chunk of land, not a bunch of separate bits. It was situated in the north-east of South Africa, just south of Zimbabwe. The Venda people under Chief Mphephu had fought the Transvaal Boers in the nine-teenth century, and when Venda was declared independent in 1979, Patrick Mphephu became its president and Thohoyandou became its capital. Like Ciskei and Bophuthatswana, Venda had its own stamps – Venda's pet topic was the history of writing, of which seven issues appeared between 1982 and 1990. Venda too saw a coup, this time in 1990, and like the other homelands it was reintegrated into South Africa in 1994 when apartheid was dismantled.

The last of South Africa's homelands to be declared inde-pendent was Ciskei. Like Transkei, it was a homeland reserved for Xhosa-speaking people. And as Transkei means 'on the other side of the Kei', so Ciskei means 'on this side of the Kei', referring to Xhosa land west of the Great Kei River. The lands of Ciskei and Transkei, however, did not touch. In between them was a strip of South African land that included the important port of East London. Ciskei had its own stamps as well: as with the other homelands' stamps, many of them seem to have little to do with Ciskei and its life, but at least there were four issues featuring local folk tales.

Lennox Sebe became its first president after 'independence'. Despite both being Xhosa homelands, the rulers of Ciskei and Transkei had disputes with each other, and in 1990 Brigadier Oupa Gqozo of the Ciskei Defence Force took power. Other coup attempts followed. In 1992, a number of ANC demonstrators were killed in Bisho, then the capital of Ciskei. Finally Gqozo resigned and like the other homelands Ciskei was reintegrated into South Africa.

There were six other self-governing homelands, Gazankulu, KwaZulu, Lebowa, KwaNdebele, KaNgwane and Qwaqwa. However, after Ciskei, no other homeland would go 'independent'. The South African government gave up its plans to make them separate countries as the apartheid system experienced a series of crises in the 1980s prior to its final collapse in the 1990s.

Tripolitania

TRIPOLITANIA IS NOT familiar to that many in the UK as the name of a geographical entity and yet the first element of the name will be familiar. Yes, Tripoli. Tripoli is itself a name derived from the Greek for 'three cities' and somewhat confusingly there is more than just one Tripoli spread around the Mediterranean. There is, for instance, a Tripoli in Lebanon.

This, however, is the Libyan Tripoli, much in the news during the recent war there. And Tripolitania was the north-western part of what is now Libya.

In ancient times, the area saw the founding of Phoenican and Carthaginian cities among the indigenous Berber or Amazigh population and then the arrival of the Romans. Some of the architecture they created in the region is still hugely impressive today – for instance, at Sabratha and Leptis Magna. And just as Rome had an impact on the region, so the region had an impact on Rome. Emperor of Rome at the end of the second century AD and the beginning of the third was one Septimius Severus, who had been born in Leptis Magna. He was a successful military commander who scored successes in various civil wars and external wars around the empire. Among his campaigns was fighting in Britain and a campaign in Caledonia, where the weather may have come as something of a surprise to one born and raised on the shores of the Mediterranean. It may even have been too much for him. After campaigning in Caledonia he fell ill and died at York.

But northern Europe was about to get its revenge on Tripolitania. As the Roman Empire in the west crumbled, a Germanic people who had traversed Gaul and then crossed from Spain into North Africa eventually extended their control as far as Tripoli. The people were called the Vandals and history has somewhat unkindly stolen their name to characterise pointless destruction. Today they would probably sue. True, the Vandals did cause some (occasionally fairly pointless) destruction as they moved around, but they were probably no worse than quite a lot of other invaders.

Eventually, though, the Eastern Roman Empire, or Byzantines as we tend to refer to them in that period, got its revenge on the Vandals, taking control of the territory, and then finally it got invaded by the Arabs. They weren't to be the last invaders, not by any means. The Normans from Sicily would have a go in Tripolitania in the twelfth century before being kicked out again, and then in the early sixteenth century the Spanish turned up in Tripoli. They weren't to last very long either. They handed over to the Knights of St John, who then in turned handed over, or in fact surrendered, Tripoli to Ottoman forces in 1551. For the next few hundred years, Tripolitania was controlled by the Ottomans. Well, sort of.

In fact, the Ottoman rulers in Istanbul often had little real control over what actually went on in Tripolitania, which was then part of an area known in the West as the Barbary Coast. The name Barbary here basically comes from westerners using the name 'Berbers' for the Amazigh. However, some of what went on on the Barbary Coast during the (nominally) Ottoman period was also pretty barbaric in the negative sense, because the Barbary Coast became famous, or in fact infamous, for the Barbary Pirates.

When most people think of pirates today, they tend to think of Europeans waving cutlasses, wearing tricorn hats and big belts and going 'Aaar' a lot. Which tends to ignore the fact that piracy has been a phenomenon experienced across a wide range of cultures, across a wide range of time periods, in a wide range of locations around the world. And few pirates have been more ruthless and had more success than the Barbary Pirates. From the sixteenth through the nineteenth century, pirates from the North African coast ranged around the Mediterranean and as far north as places like the British Isles, taking prisoner and enslaving, over the centuries, hundreds of thousands. Tripoli and Tripolitania was a major base for these pirates, and so it became a major target for Western nations trying to stop them. For instance, English and then British warships 'visited' Tripoli a number of times during the Barbary Pirate years. Warships from other nations also attacked. However, these days perhaps the best-known operation against the pirates was carried out by the young United States, just a few years after its foundation.

In 1801, war broke out between the USA and the forces of Tripoli. It was not an entirely one-sided war. The capture of USS *Philadelphia* when it ran ashore near Tripoli in 1803 necessitated a daring US commando raid to destroy the ship. But in the end, the advance of US-led forces along the Libyan coast from the east produced negotiations that ended the war.

In 1911, however, Western forces mounted an even more determined attack on the area. In 1911, Italian forces invaded Libya and bitter and brutal fighting followed in Tripolitania and elsewhere. Eventually, the Italians managed to impose their control and colonial administration, and for a time, before being integrated into Libya in 1934, Tripolitania was an Italian colony, an Italian colony with stamps. Most are overprints or standard Italian colonial issues inscribed with the colony's name, but there are special Tripolitania issues, too. A 1931 Airmail set shows Roman ruins in the area and an Arab horseman (possibly pointing up at an aeroplane that has scared his horse). Mussolini was fascinated by aeroplanes, as weapons of war but also as prestige symbols. Several Tripolitanian stamps show planes flying over the desert and its inhabitants – an attempt, surely, to literally look down on the local people and claim a cultural superiority.

However, Italian control of Libya was not to last long. After entering the Second World War, Mussolini made the mistake of invading neighbouring British-controlled Egypt and starting a desert war that eventually saw Axis forces thrown out of Libya and left most of Tripolitania under British administration. It would remain like that – using British stamps, now, with various over-printings – until 1951, when it became part of the Kingdom of Libya. The area has seen plenty of fighting since the Libyan Civil War started in 2011, but today Tripolitania remains part of Libya.

Tuva

RUSSIA IS DIVIDED into eighty-two administrative regions, which vary in size from Moscow, which has over 10 million inhabitants, to the Nenets Autonomous Okrug, which is home to just over 40,000. Twenty-two of these regions are 'republics', semi-autonomous entities defined by a strong, non-Russian cultural identity. Troubled Chechnya is one of these. Another is Tuva.

Tuva lies on the western end of Russia's long border with Mongolia. It is also right at the centre of Asia – you can visit an obelisk in the capital, Kyzyl, that claims to be the precise geographical heart of the continent. In 1992, a group of Chinese geographers calculated that the centre of Asia wasn't in Tuva at all, but – surprise, surprise – in China. You can now also visit the 'Heart of Asia' monument in Yungfen, near Urumqi. The truth, pleasingly, is that there is no exact centre of Asia because determining such a centre depends on defining exactly where Asia begins and ends. The Chinese calculation included Cyprus, which is a member of the European Union.

Tuva has its own language and culture, heavily influenced by Mongolia. Tuvan throat-singing is truly extraordinary, combining the deepest resonances from the back of the throat – try opening your mouth as wide as possible, then make the deepest sound you can – with overtones that sound like someone is playing a flute in the background.

Over the years, Tuva has been part of various empires (while its people got on with their largely nomadic lives): Mongol, Dzungarian, Chinese … Russians began arriving in the early nineteenth century. Some were traders, others 'Seekers of White Waters', a sect of Russian Orthodox Old Believers who thought that a paradise was waiting for them across the Zapadny Mountains (Old Believers refused to recognise the liturgical changes to Orthodoxy made by Patriarch Nikon in 1653, and were then regarded as heretics). Heretics of a newer kind joined them in the mid-century, as political dissidents fled the tsarist regime.

In the first part of the twentieth century, Tuva was controlled by various powers: tsarist Russia, 'White' (anti-Bolshevik)

Russia, the Red Army, Qing China, the Red Army again …
In 1921, the Agrarian Republic of Tannu Tuva was declared
an independent state, though nobody apart from Russia and
Mongolia recognised it.

Tuva did have a measure of independence, however. Its leader
Donduk Kuular was a former lama turned Communist. He
sought to strengthen ties with Mongolia and make Buddhism
the state religion. Tuva's first stamps, issued in 1926, reflect
this. They feature the Buddhist 'wheel of life' and the text is in
Mongolian script only. A second set, from 1927, lean more to
the West, with pictures and Western script. The 8 kopek stamp
continues to show the country's independent spirit; however, it
shows a map of 'Touva' with the clear implication that it is part
of Mongolia, not the USSR.

Stalin was not having this. A coup was organised: five gradu-
ates of his 'University of Toilers of the East' (a cadre school in
Moscow) deposed Kuular in 1929, and he was executed. From
then on, Tuvan stamps show only Western and Cyrillic writing (the new rulers insisted that Cyrillic be the nation's official
script, even though it is totally inappropriate for the Tuvan language). The stamps do at least try and show scenes from Tuvan
life, but they were designed and printed in Moscow, with a clear
eye – or maybe two clear eyes – on the global market for 'collectable' stamps. Over the next decade, around a hundred stamps
would appear from the tiny republic, many with strange shapes:
lozenges, triangles and tall, 'portrait' rectangles. Later ones featured creatures like badgers and capercaillie that weren't found
anywhere near Tuva. Another featured a camel racing a steam
engine, despite the fact that there were no railways in Tuva at
that time.

It's easy to denigrate these stamps, but most of them do at
least attempt to depict local life, even if it is local life filtered
through the imagination of a designer in Moscow. They also
inspired at least one remarkable young man. As a boy, Richard
Feynman collected stamps, and was enchanted by the Tuvan

ones. Feynman later worked on the Manhattan Project and won the Nobel Prize for Physics. Later still, a family conversation made him determined to visit the land of those strange-shaped stamps. As this was at the height of the Cold War, he was unable to do so (official permission arrived the day after he died). His attempts to make the journey were immortalised in the book *Tuva or Bust!*, where Feynman's determination to see Tuva becomes a metaphor for the scientific imagination, fascinated with learning strange new things and prepared to do whatever it takes to pursue that curiosity.

Tuva itself had been gobbled up by Stalin in 1944 and was a part of the Soviet Union. It was run by Salchak Toka, one of the five successful power-seizers back in 1929, who had then elbowed his colleagues aside and taken supreme power in 1932. He would retain this power until his death in 1973. Accounts of his reign involve the usual dismal stories of Stalinist leadership: disastrous attempts to collectivise agriculture, suppression of religion, a weird personality cult (though at least Toka didn't plaster himself all over Tuva's stamps). Toka was also a writer, and his works received numerous literary prizes in Soviet Russia, though for some reason his brilliance didn't seem to be appreciated anywhere else.

As the Soviet Union began to fall apart, the Tuvan Democratic Movement began campaigning not just for democracy but for fresh respect for Tuvan culture. Political violence against ethnic Russians, unfortunately, accompanied this.

Soon after, the Soviet Union voted itself out of existence. Tuva was now part of the Russian Federation. A debate followed about what this meant exactly. How independent were the republics? In 1994, Tuva decided to issue its own stamps again. Three designs (one featuring the 'centre of Asia' obelisk) were prepared, printed and delivered to the capital – but then the authorities in Moscow forbade their issue as part of a general clampdown on republics' drive for autonomy (a reaction to the violence happening in Chechnya at this time). Some philatelists argue that these should be regarded as legitimate stamps. Others, including the authoritative Stanley Gibbons and Scott catalogues, do not. More recently, a flood of unambiguously fake Tuvan stamps has followed, purely made in the West for the gullible end of the philatelic market – subjects include kittens, dinosaurs, Xena Warrior Princess and an eight-stamp mini-sheet showing Laurel and Hardy playing golf.

The three 1994 Tuva stamps raise a genuine question, however: when is a stamp 'legitimate'? Like finding the exact centre of Asia, the question turns out to be more complex and debatable than it first seems.

United Arab Republic

THE CREATION OF the United Arab Republic was an ill-fated attempt to merge two countries that shared no common border – rarely a good idea. One was six times larger (in terms of population) than the other – not a recipe for an equal partnership. The two countries were Egypt and Syria.

In 1958, Egypt was led by Colonel Gamal Abdel Nasser. Nasser was the hero of the Arab world, and arguably of the whole 'non-aligned' world, by virtue of his having totally out-manoeuvred the West over the Suez Canal two years earlier. His dream was to have one Arab nation – with him as boss.

Syria, by contrast, was in a state of political crisis at that time. It had been veering to the left for a while, partly thanks to overtures from the Soviet Union and partly due to inept attempts by the CIA and MI6 to interfere in its politics. In 1957, its government expelled three US diplomats and appointed Afif al-Bizri, a Communist sympathiser, as army chief of staff. The country's neighbours became ever more afraid of a full Communist takeover: this was less than a year after the Soviet invasion of Hungary.

Turkey began to mass troops on Syria's border, whereupon the Soviet premier, Nikita Khrushchev, said he would launch missiles at Turkey if it used these troops to invade. America didn't formally threaten retribution if Khrushchev launched his missiles, but looked prepared to do so – it was a classic Cold War escalation. Egypt also joined in, gathering troops on its border and promising to defend Syria if any invasion took place.

Fortunately, diplomacy won the day and outright conflict was avoided. However, the affair boosted pan-Arab sentiment in Syria – which had already been strong beforehand: the Ba'ath Party, which wanted a united Arab state across North Africa and the Middle East, had been the second-largest party in Syria's 1954 election.

In November 1957, Anwar al-Sadat, then speaker of the Egyptian parliament, visited Syria's parliament, which voted that the two countries unite. Syria's traditionally minded leaders tried to prevaricate, but in January 1958, a group of young Syrian army officers, led by al-Bizri, flew to Cairo – without permission from the nation's president – to negotiate a deal with Nasser. Nasser, sensing their eagerness, drove a hard bargain. In a new, joint state, political parties would be abolished and he would be president. The officers accepted, then returned to Syria with a de facto deal. The president, Shukri al-Kuwatli, found himself unable not to sign up to it, given the strength of public, parliamentary and military opinion. The United Arab Republic came into being on 1 February 1958. Later that month, Nasser visited Damascus, and was welcomed by huge, cheering crowds.

Most new nations quickly issue stamps. The UAR did this more hesitantly. Early issues are inscribed UAR Egypt and UAR Syria. Some later issues are common to both countries; others are not.

Later in 1958, a revolution in Iraq deposed and killed the pro-Western king. The country's new leaders were keen to join the UAR. However, Iraq's new government was unable to cement its power, and the country soon collapsed into civil strife: it never joined.

It was probably wise not to. Cracks soon began to show in this hasty marriage between two very different countries. The top jobs in Damascus were quickly filled by Egyptians or with pro-Nasser locals, most prominent of whom was Abdel Hamid Sarraj, an ambitious young man who was made minister of the interior and who soon developed a reputation for ruthless policing of political dissent. In 1961, Nasser began to introduce a series of Socialist measures. Import-export businesses were nationalised, then banks and heavy industry. Syria was not consulted about this. The by now deeply unpopular Sarraj was made vice president. The final straw came in August of that year, when Syria's regional government was moved to Cairo, making Syria effectively just another Egyptian province.

On the morning of 28 September, a group of Syrian army officers seized the capital's airport and radio station, and announced that they had taken power. Nasser replied by ordering the rest of the Syrian army to resist them, but these orders were ignored. He ordered Egyptian paratroops to take army bases in the north-west of the country; they obeyed, but were quickly captured. He continued to refuse to negotiate with the rebels, however. By the evening, the coup had succeeded. When it closed down that evening, Syrian TV played its old national anthem. The United Arab Republic was history.

There was another coup in Syria in 1963, and the idea of the UAR was briefly discussed, with Iraq as a third partner, before being abandoned later the same year.

In Egypt, the dream continued. All Egypt's stamps continued to bear the UAR name, and a 1971 one showed a map with the Ba'athist ideal of an Arab state from the Atlantic to the Gulf. However, in September of that year it was finally decided to change the country's official name to the Arab Republic of Egypt. Ironically, the last stamp with UAR on is of Colonel Nasser, who had died the year before.

Syrian politics remained insecure, with a series of coups until 1970, when (in yet another coup) Hafiz al-Assad became president. He died in 2000 and was replaced by his son, Bashar al-Assad, who, at time of writing, is still clinging to power in what is now a war-ravaged country.

United States of the Ionian Islands

IF YOU THOUGHT there had only ever been one United States then you'd be wrong. Because, for instance, only a few decades after the United States of America was created, a new United States, the United States of Ionia, came into being. And a few decades after, stamps with the head of Queen Victoria on them were printed for the territory.

Somewhat confusingly, Ionia and the Ionian Islands are in two completely different places. Ionia is the classical name for part of what is now Turkey. The Ionian Islands are seven islands situated to the west of the main Greek mainland. The most widely known of the islands are Ithaca, Cephalonia and Corfu, though again somewhat confusingly, Corfu's actual Greek name is Kerkyra.

In Homer, Ithaca is the name of the home island of the intrepid and wily Odysseus, who, after many years wandering the Mediterranean trying to get home from the Trojan War, managed to slip in unrecognised and slaughter all the annoying suitors who'd been chatting up his wife in his absence.

The islands have a long and varied history and have seen various empires and kingdoms come and go in the region, including the Roman, the Byzantine, the Normans, the Genoese and even a spell under the House of Anjou. The Ottomans gained the

occasional foothold on the islands, but the real power that domi-
nated the Ionian Islands for centuries was Venice.

It's not perhaps surprising if you look at a map. We tend these
days to see the Ionian Islands as inextricably a part of Greece.
And yet they are also inextricably a part of the Mediterranean,
situated just to the south of the Straits of Otranto, that mark the
entrance to the Adriatic, the Venetian empire's home sea. And in
an era when sea travel was often easier and quicker than travel
by land, the links between Venice and the Ionian Islands were
strong and convenient. The name Corfu, for instance, is itself a
Latin variant of a Greek name. Plenty of old Venetian fortifications remain and Venetian influence can still be seen even in the
cuisine, in, for instance, the famous Pastitsada cooked with pasta.

However, just as Venetian sea-power would not last forever,
neither would Venetian control of the Ionian Islands.

In 1797, Napoleon defeated the Venetian Republic and the
Ionian Islands became French. But almost before the French had
had the opportunity to raise the tricolour, the Russians arrived,
along with the Turks. In some sense, it's now geographically
hard to believe that a Russian army was campaigning in Italy
and Switzerland in 1799–1800, but it was, and as a precursor the
Russians wanted the Ionian Islands as a strategic base. After a
four-month siege, the French said *au revoir* to Corfu and handed
it over to the Russians and Turks in March 1799.

What emerged from the joint Russian and Turkish capture
was an entity that was officially part of the Ottoman Empire,
but, under Russian protection, was also in some sense the birth
of modern Greece. The entity is known as the Septinsular
Republic, Septinsular being a somewhat posh adjective meaning
'having Seven Islands', and it saw Greeks basically running their
own administration for the first time in the modern era. One of
the key figures of the republic, Ioannis Kapodistrias, would later
go on to become the first head of state of free Greece.

The French weren't entirely finished with the islands yet, but
they would be soon.

After Napoleon's victory at the Battle of Friedland in 1807, the Russians signed a peace deal at Tilsit and the French took control of the Ionian Islands again. But, of course, it wasn't only the Russians who fought Napoleon. Enter the Royal Navy to loud, patriotic cheers. From 1807 to 1814, British ships fought a determined campaign in the Adriatic against the French and their allies. Part of this campaign were moves which led eventually to British control of all seven islands. In October 1809, for instance, British forces landed on Cephalonia and swiftly captured it. Ithaca and Zante were taken from the French soon after. And just as Russia had encouraged Greek thoughts of independence, so did Britain, forming a Greek military unit, the 1st Greek Light Infantry. In 1814, Napoleon's garrison on Corfu surrendered and the Congress of Vienna placed the islands under the friendly protection of Britain. The United States of the Ionian Islands was born.

Britain brought many fine elements of its culture to the Ionian Islands including, of course, cricket, which is still played there today.

However, even while cricket was being played on Corfu, revolution and a war for independence from the Ottomans broke out on the mainland. And by 1832, much of mainland Greece was an independent kingdom. Even the attractions of cricket were not sufficient to prevent the growth of calls for the Ionian Islands to become part of the new independent Greece.

The new king of Greece was called Otto and was the son of King Ludwig I of Bavaria. Britain was not hugely keen on the idea of handing the Ionian Islands to Otto. But in 1862, the unpopular Otto was toppled and replaced in 1863 by a king much more to Britain's liking, the formerly Danish prince and now the new King of the Hellenes George. Britain decide to give the new king a present to celebrate his accession and instead of a deluxe leather-bound collection of the Complete Works of Shakespeare or similar, they decided to give him the Ionian Islands. Thus, on 28 May 1864, the Ionian Islands were united with Greece and the United States of the Ionian Islands were no more.

Its stamps disappeared, too. Issued in 1859, these had featured a depiction of Queen Victoria by Henry Corbould, who drew the royal image for the Penny Black. The stamps are unusual for having no denomination on them – you were expected to know what each of the three stamps, in orange, blue or red, was worth. When they were taken out of use (they were replaced by Greek ones), unused examples were sold to London stamp traders. At one time, they were so plentiful that one dealer covered his walls with them as an advertising gimmick. Then, suddenly, they were rare; genuine ones, especially used, now command healthy prices at auction.

Italian forces returned to the islands under Mussolini, and after a brief time when the Germans were there, British forces returned in 1944 to help liberate the islands.

Upper Yafa

UPPER YAFA WAS a sultanate in what is now Yemen – a small state and a remote one, named after the proud, important and often warlike Yafa'i people.

As they expanded their area of influence from the port of Aden in the nineteenth and twentieth centuries, British colonial authorities found that getting into Lower Yafa was often tough enough, but that getting permission from the fiercely independent locals to enter the wild, remote and mountainous area of Upper Yafa was basically impossible. The area may have appeared on maps as part of the British Empire, but it basically wasn't, and if they wanted cooperation from the locals, British administrators found they would usually have to pay for it with silver or guns, or both.

One of the first Europeans, perhaps the first European to make it into Upper Yafa, was Lieutenant Colonel M.C. Lake, seconded to Aden from the Indian army in 1925. And even then, he only managed to enter the area because the Yafa'i had started to get nervous about encroachments into their territory by Yemenis to the north. They wanted the RAF to do a flag-waving exercise, an aerial show of force, to deter the Yemenis, and the British pointed out to them that, in order to do this, someone would have to enter the area to scout for potential landing grounds.

During the inter-war years, the RAF would occasionally get involved with matters in Upper Yafa. For instance, on one occasion, after tribesmen had invaded the village of Shuku in Upper Yafa, the RAF dropped a letter on the relevant sheikh advising him to withdraw his men and he did so. In 1933, the RAF carried out operations against some villages in Upper Yafa.

Comparatively little would change in the area over the next few decades. Upper Yafa was, in reality, regarded as something of a buffer zone between territory that was actually controlled by Britain to the south and the kingdom of Yemen to the north. As long as neither side took too much interest in Upper Yafa, everybody was happy.

However, in the period after the Second World War, events would eventually make Upper Yafa a little better known to people other than the Yafa'i, and again it would involve encroachment from the north and the RAF.

In 1956, Britain's Suez adventure ended in humiliation for Britain and a massive popularity boost for President Nasser of Egypt. And in the years following, he made efforts to spread his anti-colonial, socialist, pan-Arabist message across the region. One area he took particular interest in was the kingdom of Yemen, situated not far from Egypt on the other side of the Red Sea. Here, with Egyptian support, a republican coup attempt in 1962 would set off the Yemen Civil War.

To the south, the security situation had already started to deteriorate. Muhammad Airdrus, a son of Sultan Airdrus of Lower Yafa, led a rebellion against British rule, and he developed supply lines south from Yemen, through Yafa'i territory down into Aden. In October 1960, the RAF was sent in to target two of his houses. Hawker Hunters of 8 Squadron armed with rockets and cannon attacked and severely damaged the two targets. More air raids against targets in the area would follow until, in 1962, bombing forced Muhammad Airdrus to flee across the frontier. And once again, Britain would send bribes of money and weapons to the tribal leaders in Upper Yafa to try to dissuade them from joining in any subversion prompted by Yemenis from the north.

But Britain also had another plan to try to stabilise the area politically and keep it under British control. In 1962, it launched the Federation of South Arabia which eventually incorporated all the local rulers and their states – all, that is, except Upper Yafa. Upper Yafa would never join the Federation of South Arabia. And 1962 also saw the creation of the National Liberation Front, the NLF, aimed at driving Britain out of Aden and the surrounding territory. The NLF, at this stage, had Egyptian support and in the summer of 1963, the NLF's anti-British campaign came to Upper Yafa, with NLF fighters aiming to coordinate tribal rebels against Britain. In the autumn, their campaign spread west into neighbouring Dhala and the Radfan area. Tribesmen began targeting the main road from Aden to Yemen which ran through Dhala, resulting in some bitter fighting as security forces fought to keep the road open.

But the end of British rule in the area was not far off. The emergence of a second guerrilla group, the Front for the Liberation of Occupied South Yemen, which fought the NLF as well as the security forces, made the situation even more violent and chaotic. And heavy fighting in Aden in 1967 was too much for the British government. In November, British forces withdrew from Aden and the area – including Upper Yafa – became part of the new People's Republic of Southern Yemen. The sultanate was abolished. Muhammad Airdrus returned from exile the same year. The NLF arrested him and executed him.

The Yafa'i tribe, however, remain important in Yemen.

Upper Yafa's stamps date from its last days, in late 1967, when it produced a flurry of issues. One set was for genuine postal use and bears the sultanate's flag and a map. Other stamps in the name of Upper Yafa were aimed purely at collectors and cover standard themes of football, old masters and flowers, and are of no interest to serious philatelists.

Victoria Land

IN JANUARY 1909, a team led by British explorer Ernest Shackleton got within 100 miles of the South Pole. They nearly failed to return alive. The expedition's mother ship, the *Nimrod*, had orders to leave by 1 March. Slowed by illness and by bickering, the four-man party made it back to the ship on 28 February. They had shattered the previous record for the furthest south anyone had been. Soon, someone would reach the pole itself. Who?

The most likely candidate was another Briton, Captain Robert Falcon Scott, who began assembling an expedition on Shackleton's return. The aim was partly scientific, but also political. Scott wrote: 'The main objective of this expedition is to reach the South Pole, and to secure for The British Empire the honour of this achievement.' By 1910, he was ready to set off. His ship, the *Terra Nova*, reached Melbourne, Australia, in October of that year.

Another candidate was Norway's Roald Amundsen. In 1905, Amundsen had become the first man to sail the North West Passage across the top of Canada (learning a great deal about Arctic survival from the Inuit people that he met in the process). However, he was more interested in the North Pole, and began preparing an expedition to reach it. In 1909, American explorer Robert Peary got there first. Amundsen decided to head south instead. He played his cards close to his chest, however. The first thing Scott knew about his rival's new plan was a telegram that reached him in Melbourne: 'Beg leave to inform you *Fram* proceeding Antarctic Amundsen' (*Fram* was the boat in which Amundsen was sailing, formerly used by polar pioneer Fridtjof Nansen). The race to the South Pole was on.

Scott left the New Zealand port of Lyttelton on 26 November. Before he left, he was sworn in as a New Zealand postmaster and took possession of 24,000 ½*d* and 1*d* New Zealand stamps, overprinted with 'Victoria Land'. These were for expedition members to send mail from base camp, which would be supplied (ice permitting) from Lyttelton. Used examples of the stamps now command a small premium over mint – both are valuable – so it is reasonable to assume that nearly half the stamps saw postal use.

Both parties arrived in Antarctica in January 1911. They set up base camps and began laying out 'depots', pre-arranged places with supplies and shelter along the route to the pole, for use on the way out and, even more important, on the way back. The sun then set; it would not be visible for four months. Both teams would sit out the winter in their base camps, then head south as soon as spring began.

Amundsen made the first move – a mistaken one, setting off in early September. The weather soon drove him back. He set off again on 19 October. Scott followed on 1 November. As his base camp was 60 miles further from the pole than Amundsen's, this was probably too late.

In addition, Scott's expedition ran into more problems. Both he and Amundsen had been advised by Nansen to use dogs for transport. Scott ignored this advice, in part anyway, also taking ponies and three motorised sledges. However, the machines soon froze up, and the ponies turned out not to be suitable for the extreme conditions. Valuable time was lost. Amundsen, by contrast, took only dogs, having first recruited expert dog-handlers to drive them.

As a result, Amundsen had a relatively untroubled journey – by polar standards; at one point, he nearly fell into a crevasse. At other points his diaries tell of how much he was enjoying the skiing. He and his three-man team reached the pole on 14 December, after which they spent three days double-checking that it really was exactly 90 degrees south. Finally convinced, they headed for home, leaving a flag, some supplies and a message for Scott to deliver to King Haakon of Norway in case they failed to make it back and Scott did.

Scott had a harder journey, and reached the pole on 17 January 1912. He wrote in his diary, 'Great God! This is an awful place and terrible enough for us to have laboured to it without the reward of priority. Well, it is something to have got here.'

The return journey was hellish. Scott's second-in-command, Edgar Evans, died from wounds falling into a crevasse. Exhausted, they then reached a depot where Scott had instructed a support team with dogs to rendezvous with them, to find nobody present. After waiting a few days for this team to appear, Scott had to accept that they weren't going to, and that he would have to battle on to the next depot unaided. If this wasn't misfortune enough, the weather turned suddenly even colder than expected. On 16 March, another of the party, Captain Oates, succumbed to frostbite – knowing he was doomed, Oates left the tent with the immortal last words that he 'might be some time'. Four days later, a massive blizzard marooned the three remaining explorers, Scott, Henry Bowers and Edward Wilson, in a tent which they were never to leave. It is reckoned that they actually died on 29 March.

Bizarrely, the other great tragedy of the pre-Great War era (in British life, anyway) happened two weeks later, when the *Titanic* struck an iceberg in the North Atlantic.

Scott's reputation has been on something of a roller-coaster ride since then. For some people, the image of the English gentleman giving his all for the Glory of the Empire didn't survive the First Battle of the Somme in 1916. For others, he remained a hero until the late 1970s, when a new biography by Roland Huntford criticised his mismanagement of the expedition. For a while it became fashionable to regard Scott as an autocratic amateur, out of his depth. More recently, however, his star has been rising again. Fellow explorer Ranulph Fiennes has leapt to his defence.

The debate seems to hang on whether Scott gave clear orders for the dog team to meet him at the depot on the way back. Critics say he didn't, so it was his fault that they weren't there. However, more recently a written order to that effect has been found. The implication is that he was let down by his subordinates. But they, too, had difficulties to contend with. Modern computer analysis of weather patterns around the time of Scott's death highlights the freak nature of the blizzard that hit that part of Antarctica at that time. Scott might not have had the focus and flair of Amundsen, but he was clearly unlucky. And nobody can deny his bravery.

Zapadna Bosna

OF THE LEADERS in the Balkan Wars, Tudjman of Croatia is dead, Izetbegović of Bosnia is dead, Milosevic of Serbia is dead, Mate Boban of the Bosnian Croats is dead, Milan Babić and Goran Hadžić of the Croatian Serbs are dead, Karadžić of the Bosnian Serbs is in prison, and Milan Martić of the Croatian Serbs is also in prison.

However, one man who is currently still very much alive and who has just been elected mayor of Velika Kladuša, the heart of his old power-base, is Fikret Abdić of Zapadna Bosna, the entity at the heart of the little Bosnian war that very few people outside Bosnia have even heard of. It's an extraordinary story. And it has stamps as well. At the end of the war, Abdić looked very much like a loser, but now, with him still alive, free and in (some) power again, it's a somewhat, in some sense, changed situation.

Zapadna Bosna just means West Bosnia, but in this chapter we're not concerned with the whole of western Bosnia, but just a little chunk of it in the top north-west corner of Bosnia, next to Croatia, centred round the little old town of Velika Kladuša. Velika Kladuša has a pretty castle on a hill. Not a huge distance to the south of Velika Kladuša is the city of Bihać. Velika Kladuša has not played a huge part in history but it did get involved in the 1950 Cazin rebellion against Tito, perhaps something of a sign of the remoteness and independence of spirit of the region.

Tito's Yugoslavia was, of course, socialist, but that didn't mean it was impossible to get rich in it. One man who did make money in it and made others affluent too was Fikret Abdić. Born into a Muslim family near Velika Kladuša in 1939, Abdić became the director of local agricultural cooperative Agrokomerc. Agrokomerc grew to be a business employing thousands of workers and spreading wealth across the region. Not surprisingly, Abdić became very popular locally. The rise of Agrokomerc did not, however, happen without controversy.

Nonetheless, in 1990, as Yugoslavia began to fall apart, Fikret Abdić stood for election to the Bosnian presidency and might have ended up president. Instead, however, of the cosmopolitan businessman and dealmaker Abdić, the position of Bosnia's president ended up being taken by the somewhat less flexible Alia Izetbegović. How much history might (or might not) have changed if Abdić had become president instead of Izetbegović we will now never know.

Instead, Fikret Abdić returned to his power-base and as Bosnia started to fall apart, he started to make moves. In spring 1993, it seemed to many that Bosnia and Herzegovina was basically finished. The Serbs had seized control of vast swathes of eastern and northern Bosnia, in the process isolating the area around Bihać, creating the Bihać pocket sandwiched between Serb-held territory in Bosnia and in Croatia. Not only that, but war had broken out between former allies the Bosnian Croats and the Bosniaks, as the Bosnian Croats saw the chance of carving out their own territory within Bosnia, which could then develop closer links with neighbouring Croatia.

Abdić had also seen a chance of carving out his own territory, based on his power-base around the home of Agrokomerc, Velika Kladuša. The little Bihać pocket was split in two, with the Bosnian army's 5th Corps still operating out of Bihać, and in the north, Abdić, accusing Izetbegović of fighting a 'holy war' and declaring the grandly named Autonomous Province of Zapadna Bosna, Western Bosnia, with its own army. At first, he did not declare full independence and his 'state' and his army often used symbols and badges based on the Bosnian lily symbols of the Sarajevo government and therefore, rather confusingly, somewhat similar to some of the badges and symbols being used by the Bosnian 5th Corps in the other half of the pocket. Stamps were also issued – or at least overprints on old Yugoslavian stamps.

As fighting raged elsewhere in Bosnia, Abdić's Autonomous Province of Zapadna Bosna, Western Bosnia reached a truce in autumn 1993 with the Bosnian Serbs. But there was to be no peace with the Bosnian 5th Corps led by the talented Atif Dudaković. In Operation Tiger in the summer of 1994, the 5th Corps destroyed Abdić's forces and sent a stream of refugees fleeing from the area around Velika Kladuša. However, Abdić retaliated against the 5th Corps in December 1994, and re-established himself in his old power-base. In 1995, he opted for full independence from the Bosnian government and declared the Republic of Zapadna Bosna. But total victory was not far off for the Bosnian 5th Corps. In August 1995, the Croatian army's Operation Storm smashed through the Republic of Serbian Krajina and ended the siege of the Bihać pocket. The Republic of Zapadna Bosna collapsed, too, and, soon after, the Bosnian 5th Corps started pushing east, deep into Bosnian Serb-held territory, as the war reached its final stages.

Abdić had lost his power-base, but from all his years of wheeler-dealing he still had some friends. Abdić escaped to Croatia, where President Tudjman gave him political asylum and citizenship. Then, in 1999, Tudjman died. Since he was a Croatian citizen, the new Croatian authorities would not extradite him to Bosnia to stand trial, but they did put him on trial in Croatia for war crimes. In 2002, he was sentenced to twenty years in prison. But the extraordinary story of Abdić did not finish there. His sentence was reduced to fifteen years and he eventually got out of prison in 2012 after serving ten years.

Now, after standing in mayoral elections in Velika Kladusa in 2016, Fikret Abdić is once again in power in his western Bosnian power-base.

Appendix: The Story of Stamp Collecting

Stamp collecting is a hobby almost as old as stamps themselves. Even older, perhaps, as people collected revenue stamps in the eighteenth century. The world's first postage stamp was Britain's elegant Penny Black, which was issued in May 1840. The collecting began at once, though not always in the modern way: an 1841 advert in *The Times* asked for used stamps so that the advertiser could paper a wall.

During the next two decades, many countries began issuing stamps, and the hobby really took off. By the mid-1850s, entrepreneurs were making a living buying and selling stamps: William S. Lincoln in London, the teenage Stanley Gibbons in Plymouth. The 1860s saw the first books on how to spot forgeries; the Royal Philatelic Society, dedicated to stamping out such roguishness, was founded in London in 1869.

The world's first printed stamp album for collectors dates from 1862. It was produced by Justin Lallier, a Parisian dealer, in August of that year. It was in French; an English edition followed in time for Christmas. The Lallier album is divided into continents, under which category countries are listed alphabetically. There is a marked space for each stamp on the right-hand page, and stamp information on the left-hand one. The album has room for 1,200 stamps. In 1862, collectors would have pasted the stamps in – tiny, gummed stamp 'hinges' were a later development.

Some Victorian albums are works of art in themselves, with beautiful engravings of national emblems or of stamps. Others are 'entry level', simply with country names at the top of the page (though always in elegant lettering). In 1900, you could buy a beginner's Lincoln album for a shilling, or fork out 70*s* for the company's top-of-the-range Number 3 album, 'bound in best Turkey Morocco … handsomely lettered in gold and with two superior gilt clasps'. (A skilled labourer earned around 30*s* a week at that time.)

The first Stanley Gibbons stamp catalogue, listing stamps and their prices, came out in 1865, and was issued monthly. At that time, Gibbons was still running his business from Plymouth. He moved to London in 1874, and the first Gibbons shop in the Strand opened in 1891. (Gibbons, a colourful character, didn't just collect stamps. He married five times and, when he died, left his large Richmond home not to his estranged fifth wife but to a 'dear friend', Mabel Hedgecoe.)

The hobby kept booming in the twentieth century. For many children in a pre-TV age, a stamp collection was a window into the world. Many continued with the hobby into adulthood. King George V was a keen collector, as was US President Franklin D. Roosevelt, who once said, 'I owe my life to my hobbies, especially stamp collecting.' FDR always found time to work at his collection, even – or maybe especially – at times of great stress. Young collectors are rarer now – there are more accessible world-windows – but it is estimated that there are still 60 million people around the world who collect.

Acknowledgements

We would like to thank the team at The History Press: our commissioning editor, Mark Beynon; editors, Lauren Newby and Rebecca Newton; marketer, Caitlin Kirkman; and designers, Katie Beard and Martin Latham. Thanks, also, to Stanley Gibbons for their help in providing many of the images used in the production of this book, to Andrew Thompson for photographing some other images, and to Ingolfson and Arno-nl for posting images online for Creative Commons use.

We have used many sources for researching this book. Among these are some informative websites: dcstamps, Big Blue 1840–1940, and StampWorldHistory. Thanks to the creators of these.

Chris would like to dedicate the chapters of the book that he wrote to his late uncle, Frank Peddar, who got him interested in collecting.

Index

Abdić, Fikret 254–7
Achilles 76–7
Addis Ababa 101
Adrianople 64, 73
Adriatic Sea, the 25, 73, 92, 91,
    112, 246
Aegean, the 118–9
Afghanistan 28, 222
Africa 83, 99, 110, 128, 134,
    156–7, 159,165–7, 169, 171–4,
    183, 186, 215, 229–30; British
    East Africa 158, 231; British
    South Africa Company 169;
    Central Africa 214–5; East
    Africa 80, 101, 159, 166, 231;
    East Africa Protectorate 230;
    German East Africa 132,
    156–7; German South-West
    Africa 131; German West
    Africa 132; Horn of Africa 99,
    158, 161; Italian East Africa
    231; North Africa 55, 236,
    243; Organisation of African
    Unity 37; South Africa 156–7,
    170, 216, 229, 232–5; South
    African Republic (modern
    Transvaal) 214; sub-Saharan
    Africa 172; West Africa 187
Alaouites and Hatay 15–18
Albania 72, 76–7, 226
Albreda 185
Alexandroupoli 63–6; Dedeagh 63
Allenstein and Marienwerder
    18–21
Allied Forces, the 15–16, 20–1,
    28, 33, 40, 46, 61–2, 79, 86–7,
    93–5, 102–5, 124–6, 138–40,
    145, 155, 158, 173, 200, 203,
    208, 218, 221, 232
America/United States, the 9, 24,
    42–4,47–9, 58–9, 83, 87–9, 94,
    103, 105, 108, 120, 126, 139,
    161, 170–2, 174, 176–8,183–4,
    186, 192, 205, 207, 208, 238,
    242–3, 245, 251, 259
American Civil War, the 47, 49,
    215; South America 41, 50, 51,
    121, 140, 171–2

Amoy 21–5
Anatolia 44–5
Andaman Islands 30–1
annexation 38, 61–2, 77, 94–5, 102, 140, 146, 154, 176, 218, 222
Antarctica 252, 254
Antioch 15, 17
Aouzou Strip 91–2
Arabia 16, 73, 79–81, 147, 159 *see also* Federation of South Arabia
archipelagos 30, 108, 111, 207, 210–1
Armenia 33, 45–6, 227–9
armistice 16, 46, 79, 98, 101, 103, 139, 232
Armistice of Mudros 16, 33, 228
Asia 44, 63–4, 73, 76, 133, 142, 183, 194, 239, 241–2
Assyrians 15, 44
Atlantic Ocean 41, 86, 136, 138, 184, 244; Wall 86
Atlantis 53, 184
Auckland 105–8
Austerlitz 221–2
Australia 16, 105, 110, 142, 183–4, 219, 251
Austria 25–8, 38, 93, 102–5, 149, 199, 202–3, 205–6, 220–22
Austria-Hungary 43, 102–04, 188
Austrian Empire 25–7
Austrian Italy 25–8
autonomy 29, 44, 55–6, 60, 130, 151, 161, 164, 174, 225, 241
Axis Forces, the 124–5, 238
Azad Hind 28–31
Azerbaijan 227–29

Bab-el-Mandeb 80, 99, 159
Baghdad 44–5, 73
Balkans, the 55, 75; First Balkan War, the 65, 78; Second Balkan War, the 65
Baltic, the 18, 60–61, 66, 134–6, 144, 154–5, 185
Barentsburg 209–10
Batum 31–4
Beijing 23, 141, 143, 224–5
Belgium 10, 84, 128–31
Berbers, the 89, 237
Berlin 30, 75, 156
Bessarabia 147–50
Biafra 34–7
Bioko 83, 172–4
Black Sea, the 31, 68, 109; Coast 45
Bohemia and Moravia 37–40
Bolsheviks 33, 67–8, 152, 195–6, 239–40
Bombay 70, 163
Bosnia 34, 72–3, 111– 5, 188–91, 254–7; Bosniaks 111–5, 256; Bosnian Croats 113–5, 254–6; Bosnian Serbs 111–4, 254–6; Bosnian War 111–3, 191, 254
Bosnia Herzegovina 112–5, 255 *see also* Herzegovina
Botswana 216, 233–4
Brazil 83, 121, 172
Breslau (Wrocław) 198–200
British Empire 81, 131, 216, 218, 248, 251
Brittany 86–7
Brest 33, 87
Brussels 128, 220
Budapest 73, 206–7

Buddhists 223, 240

Bulgaria 64–6, 73–5, 77–8, 109

Burma 30, 142, 191–4,

Byzantine Empire 45, 64, 77–8, 119

Byzantines 45, 64, 73, 77, 112, 236, 245–6

Byzantium 45, 64

Cambodia 85, 124

Cameroon 83, 173

Canada 183, 209, 251

Canal Zone 41–4

Cape Colony 157, 214, 216

Cape of Good Hope, the 100, 155, 165, 172, 217

Cape Town 166, 168–9

Caribbean, the 56–8, 135

Carthaginians 89, 236

Caspian Sea, the 32, 73

Caucasus 32–4, 226–28

Cayenne 122–4

Cephalonia 245, 247

Charminar 115, 116–8

Chechnya 239, 241–2

China 21–5, 72, 80, 131–4, 140–3, 161, 175–7, 191–3, 196, 222–5, 239; Cochin-China 182; Qing Dynasty 21, 141, 223–4, 239–40

Christmas Island 218–9

Cilicia 44–6

Cold War, the 43, 79, 102, 167, 170, 206–7, 241, 243

Colombia 42, 50, 52

colonialism 84, 134–5; colonial warfare 96

Columbus, Christopher 51, 59, 172

Communists 23, 29, 40, 66, 104, 121, 143, 170, 189, 193, 206, 224, 228, 240, 242–3; anti-Communist 68

Confederate States of America 47–9

Congo, the 128–31; Belgian Congo, the 128; Congo Free State, the 128; Congo National Movement (MNC) 128

Congress of Vienna, the 25, 247

Corfu 78, 245–7

Corsica 119, 221

Cossacks 67–9, 100, 160

coups 35, 41, 51, 56, 76, 81, 85, 129–30, 194, 211, 234, 240, 244, 249

Courland 134–6 *see also* Kurland; Courland Empire, the 135; Courland Pocket, the 135; Courlanders 185; New Courland 135

Crete 54, 83, 118, 212

Crimea 67, 119; Crimean War, the 75, 149

Croatia 92, 95, 112–4, 187–91, 254–7

Crusaders 15, 45, 64, 77

culture 25, 53, 67, 85, 162, 237, 239, 241, 247

Cundinamarca 50–3

Curonians 134

currency 26–7, 29, 114, 116, 125, 146, 181–2, 190

Cyrenaica 53–6, 212

Cyrillic 34, 240

Czechoslovakia 38–9, 40, 103, 146, 199

Czech Republic 37, 198, 221

Damascus 15–6, 243–4
Danevirke, the 201, 203
Danish West Indies 56–9 *see also* West Indies
Danube, the 73–4
Danzig/Gdańsk 59–62, 145
Dedeagh 63–6
Denmark 56–9, 108–9, 201–4
Devil's Island 122–4
disease 41–2, 57, 83, 86, 123, 166, 173
Djibouti 99, 101–2, 159–60; Djibouti Civil War 160
Don and Kuban Republics and United Russia 66–9

East Prussia 20, 60
Eastern Rumelia 72–5
Edirne 64, 73–4
Egypt 15, 53, 55, 63, 80–1, 99–100, 159–60, 238, 242–4, 249–50
elections 40, 62, 66, 128, 170, 184, 196, 216, 243, 255, 257
England 41, 57, 144, 162, 201
Epirus 76–8
Ethiopia 99–100, 140, 159, 231
Europe 17–18, 20–1, 25–7, 41, 48–51, 56–8, 63–5, 72–3, 81, 83, 86–7, 90, 96–100, 105, 116, 119, 121–2, 124–6, 128, 131–4, 137–40, 144, 147–9, 153, 156, 158, 165, 167, 172, 182, 185–6, 194, 201–6, 219, 221–3, 229, 236–7, 239, 248; Eastern Europe 86, 147, 204–5; Western Europe 74, 206
European Union 121, 137, 239
expeditions 41, 51, 80, 90, 100, 132, 165–6, 176, 184, 207, 223, 251–4

explorers 50, 83, 99, 168, 172, 183, 194, 207, 250–1, 254

fascism 94, 124–6, 192
February Revolution, the 33, 67
Federation of South Arabia 79–83
Fernando Poo 83–6, 172
Festung Lorient 86–9, 126
Fezzan 89–92, 212
Finland 66, 151–2; Finnish Civil War 151; Finnish War of 1808–09 151
First World War, the 15, 19–20, 27, 32, 38, 43, 46, 49, 55, 61, 65–6, 79, 88–9, 91, 93–4, 102, 123, 131, 135, 138, 145, 150, 157, 162, 173, 188, 227, 230
Fiume 92–5
Fort James 185
fortifications 61, 73, 86, 110, 126, 246
Fourteen Points 103, 139
Free French 87–8, 91, 99, 101, 160; French Guiana 121, 124; Vichy 86–7, 91, 98–9, 101–2, 155, 160
Free City 61, 222
French India 95–9
French Territory of the Afars and Issas 99–101

Gambia, the 185–7
Gambia River, the 135, 185, 187
Garamantes 89–90
Geneva Convention 27, 137
Georgia 31–4, 49, 226–8
German Austria and Carinthia 102–5
German Empire, the 19, 91, 131, 203

Ghadames 91

Goa 70, 117

Gorée 186

Goschen 214–5

Great Barrier Island Pigeongram
    Service 105–8, 181

Greece 31, 44–5, 53–4, 63–6,
    73–4, 76–9, 89, 118–9, 121,
    149, 184, 210–3, 236, 246–8;
    Greek Civil War 65, 79

guerrillas 52, 82, 126, 170, 189,
    193, 251

Gujarat 70, 162

Gukurahundi, the 171

Gulangyu 22–3

Gustav Line, the 126

Habsburg Empire, the 38, 188, 205

Hanseatic League, the 61, 208

Hatay, Republic of 17–8 *see also*
    Alaouites and Hatay

Heligoland 108–11

Herceg Bosna 111–5

Herzegovina 74, 112–4, 255 *see
    also* Bosnia Herzegovina

Hindus 99, 115, 117–8, 161

Holy Land, the 46, 77, 211

Hong Kong 21–2, 132–3, 182
    New Territories 132–3

Hungary 72, 102–3, 150, 188, 198,
    204–5, 243 *see also* Austria–
    Hungary

HVO (Hrvatsko vijeće obrane,
    Croatian Defence Council),
    the 113–4

Hyderabad 115–8

Icaria 118–21, 181

Idris 55–6

Imperial Japanese Army 23, 140,
    177

independence 30, 33–4, 36–7, 51,
    67, 74–5, 81, 85, 98, 102–3,
    116–7, 128–30, 137, 139,
    145, 146, 150, 151, 163, 190,
    193, 197, 214, 225, 228, 232,
    234, 240, 247, 255–6

India 28–31, 57, 69–72, 80, 95–8,
    105, 115–7, 161–5, 169, 192–3,
    216–9, 224–5; East India
    Company, the 69–72, 169,
    216–8; East India Postage 69–
    72; Union of India 117, 164

Indian National Army (INA) 28–31

Indian Ocean, the 80, 155–6, 159,
    217–9, 233

Ingria 151–2 *see also* North Ingria;
    Ingrian War 150

Inini 121–4

invasion/invaders 15, 20, 24, 39,
    44, 55, 58, 79, 86, 90, 92, 94,
    117, 130, 141, 153, 155, 176,
    177, 179, 192, 198, 206, 209,
    212, 215, 218, 231, 242

Istanbul 64, 73, 75, 237

Isthmus, the 41–2, 152

Italian Social Republic (the Salò
    Republic) 124–7

Italy 10, 25–7, 38, 54–5, 76, 79,
    90–1, 93–5, 101, 120, 124–6,
    150, 192, 210–2, 220, 229–31,
    246 *see also* Austrian Italy

Japan 9, 23, 29–30, 133, 140–3,
    154, 175–7, 192–3, 197

Kalikata 70, 72

Katanga and South Kasai 127–130

Kiautschou 131–3

Kingdom of the Serbs, Croats and Slovenes, the 94–5, 105, 188 *see also* Yugoslavia

Kismayu 229–31

Klaipėda 144, 145–6 *see also* Memel; Klaipėda Revolt, the 145; Klaipėda Convention, the 146

Knights Hospitaller 119, 211

Korea 140, 154; North 171

Koxinga 21, 24

Kurland 134–6 *see also* Courland

Kwidzyn 18–9, 21

Labuan 217–8

Lake Chad 90

Lake Nyasa 156–7

Land of Punt, the 99, 158

Latin 43, 90, 147, 246

Latvia 134, 135–6

leadership 29, 113, 135, 202–3, 241

League of Nations 137–40

Lebanon 16, 235

Léopoldville (Kinshasa) 128, 131

Lhasa 223–5

Libya 53–6, 89–92, 212, 235, 238; Libyan Tripoli 235

Lithuania 20, 144–6

Lombardy 25–6

London 13, 48, 70, 81, 97, 106, 170, 203, 235, 248, 258–9

Lower Yafa 248–9

Madagascar 153–6, 160

Madras 70, 133

Mafeking 215, 233

Maharajas 118, 192

Malacca 216–9; Malacca Straits, the 216

Malaya 28, 218

Manchuria Manchukuo 140–3

Mankuroane 214

Mediterranean, the 54, 66, 73, 89, 119, 159, 170, 235–6, 245

Memel 136, 143–6 *see also* Klaipėda

Mercury 26, 88

Merina 154

Metz 178–9

Middle Ages, the 38, 64, 77, 90, 99, 165

Milan 25, 127

Mississippi 47–8

Moldavia and Wallachia 147–50

Molossians 76–7

Mongolia 16, 198, 239–40

Montenegro 73–4, 112

Moscow 67, 150, 196–7, 206–7, 238–41

Mostar 112–4

Mosweu 213–4

Mozambique 156–8, 165, 167, 170; Mozambique Liberation Front (FRELIMO) 167

Mughals, the 70, 116, 161

murder 13, 40, 68–9, 85, 123, 176, 195

Murzuq 90–1

Muslims 45–6, 99, 112, 114, 117–8, 255–6

Nanking (Nanjing) 22–3, 31

Napoleonic Wars, the 61, 93, 109, 144, 186, 199, 202

nationalism 25, 46, 74, 85, 119, 189

NATO 139, 206

Nazi Party, the 39–40, 62, 69, 86–8, 91, 98, 102, 124, 126, 134, 135, 142–3, 158, 189

Netherlands, the 57, 84, 185

Nicobar Islands 29–30

Niger 187
 Delta 36; Niger Coast Protectorate 34

Nigeria 34–7

Nizams, the 116–7

Normandy 86–7

North Ingria 150–3 *see also* Ingria

North Sea, the 61, 108–11, 155, 183, 201, 230

Norway 86, 207–10, 251–2

Nossi Be 153–6

Nyassa Company 156–8

Nyassa District 156, 158

Obiang, Teodoro 85–6

Obock 100, 158–61

October Revolution, the 33, 66–7

Odysseus 120, 245

Okinawa 174–8

Olsztyn 18–9, 21

Oltre Giuba 229 *see also* Trans-Juba

Organisation Todt 86–7, 126

Ottoman Empire, the 15–6, 32, 46, 54, 65, 72–3, 90, 119, 149, 188, 212, 246; Ottomans, the 16, 73–5, 77–9, 99, 119, 148–9, 237, 245, 247

Pacific Ocean, the 42, 131–2, 138, 142

Palace of Nations, the 138, 140

Palestine 15–6

Panama 41–4, 51; Canal 42, 44

Paris 38, 106, 173, 258

Paris Peace Conference 139, 145

Patiala and Nawanagar 161–4

peace 19, 25, 28, 32–3, 35, 39, 52–3, 55, 65–6, 75, 78, 91, 96–7, 105, 109–10, 114–5, 130, 139–40, 144, 180, 186, 190–1, 199–200, 203, 215, 221, 228, 247, 256; Nobel Peace Prize 52, 139, 225

Pearl Harbor 23, 155, 192, 218

Penang 133, 216–8

philately 11, 47, 52, 157, 182–4, 197, 219, 242; philatelists 11, 20, 48, 120, 142, 181, 242, 251; Royal Philatelic Society 258

Piedmont 26, 150

plebiscites 20–1, 28, 105, 139, 179–81, 199–200, 203–4

Plovdiv 73–4

Poland 18, 20, 40, 59, 63, 66, 103, 145, 148, 192, 198–200; Polish Corridor, the 61–3; Polish crown, the 18–9

politics 15, 25, 28–9, 36, 39, 46, 64, 71, 72, 74, 85, 93, 112, 115, 118, 120, 122, 126–7, 138–9, 141, 169, 184, 187, 191, 193, 201, 206, 216, 224, 240–5, 249, 251, 257; geo-political 65, 83, 135

Pondicherry 96–9

Portugal 84, 122, 156–7, 167, 172–3

post 11, 13, 22, 26, 49, 75, 87, 96, 105–8, 165, 181, 186, 205, 220–1, 222; post horn 104, 149 post offices 11, 17, 22, 62, 65, 87, 106; New Zealand Post Office, the 103; Polish Post Office, the 62

postal services 13, 107, 221–2 ; US Postal Service 47, 105

Prague 38, 40, 103

propaganda 24, 29, 47, 86, 88, 94, 141–2, 189

Prussia 19–20, 27–8, 61–2, 106, 132, 144, 179–80, 199, 202–3, 222; East Prussia 20, 60; Prussian Confederation, the 19

puppet states 124, 140, 142–3

Quelimane 164–8

Rákozi, Mátyás 204–5

Rangoon 193

Red Army, the 62, 66–8, 136, 146, 195, 197, 206, 228, 240

Red Sea, the 80–2, 99, 159, 249

referendums 34, 52, 102, 181

Reformation, the 134, 198

Regensberg 220–1

religion 112, 117, 134, 174, 240–1

Rhodesia 110, 168–71

Rijeka 92–5

Rio Muni 84, 171–4

Roman Empire 32, 54, 64, 73, 77, 119, 211, 235; Eastern 45, 64, 77, 236; Holy 25, 198, 201–2, 220–1; Western 45, 64, 77

Romania 67, 73–4, 147–50

Rome 54, 76, 124, 126, 236

Royal Navy, the 84, 111, 135–6, 144, 156, 247

RSK, the 190–1

Russia/Soviet Union/USSR, the 18, 20–1, 29–34, 36, 60–1, 65–9, 72–4, 94, 100, 130, 133, 135–7, 140–1, 144–6, 148–53, 155, 160, 194–7, 200, 202, 205, 207–10, 221, 223, 226–9, 238–42, 246–7; Russian Empire, the 31–4, 135, 144, 152, 227–8; 1828–29

Ryukyu Islands 174–8

Saar 178–81

Saarbrücken 178–9

Sagallo 100, 160

Sardinia 26, 119

Satsuma 176

Schleswig 201, 203–4 *see also* Slesvig; Schleswig-Holstein 109, 201, 203

Scotland 41, 209

Sealand, the Principality 183–4

Second World War, the 18, 39, 55, 59–60, 65, 69, 81, 86, 95, 101, 111, 126, 136–7, 146, 160, 169, 183, 188–9, 192, 204, 206, 209, 210, 212, 218, 230, 238, 249

Sedang 181–5

Senegal 185–7

River 185–6

Senegambia 185–7

Serbian Krajina 187–91

Seven Years' War, the 144, 199

Shan States 191–4

Shangai 22–3

Shona 168–70, 215

Siberia, Far Eastern Republic and Priamur 32, 68, 194–7

Silesia 198–201 *see also* Schleswig

Singapore 28–31, 142, 216–9

slavery 48, 51, 58, 77, 84, 87, 142, 154, 165, 173; abolishment 48, 154, 166; slave trade 83–4, 165, 230

Slesvig 201–4

Slovakia 38, 40

Sofia 64, 74

Somalia 99, 101, 229–32

Somaliland: British 100, 231; French 99, 101; Italian 231

Sopron 204–7

South Pole, the 251–2

Spain 41, 51, 83–6, 122, 130, 171–4, 226, 236

Spanish Civil War, the 84, 140, 173; Spanish Guinea 84, 171–2, 174

Spitsbergen 207–10

stamps: Airmail 43, 62, 108, 238; albums/catalogues 9, 13, 23, 32, 33–5, 58–9, 61, 72–3, 93, 108, 111, 124, 164, 175, 182, 194, 209, 242, 258–9; Scott catalogue 13, 124, 242; Stanley Gibbons 13, 124, 181, 210, 242, 258; Cinderellas 13, 181–2, 184–5, 225; commemorative 11, 43, 82, 105, 108, 126, 130, 137–8, 177, 190, 230; definitive 11, 43, 56, 62, 68, 78, 82, 95, 104, 116, 124, 125–6, 130, 141–2, 145, 152, 160, 174, 180, 187, 190, 204; denomination 13, 17, 20–1, 22–3, 26, 48, 58–9, 65, 87, 91–2, 107, 114, 136–7, 146, 149, 160, 182, 190, 200, 204, 224, 248; image 13, 35,
39, 47, 52, 94–5, 120, 219, 248, 253–4; inscription 13, 20–1, 26, 35, 39, 68–9, 120–1, 130, 219; overprints 13, 16–8, 21, 23, 28, 34, 39, 43, 46, 55, 62, 65, 68, 75, 79, 87, 91–2, 98, 104–5, 107, 124, 125, 130, 136–8, 142, 145, 150, 154, 157, 160, 163, 167, 169, 180, 190, 193, 196–7, 200, 204–7, 210–12, 219, 230, 238, 252, 256; postmark 13; used 22, 163, 258

Stampalia and the Dodecanese 210–3

St Croix 57, 59

Stellaland 213–6

St Nazaire 87

St Petersburg 135, 150–1

Straits of Otranto 93, 246

Straits Settlements 216–9

Suarez, Diego 155, 160

Suez Canal, the 42, 81, 100, 155, 159, 242

Sumatra 29, 217

Surat 70, 96

Surinam 121–2

surrender 37, 58, 79, 88, 95, 200, 210, 218

Svalbard 207–9

Sweden 144, 150–1, 202, 209

Switzerland 137–8, 246

Syria 15–8, 46, 140, 212–3, 242–5

Syrian Civil War, the 15, 17

Tadjoura 100–2; Gulf of 100, 159

Taiwan 21–4, 30, 140, 175, 176, 193

Teutonic Knights, the 18–20, 60, 144, 150
Thailand 191–3
Thessalonica 64, 77
Thirty Years' War, the 56, 198–9
Thrace 63, 65
Thurn und Taxis 219–22
Tibet 222–5
Tobago 135
Tordesillas, Treaty of 122, 172
traditionalists 67, 69, 84, 88, 197
Transcaucasian Socialist Federative Soviet Republic 226–9
Trans-Juba 229–32 *see also* Oltre Giuba
Transkei, Bophuthatswana, Venda, Ciskei 232–5
Transylvania 148–50
Tripoli 91, 235–7
Tripolitania 90, 235–8
Tshombe, Moïse 129–30
Tsingtao (Qingdao) 131–3
Tudjman, President 254, 257
Turkey 6–18, 31–4, 44, 46, 54–5, 63, 68, 73–5, 79, 94, 118–20, 148, 188, 212–3, 227–8, 242–3, 245–6, 259
Tuva 238–42

Uganda 37, 85, 230
Ukraine, the 66, 147, 185, 188
Union, the 47–9, 117
United Arab Republic 242–5
United Nations, the 128–9, 137, 140, 146, 184, 231
United States of the Ionian Islands 245–8

Upper Yafa 248–50
Ustasha, the 189

Vandals, the 236
Vasco da Gama 156–7, 165, 167, 172, 217
Venetia 25–7
Veneto 25, 27
Venezuela 51
Versailles 21, 180, 199
Vicksburg 48–9
Victoria Land 251–4
Vienna 25, 73, 94–5, 104, 221, 247
Vikings, the 56–7, 134, 201, 207
Vladivostok 195–7
Vryburg 213–6
Wanrong 142–3
Washington 49, 114–5, 129
Westerplatte 62–3
West Indies, the 56, 135, 184
White Army, the 67–8, 152, 195–6

Xhosa 233–4
Xiamen 21, 24–5

Yekaterinodar 67–8
Yemen 73, 79, 81, 99, 159, 248–50; Civil War 81; Occupied South 81, 250; South 82
Yi, Pu (Kangde) 141–3
Yugoslavia 94–5, 105, 112, 188, 255–6 *see also* the Kingdom of the Serbs, Croats and Slovenes

Zagreb 103, 189–91
Zanzibar 80, 110, 166, 229
Zapadna Bosna 254–7